Leila Simona Talani is Lecturer in International Political Economy at King's College, London

INTERNATIONAL LIBRARY OF MIGRATION STUDIES

Series ISBN 978 1 84885 225 9

See www.ibtauris.com/ILMS for a full list of titles

1. *Migrating to America: Transnational Social Networks and Regional Identity among Turkish Migrants*
Lisa DiCarlo
978 1 84511 646 0

2. *Homelands and Diasporas: Greeks, Jews and Their Migrations*
Minna Rozen (ed.)
978 1 84511 642 2

3. *The Iraqi Refugees: The New Crisis in the Middle East*
Joseph Sassoon
978 1 84511 919 5

4. *Immigration and National Identity: North African Political Movements in Colonial and Postcolonial France*
Rabah Aissaoui
978 1 84511 835 8

5. *From Egypt to Europe: Globalisation and Migration Across the Mediterranean*
Simona Talani
978 1 84511 669 9

6. *Creative Diaspora: Women, Art, Migration*
Suzanne Chan
978 1 84885 337 9

7. *Refugee Status in the Arab and Islamic Traditions: Concepts of Protection and Safe-Conduct and the 1951 Geneva Convention Relating to the Status of Refugees*
Arafat Shoukri
978 1 84885 390 4

From Egypt to Europe

Globalisation and Migration Across the Mediterranean

Leila Simona Talani

TAURIS ACADEMIC STUDIES
an imprint of
I.B.Tauris Publishers
LONDON • NEW YORK

Alla mia mamma ed al suo nipotino Gabriel

Published in 2010 by Tauris Academic Studies
An imprint of I.B.Tauris & Co Ltd
6 Salem Road, London W2 4BU
175 Fifth Avenue, New York NY 10010
www.ibtauris.com

Distributed in the United States and Canada
Exclusively by Palgrave Macmillan
175 Fifth Avenue, New York NY 10010

International Library of Migration Studies 5

ISBN 978 1 84511 669 9

A full CIP record for this book is available from the British Library
A full CIP record for this book is available from the Library of Congress

Library of Congress catalog card: available

Printed and bound in India by Thomson Press (India)
Camera-ready copy edited and supplied by the author

Contents

Acknowledgements

The author would like to thank the British Academy for financing much of the field work through its research grants.

The author is also grateful to Graziella Rizza, Dalia Bayoumi, Alan Cafruny, Steve Green, Henk Overbeek, Luciano Bardi and Antimo Verde, for their help, support, comments, information, suggestions and, most important of all, friendship.

Illustrations

Tables

Figures

Introduction

September 11, 2001 certainly marked a watershed in the modalities of interaction with Muslim countries and modified the perception and the reception of Muslim migrants in the Western world. In this context, the question of how these events impacted on further developments in the process of migration from the Middle East to Europe becomes unavoidable. One of the most controversial effects of September 11 on migration is the acceleration of the process of 'securitisation'.[1] It is certainly difficult to deny that the terrorist threat from Muslim fundamentalism reshaped the EU attitude towards Muslim migration in a much more security-oriented fashion and reinforced phenomena such as anti-Muslim behaviour (Islamophobia), social unrest of Muslim communities[2] and right-wing extremism.[3]

However, the problem of Muslim migration from the Middle East–North Africa (MENA) to the EU precedes the more recent security concerns and has become, in the last decade, one of the first priorities to be tackled by policy-makers in both countries of origin and host countries. The dimensions acquired by the phenomenon of mass migration, the degree of involvement of organised crime groups in the smuggling of migrants, the appalling conditions in which immigrants often find themselves in the hosting countries, pose a number of questions which make it imperative to investigate the underlying causes and consequences of the problem.

There seems to be a certain degree of consensus in the literature on the fact that the process of globalisation has indeed modified the terms within which migratory processes take place.[4] However, scholars are still divided on the assessment of the 'hows' and 'whys' of the impact of globalisation on migration. This is partly due to the fact that the issues relating to migration tend to be interdisciplinary by their very nature, covering the most various academic fields, from urban studies to anthropology, and from sociology to political economy.[5] Moreover, the definition itself of globalisation seems surrounded by a certain degree of mystery, being often invoked in different contexts or debates without a proper systematic attempt to define it.[6]

The main objective of this book is to study the impact of globalisation on migratory flows from a distinct International Political Economy (IPE) perspective, with particular attention on the dynamics of migration from the MENA area, especially Egypt, to the EU.

The theoretical aim of the book is, first, to understand the problem of migration, both legal and illegal, in the context of globalisation; and, second, to assess the relation between globalisation, marginalisation and the EU response to threats of mass immigration from less developed countries. The book therefore focuses on the following theoretical questions:

- How is the process of globalisation related to the increase of migratory flows from less developed countries to Western ones?
- What are the main political and economic causes and consequences of migration, in general, and illegal migration, in particular?
- Is there tension between legal and illegal migration?
- What is the reaction of host societies to Muslim migration and how is it possible to address it?

From an empirical point of view, the book presents the case of Egyptian migration. The related research questions are:

- What are the dynamics of migration from Egypt?
- What is the profile of the Egyptian migrant?
- Is economic migration prevailing over political migration?
- How might we explain Egyptian migration?
- Is there a relation between globalisation and Egyptian migration?
- What do Egyptian migrants do in receiving countries?

The empirical analysis is based on the results of surveys carried out by the author on motivations for migration at the point of origin.[7]

To sum up, this book comprises an enquiry into the impact of globalisation on migration from the point of view of marginalised countries. To be sure, many contributions have been published on the general, broader analysis of globalisation and its relation to migratory flows.[8] However, as far as the author is aware, none of these scholarly interventions has focused on the Middle East as a marginalised area and on the related consequences of this marginalisation from the process of globalisation in terms of both brain drain and mass migration. The only partial exception in this panorama is represented by Dodge and Higgot (2002) and Hakimian and

Moshaver (2001); however, both are mainly concerned about the economic dimension of marginalisation and ignore the socioeconomic consequences of the phenomenon, including its impact on the decision to migrate. The study proposed here, on the contrary, integrates the economic, the social and political dimensions of the phenomenon to produce an overall vision of the consequences of globalisation on the motivations for migration.

The notion of globalisation is by no means an uncontroversial one in the academic debate as well as in the wider public discourse. It seems possible, however, to classify the positions adopted by scholars on the subject into three broad groups:[9] those who deny the existence itself of the phenomenon of globalisation;[10] those who admit it, but tend to give only a quantitative definition of globalisation;[11] and those who adopt a qualitative definition.[12] The theoretical background of this book is represented by the traditional qualitative [13] definition of globalisation. This identifies the process of globalisation as a qualitatively new phenomenon, characterised by the dramatic increase of foreign direct investment (FDI), by the transnationalisation of social groups, including labour and business, and by an unprecedented interdependence of financial markets.[14]

Technological transformation is an exogenous component of the qualitative definition of globalisation, and it is the factor which brings about transformation in the realms of financial transactions and production. This, in turn, triggers related changes in the economic, social and political spheres. Technological transformation is also the driving force behind the process of transformation of global production and the related global reallocation of production alongside the lines of the dramatic increase of FDI and mergers and acquisitions, and the creation of the export processing zones.

As a consequence of the restructuring of production, the labour structure also changes, with a substantial reallocation of labour-intensive production to Third World countries. However, this outcome is compounded by the opposite effects of technological development in terms of the increase of distant work, and of the increase of labour mobility, including mass migration.

Indeed, on the one hand, production tends to move to some specialised regions of the globe,[15] where it is possible to exploit the advantages of lower production costs both in the form of lower labour costs and/or in the form of lower costs of primary resources. This phenomenon gives rise to the paradox of regionalisation within globalisation, characterised by the creation of economically integrated regions. On the other hand, however, the populations of those marginalised zones of the globe, whose economic conditions are deemed to worsen as a consequence of the process of globalisation, experience an increased incentive to leave their home countries and move to the more developed regions of the world in search of better life standards. This produces the two interrelated phenomena of the 'brain drain', when skilled or highly educated labour flees the country of origin, and 'mass migration', when migratory flows interest unskilled labour.

Moreover, migration, both legal and illegal, acquires regional patterns, due to historical, geographic, social or cultural reasons. All responses to migration, therefore, take the form of regional policies, such as the US or the EU immigration policy. Here a fundamental paradox arises. This paradox lies in the advantages of immigration in terms of reduction of the costs of production and of contribution to the sustainability of the welfare state (particularly given the ageing problem in the more developed world), and the implementation of stricter migration policies at the regional level. In Europe, for example, despite the fact that the implementation of a common migratory policy is still far from being achieved, the outlook of public policy responses to mass migration has accredited the idea of the creation of the so-called 'Fortress Europe', an area where internal mobility is promoted while barriers are erected vis-à-vis countries outside the EU.

Of course, the main reasons for the adoption of similar responses to mass migration are the traditional concerns over political unrest, social conflict, cultural clashes or religious struggles. However, a further aspect of the issue is represented by the politico-economic consequences of 'illegal' migration (as opposed to legal migration), in terms of cost reduction and loss of bargaining power compared with organised labour.[16]

To conclude, from the theoretical point of view, the following issues appear particularly relevant:

- The paradox of regionalisation within globalisation and its consequences in terms of the increase of intraregional temporary migration.
- The paradox of marginalisation within globalisation and its consequences in terms of the increases of brain drain and mass migration.
- The paradox of 'Fortress Europe', and its consequences in terms of the increase of illegal migration.

Egypt is considered here as a clear case of marginalisation within globalisation, the MENA area as a case in which the process of regionalisation within globalisation failed to happen, and the creation of 'Fortress Europe' as the factor inducing Egyptian migrants to enter the EU illegally.

The book argues that the case of Egypt is one in which the lack of regionalisation and the progressive marginalisation of the region and, in particular, of the country under analysis, do explain the increase in permanent migration to more developed countries. Moreover, although the data collected do not allow for definitive conclusion on the subject, the fact that the main destination countries of Egyptian migration to Europe have adopted very strict migratory policies, in line with the paradox of Fortress Europe, allows for legitimate suspicion that the bulk of these migratory flows is illegal.

Finally, there is no doubt in the author's mind that the impact of September 11 on the Southern Mediterranean, and Egypt in particular, has been to increase its marginalisation; and there is no doubt that this effect, far from discouraging it, will prompt new waves of Muslim migration to the EU, with all the problems that this might provoke.

The book is divided into two sections. The first section provides an overview of the main political science approaches to migration and globalisation. It addresses the debate over the definition of globalisation and deepens the qualitative approach to draw conclusions about the impact on migration from marginalised countries. It also sketches the notion of 'Fortress Europe', its origins and its relations with the issue of securitisation from a theoretical standpoint. Whereas the first section is devoted primarily to theory, the second section is essentially empirical. It tests a number of hypotheses derived from the theoretical context of the specific case of migration from the MENA area and from Egypt in particular. After verifying to what extent the area can be classified as marginalised from the process of globalisation, it describes the characteristics of migratory flows from the region, referring to the data collected by the author. It finally analyses the question of the integration of migrants into the labour markets of the receiving countries and, more in general, the problems stemming from the integration of Muslim migrants in European societies, from "Islamophobia" to social unrest. It also suggests how the concept of social capital may prove relevant to facilitate communication between host and migrant communities.

The book consists of nine chapters. Chapter 1 sets the theoretical approach within the debate about migration theory in general and, in particular, the political science discussion focusing on the role of the State in addressing modern migration. Theories of international migration are far from clustered in a well-defined theoretical paradigm. On the contrary, although there seems to be a sort of consensus in the social sciences on the kinds of questions being asked, the perspectives from which those questions are answered within the various disciplines differ substantially. This contribution is firmly set within the political science approach to international migration and, in particular, within the international political economy tradition.

Chapter 2 clarifies the state of the debate in international relations/international political economy with regard to international migration. Before proceeding headlong to the consequences of globalisation on migration, it defines what globalisation is from the different IPE perspectives, and what the implications are of the different definitions of the concept on the capacity of the nation state to produce relevant policy-making. Once again, it is important to explore what role the state has in this debate.

Chapter 3 deepens the analysis of 'Fortress Europe' and relates it to the process of European integration as well as to the notion of 'securitisation'. In Europe, despite the fact that the implementation of a common migratory policy is still far from being achieved, the outlook of public policy responses to mass migration has accredited the idea of the creation of the so-called 'Fortress Europe', i.e. an area where internal mobility is promoted while barriers are erected vis-à-vis countries outside the EU.[17] The origins of 'Fortress Europe' have been traced back by scholars to Council Regulation 1612/68, which distinguished between the right to free movement by nationals of member states and the right to free movement by nationals of Third countries.[18] The establishment of freedom of movement for EU citizens has only exacerbated this divide. This was initiated by the Single European Act in 1986 and continued in by the 'EU citizenship' provisions of the Maastricht Treaty in 1992. Third country nationals' rights of access to the EU were, on the other hand, progressively but steadily restricted by the Schengen agreements, the Third Pillar on Justice and Home Affairs, the Dublin Convention, and the few legislative provisions more recently adopted under the new title on migration instituted by the Amsterdam Treaty. The consequences of the adoption of this extremely tight approach to migration from third countries, at both the EU and national level,[19] have been an increase of irregular migration and the progressive 'securitisation' of migration. By 'securitisation', the experts mean the development of migration into a 'security issue', which has to be managed by security agencies such as, for example, Europol.[20] The chapter reviews the developments leading to the creation of Fortress Europe; it identifies the migratory regimes existing within the EU before and after the Amsterdam Treaty; and gives some insights about the explanations proposed to the communitarisation of migratory policy with a special attention to the debate on securitisation.

In Chapter 4, the author approaches the question of migration from a specific MENA country, namely Egypt. The chapter reconstructs the historical developments of migration in the MENA area and in Egypt. Until very recently, Egyptians had 'a reputation of preferring their own soil. Few leave except to study or travel; and they always return … Egyptians do not emigrate.'[21] Indeed, only a small number of Egyptians, primarily professionals, had left the country in search for employment before 1974. The chapter describes the different phases in the evolution of Egyptian migratory flows and of migration within the Arab world.

In Chapter 5, the author answers the question, 'Why do Egyptians migrate nowadays?' referring to the theories relating to the impact of globalisation on mass migration from marginalised countries. The chapter focuses on the lack of regionalisation of the MENA area. It provides data on the marginalisation of the area with all that follows in terms of economic incentives to migrate.

In Chapter 6, Egypt is singled out as a clear case of marginalisation within globalisation. Since the 1990s, the shift to a free market economy and the adoption of macroeconomic policy reforms and structural adjustments in Egypt have produced mixed results. Stabilisation programmes have been successful, and a series of IMF agreements along with massive external debt relief, particularly from the USA through USAID, have helped Egypt to improve its macroeconomic performance during the 1990s. However, neither the relative macroeconomic stability experienced by Egypt in the course of the 1990s, nor the substantial programme of privatisation, nor its commitment to economic reform and structural adjustment has helped Egypt in attracting FDI. Here the author provides useful evidence about the marginalisation of Egypt from the process of globalisation.

In Chapter 7, the profile of the Egyptian migrant is outlined with reference to the survey carried out by the author in Cairo during 2002/2003 and compared to the profile of the Moroccan migrant. Egyptian migrants are predominantly male, concentrated in young age groups, and with a relatively high educational level.[22] This section sheds some light on the characteristics of Egyptian migrants in general, and as emerged from the survey. Reference is made to the theory of migration as a social process to ascertain to what extent migration from the MENA area and from Egypt in particular can be defined as an instance of globalisation-induced migration.

Chapter 8 addresses some of the issues relating to the integration of the Muslim migrant in the labour markets of the destination country. It sketches the situation of the labour markets in receiving countries for Muslim workers in general and in the case of Egyptian workers. The chapter then tackles the question of the insertion of foreign-born workers into the underground economy. The aim is to verify to what extent the existence of a thriving underground economy, especially in southern European countries, may represent a strong pull factor attracting especially undocumented migrants to the EU.

Finally, Chapter 9 touches upon the complex issue of integration of Muslim migrants' communities in the civil society of European hosting countries, without any ambition to be exhaustive or even to highlight the main terms of the question. By making reference to original research on the subject, it stresses how co-habitation between Muslims and national communities was already problematic before the occurrences of September 11, to the extent that it was possible to talk about straightforward hostility against Muslims or Islamophobia. This produced the reaction of the widespread establishment of Muslim social, political and religious organisations all over Europe and the related debate of whether they constitute genuine social capital. After defining social capital and analysing the issue of how to measure it, the chapter finds out that the emergence of 'Muslim voices', instead of increasing the level of trust between Muslim communities and the local civil society, may have indeed reduced it. This, in turn, enhances diversity and multiplies the occasions of confrontation between host communities and communities of migrants. In a few words, it reduces social capital and facilitates Islamophobia and social unrest. The solution, as some scholars point out, is an increase of social capital measured in terms of trust and respect for civic norms. This is a result which might be obtained also by introducing adequate urban policies.

To conclude, the book includes theoretically sophisticated and empirically rigorous research carried out by the author, and provides a systematic account of globalisation and its impact on migration from marginalised countries with special attention to the Middle East and North African region.

Chapter 1

Migration in theory

The state of the debate or the State in the debate

1 Introduction

Theories of international migration are far from clustered in a well-defined theoretical paradigm. On the contrary, although there seems to be a sort of consensus in the social sciences on the kinds of questions to ask in approaching international migration, the perspectives from which those questions are answered differ substantially among the various disciplines. Brettell and Hollifield,[1] in an extremely useful compendium of migration theories, have classified such theories across disciplines according to their main research questions, levels of analysis, relevant methodologies and main hypotheses.

Historians tend to ask questions similar to those of social scientists, such as: What are the determinants and consequences of population movements? Who moves, when do they move, why do they move? Why do some people not move? How do those who do move experience departure, migration and settlement? These questions are generally answered with reference to single groups or, more frequently, individuals, thus adopting a distinct micro approach to the study of migration and traditionally using archives as their main methodological tool.[2] Anthropologists also are usually more interested in the micro-level of analysis. They often adopt a case-study approach despite their endeavouring to engage in cross-cultural comparisons to allow for broader generalisations.[3] The micro-level of analysis is predominant in economics, too. Economists, starting from the assumption of the rational actor model, and adopting methodological individualism as their main heuristic tool, ask questions relating to motivations for migration which are normally answered through maximisation models.[4]

The macro perspective, on the contrary, prevails in sociology, demography and political science, whereas lawyers are more eclectic in their choices of levels of analysis and methodology. In sociology, traditional structuralist theoretical frameworks tend to emphasise social relations as central to understanding the process of migration and integration of immigrants. The methodologies vary, implying the use of ad-hoc surveys or more aggregated data.[5] Demographers are concerned with the nature of population change, a question which is generally answered through the construction of predictive models and analysed by means of statistical tools.[6] Finally, political scientists are most often interested in the macro-level of analysis.[7] Their contributions to international migration have been grouped by Hollifield into three themes. One is the role of the nation state to control its borders; and therefore migration, which implies the whole discussion about whether in the age of globalisation the nation state is still able to exert such control. The second theme is the impact of migration on international relations, especially the institutions of sovereignty and citizenship. The third is the question of integration of migrants into the host societies, with special attention to its political dimension.[8]

This contribution is set firmly within the political science approach to international migration, in particular within the international relations/international political economy tradition. The questions addressed relate to the motivations for migration from the point of departure and the dynamics of international migration. Above all, the author tries to answer the question, why is international migration increasing in the era of globalisation?

So what is the state of the debate in international relations/international political economy with regard to international migration? And, first of all, what is international political economy? To this subject we turn in the next section.

2 What is International Political Economy?

The interaction between economics and politics has been one of the most debated topics in the study of international relations, from the seventeenth-century mercantilists to twentieth-century Marxists. However, since the first half of the twentieth century, the analysis of the international political economy has been neglected[9] and the disciplines of economics and politics have been divorced from each other. Similarly, the domestic and international levels of analysis have been separated.[10] Different scholars have traced the reasons why this occurred in different events.[11] For example, in her best-selling book of the late 1970s, *The Politics of International Economic Relations*, Joan Edelman Spero[12] analysed the main causes of the decline in the use of political-economy variables to explain international events. She puts the blame for the divorce on the liberal heritage in Western academia, which rejected the idea of a unified political and economic order, replacing it with two separate orders. Starting from the assumption that the economic system enjoys a sort of natural harmony whereas such harmony is not discernible in the political sphere, liberal theorists infer that the two fields should not interfere with one another. Such theoretical separation has led to, and has been reinforced by, the specialisation of modern academia, in which economics and politics have been treated as different disciplines, interested in different processes and studying different systems with different rules.

Furthermore, argues Spero, this formal division of analysis has been strengthened by two political and economic developments following the Second World War. The first of these was the agreement on post-war international economic relations. This was represented in the West by the Bretton Woods system and in the East by the Soviet Union hegemony, which rendered less frequent, and so less meaningful, the conflict over economic issues. The second development was the emergence of the Cold War, with all that implied in terms of primacy of security issues for international relations. Therefore, international relation theories focused on 'high' politics and security-related issues, and neglected 'low', economic politics.[13] However, by the mid-1970s, the two factors that had shaped the study of international politics in the post-war decades (economic consensus and security conflict) were becoming less relevant – hence the revival of an integrated political economy approach in the study of international relations and the emergence of 'the politics of international economic relations' (PIER).

Joan Spero's PIER approach was criticised by Murphy and Tooze in their definition of a new international political economy (IPE).[14] During the 1950s and 1960s, realists dominated US international relation theories. Consequently, the development of 'orthodox' IPE, categorised by the authors as a branch of international relations, was characterised from the beginning by the realist conceptual separations of economics and politics, and the international and the domestic. Realists borrowed this separation from the notion of 'liberal' economic order. This is an order in which economic activity is separated from political activity, both from a prescriptive and a descriptive point of view, for the purpose of maximising the commonwealth.[15] Realism not only borrowed its conception of the relations between politics and economics from liberal thought, but also helped to support the liberal elements of the international economic order. It is therefore possible to recognise a dynamic relation between the predominant theoretical perspective and the actual shaping of economic policies.[16]

Only when the liberal world economic order collapsed in the mid-1970s was orthodox IR confronted with the necessity of reconciling the academic fields of political science and economics, and analysing the 'politics of international economic relations' (PIER), or the 'political economy of international relations' (PEIR). However, this was in order to find a new body of rules and norms that would preserve the actual division between the political and the economic, and keep the world economy functioning as it had in the 1950s and 1960s.[17]

Gilpin's renewed attention to the interaction between economics and politics from a neo-realist perspective is an example of orthodoxy in IPE.[18] This was reflected in most of his 1970s works and confirmed in his *Political Economy of International Relations* (1987). Here, Gilpin justifies the need for an integrated approach to the study of international relations. This need arose as a consequence of the relative decline of the American economic leadership of the post-war liberal international economy; the shift of the world economy from the Atlantic to the Pacific; and the increasing integration of the American and Japanese economies.[19]

According to Gilpin's realist approach, the relevant questions in IPE concern the relationships between the State and the market. This happens because '[t]he tensions between these two fundamentally different ways of ordering human relationships has profoundly shaped the course of modern history and constitutes the crucial problem in the study of political economy'.[20] The interaction between the State and the market influences the distribution of power and wealth in international relations. In this context, states are the main actors in an international system which is conceptualised as 'anarchical'[21] and lacking a supranational source of legitimacy and power. International institutions provide only the framework within which states bargain to maximise their utility functions, and deals are struck at the minimum common denominator in order to minimise the loss of sovereignty. The realist approach to IPE differs from realism in IR for its focus on low politics, and its tendency to attribute heuristic primacy to economic variables. More recently, a main point of difference has been the attempt to ground the interests of the state in their domestic context in what has been called an inside-out or two-level game approach.[22]

One of the most successful attempts to find an integrated domestic–international politics model has been proposed by Robert Putnam in his article 'Diplomacy and Domestic Politics'.[23] Here, the author presents a conceptual framework of general applicability to ascertain when and how domestic politics and international relations are connected. Putnam's approach to the problem rests on the metaphor of the two-level game for domestic–international relations. The national level is the locus of a pluralist competition among interest groups trying to maximise their power by lobbying governments and building coalitions to obtain favourable policies. At the international level, states, always conceived as rational actors, seek to maximise both domestic consensus and their power and position in the international system. As national politicians act at both levels, the study of international relations cannot avoid analysing both the national and the international contexts.

The other mainstream approach to IPE is liberal institutionalism, whose main representative is Keohane. Keohane argues that Gilpin has offered a helpful working definition of the phrase 'world political economy', but the concepts of power and wealth are too static to explain behaviour. Power and wealth must be analysed within relationships and processes to provide useful information about the behaviour of actors; they have to be studied through the institutions that embody them in the international system.[24] As an alternative, according to Keohane,

> We can view international political economy as the intersection of the substantive area studied by economics – production and exchange of marketable means of want satisfaction – with the process by which power is exercised that is central to politics. Wherever, in the economy, actors exert power over one another, the economy is political.[25]

Therefore, according to Keohane, thinking about IPE in terms of wealth and power does not help to construct a strong explanatory model of behaviour. However, focusing on the 'pursuit of wealth' and the 'pursuit of power' contributes to more insightful interpretations. The emphasis on the processes through which power and wealth are acquired allows strong hypotheses about the motivations of actors and the specific interests within a given institutional framework. Defining international political economy in terms of the pursuit of wealth and power leads neo-institutionalists to analyse cooperation in the world political economy and the institutional form it takes less as an effort to implement high ideals than a means of attaining self-interested economic and political goals.[26]

As a matter of fact, wealth and power are sought by a variety of actors in world politics, but states are, in Keohane's thought, crucial actors. This is why his analysis of international cooperation and regimes focuses principally on states. At the same time, however, contrary to neo-realist perspectives, in the neo-institutional conceptualisation states do not act in a vacuum or in an anarchical system, but are constrained by the international institutional structure.[27] Both approaches are heavily rationalist and stress the importance of economic interests in defining national preferences.

Helen Milner has addressed the issue of how to identify the interests of the state from the neo-institutionalist perspective, underlying the necessity to ground states' preferences on considerations of domestic politics. This allows the determination of the pay-off structures, or national interests of states, the strategies available to states to alter systemic conditions, and the capacity of states to ratify and implement cooperative arrangements. For these reasons, domestic politics are essential in order to understand international cooperation, and international economic cooperation in particular.[28]

Not surprisingly, neo-liberal theorists focus almost exclusively on politics and policy in liberal states, where the competition among groups is relatively open and unaffected by authoritarianism and corruption. Neo-realist and neo-liberal approaches are classified within the mainstream in IPE.

The last development in the evolution of IPE is the debate between mainstream approaches and critical ones. Starting from the criticism of both the realist perspective and its subsequent PIER/PEIR development, Murphy and Tooze propose a new IPE whose purpose is to re-establish the study of IPE at the core of social science as a whole. The same perspective had already been proposed by Stephen Gill and David Law in their global approach to political economy.[29] According to these authors, the roots of the political economy approach to international relations go back centuries and may already be traced in the analyses of the mercantilists. However, the emergence of international political economy as a self-conscious field of study took place only in the 1970s. The historical gap during the early twentieth century should be explained by the increasing specialisation of social science disciplines.

The revival of IPE in the 1970s, particularly in the United States, was the consequence of the changes in world economics, with the breakdown of the Bretton Woods order and the growing impact, mainly on US policy, of interdependence. This modified the academic community's perception of the relations between economics and politics. The academic sources of the resurgence of international political economy were, in the categorisation by Gill and Law, varied in character. They included: (i) the emergence of neo-classical political economy analysis; (ii) the revival of Marxist analysis; (iii) the emergence of 'development studies' and concern over North–South relations; (iv) the analyses of international constraints on national policies as expressed by interdependence and dependency theories; and (v) the comparative socio-historical approach.[30] Given this multitude of approaches and the lack of agreement in the definition of 'political economy' itself, the boundary of the field is so confused that Gill and Law prefer to abandon the use of the term 'international political economy' in favour of the more comprehensive expression 'global political economy'. They believe that the latter could both 'facilitate a better communication among the rival theoretical frameworks and increase interdisciplinary exchanges'.[31]

Gill further clarifies his new IPE position in the essay 'Historical Materialism, Gramsci and International Political Economy',[32] where he argues in favour of a new critical historical materialist IPE analysis. This is opposed to the positivist approach, which he criticised for its non-historical nature; lack of a dynamic, dialectical quality; narrowness and incompleteness of abstractions; and tendency to extreme parsimony in explanation relative to the infinite complexity of its object of analysis, namely the international system.[33]

The last development in the field of IPE is, thus, characterised by an increasing opposition between the orthodox stream of thought, enriched by the contribution of the public choice school,[34] and the growing new critical IPE perspective. The latter tries to 'provide a common language in which to preserve the insights of otherwise separate research traditions, supporting multiple points of synthesis among different perspectives, and avoiding the establishment of one, unitary, all-encompassing theory of IPE'.[35]

Critical IPE theorists, although belonging to different schools and adopting a multiplicity of approaches, some of them pretty eclectic, display some common characteristics. Methodologically, they are open to various explanations, from historical to social ones, without being constrained by the rational actor model typical of methodological individualism in economics. They are therefore willing to recognise the subjectivity of all social sciences avoiding constraining IPE in rigid categorisations.[36] Accordingly, the interests of critical IPE scholars are more varied than those of the orthodoxy, including not only State-centric analysis, but the role of people, multinational corporations and ideas in defining international events.

Susan Strange's eclectic definition of IPE should be inserted within this context.[37] The first stage in her definition of IPE was expressed in the Preface to a collection of essays called *Paths to International Political Economy* in which she argued strongly for openness to insights from other disciplines in the development of IPE, a field that she considers a branch of international relations. In her later work, she has devised a truly eclectic approach to international political economy, encompassing different disciplines in the social sciences, from economics to sociology, and from history to international relations. The aim is to allow for a systematic dialogue between them and to overcome the limits of the traditional mainstream paradigm of the Politics of International Economic Relations (PIER). This synthesis is achieved by identifying the main 'enveloping' structures that, rather than the rational, conscious decision of any actor, determine the range of options within which 'States and other groups and individuals contest all the major who-gets-what issues of politics',[38] both at the national and at the international level.

Apart from the importance, already stressed by Marxist and Gramscian authors,[39] of the production structure in international political economy, Susan Strange draws to the attention of IPE scholars the role of the financial structure,[40] the security structure and the knowledge structure, represented, at the abstract level, by belief systems, and at the operational level, by the management of information.[41] Moreover, two other major factors, technology and markets, both exogenous to the international political system and both ignored by the orthodox scholars, are added to states as the determinants of change in the major structures. Thus an eclectic analytical framework for the study of IPE is set. The final stage in the clarification of Strange's position is represented by the insertion of a new variable in the evolution of structures and bargaining relationships: firms. Firms, like states, with which they undertake an incessant bargaining process, play a role in markets and technological development. Like states and markets, they are affected by changes in any of the four major structures and, above all, they exercise power in many ways, both domestically and internationally. Thus, she argues, if we want to achieve the main aim of IPE, which is to look for the sources of power and the consequences of the exercise of it, we cannot rationally exclude firms from our analysis.[42]

Apart from Susan Strange's eclectic contribution to a new definition of IPE, the development of a neo-Gramscian definition of IPE, based on the works of Cox[43] and well explained by Gill,[44] should not be neglected since it can be very useful in broadening the insights of an integrated political–economical approach to international events. Neo-Gramscians develop a historically integrated, dialectical form of IPE analysis with the explicit aim to 'transcend the subject/object and agent/structure dichotomies that undermine the plausibility of the generally positivist epistemologies and ontologies at the roots of the majority of studies in IPE'.[45] At a preliminary level of analysis, it is possible to underline three main differences between Gramscian and orthodox IPE. First, in international studies, the Gramscian approach is a critique of the empiricist and positivist assumptions of the prevailing orthodox tradition, to which it contrasts a specific form of 'non-structuralist historicism'.[46] Second, the Gramscian approach is also critical of methodological individualism and methodological reductionism since, for Gramsci, it is *la situazione* (the situation), defined as the ensemble of social relations configured by social structure, that is the basic unit of analysis rather than any individual actor as in modern public choice theory.[47] Third, the approach inserts a normative dimension to the analysis of social events introducing the objective of realising an 'ethical' State and a unitary society in which 'personal development, rational reflection, open debate, democratic empowerment, and economic and social liberation can become widely available'.[48]

Critical approaches to IPE have been enriched lately by neo-constructivist analyses. Neo-constructivists[49] criticise mainstream assumptions of the rational actor model, State-centrism, and the distinction between integration in 'low politics' and integration in 'high politics'. The criticism of the rational actor model is carried out by reverting to social constructivism. In particular, neo-constructivist scholars argue that social action does not only and necessarily follow an 'instrumental rationality', by this meaning the logic of rationally maximising a utility function. According to neo-constructivists, in explaining social behaviour it is imperative to consider the impact of ideas and shared beliefs, therefore rejecting the logic of instrumentality in favour of the logic of communicative action. In other words, in their decision-making, social actors are moved by their values, beliefs and views of the world, and not necessarily by their material interests ranked rationally according to their utility functions. Therefore, to understand why certain actors take a certain decision, it is important to understand the values or ideas pursued by the actors in question and to appreciate how these have been communicated to them (which is the analysis of the communicative action). The criticism of State-centrism takes place by reverting to transnationalism and transgovernmentalism.[50] Transnational relations are defined as 'transboundary relations that include at least one non-governmental actor',[51] whereas transgovernmental relations are defined as 'cross-boundary relations among sub-units of national governments in the absence of centralised decisions by state executives'. [52] By means of these two concepts, neo-constructivists reject the notion both of the State as the only actor in the international arena ('transnationalism') and of the State as a unitary, monolithic actor ('transgovernmentalism'). Finally, neo-constructivists do not accept the mainstream proposition that integration in 'low politics' (economic issues) is easier than integration in 'high politics' (foreign, defence and security policy), and this is mainly due to the lesser role they assign to material interests in explaining social action in general, and international or European integration in particular. Indeed, if the vectors of integration are represented by the profound beliefs of policy-makers and by the degree of transnationalisation and transgovernmentalism of the issue to be integrated, rather than by the maximisation of an economic or material interest, the distinction between low and high politics becomes irrelevant.

Let us see how these approaches have been applied to the issues of international migration.

3 Mainstream versus critical IPE approaches to migration: The State in the debate

3.1 The political economy of immigration in the realist tradition

Myron Weiner[53] is the most prominent representative of the realist IPE approach to international migration. His analysis starts from the consideration that the global migration crisis is mostly the consequence of state policies,[54] both in sending and receiving countries. Sending countries have strong political and economic incentives to favour migration. From the political point of view, forced migration can be used to dominate ethnic communities, to eliminate political dissidents and class enemies, or as a foreign policy tool, especially to force neighbouring countries to accept undesired policies. As a macroeconomic tool, migration can produce relief from unemployment and the costs of the welfare state, can improve the balance of payments through remittances, and allows foreign technology to be obtained. In receiving countries, the increase of migrants is not so much the consequence of labour market needs, but of ease of access. Weiner believes that every society has only a limited capacity to absorb foreigners and points to xenophobic backlashes in Western Europe as examples of the kind of security threat posed by uncontrolled migration. After all, '[s]tates will not and cannot allow others to decide who will permanently live and work in their own societies'.[55] Hence states have the right to control their borders, and, as border controls are becoming less and less efficacious as a consequence of the globalisation of information, they have the right to identify more efficient internal controls on an ad-hoc basis (identity cards, repatriation schemes, expulsions, etc.). After an analysis of the negative impact of immigration for receiving countries, Weiner concludes that Western governments have to be prepared to intervene in conflicts that are likely to produce large refugee flow.

Whereas some realist scholars[56] tend to consider migration or refugee policy as a matter of national security, others[57] encourage states to open their borders when it is in their interest to do so (i.e. when it will enhance their power and position in the international system). According to this latter interpretation, migration policy and flows are a function of internationally systemic factors – namely, the distribution of power in the international system and the relative position of the states. The decision to allow economic immigrants and refugees by governments is therefore a consequence of the desire to improve their relative position in the system and modify the balance of power. Borjas,[58] for example, although mainly an economist, proposes a similar realist political economy interpretation of migration. He equates the international immigration market with the regular labour market, stressing that migrants choose on a totally rational basis whether to move to one country or another according to which benefits countries have on offer. Starting from the assumption (empirically demonstrated and demonstrable) that immigration is an advantage to host countries (especially skilled migration), it then becomes imperative for a rational State (such as the USA) to enhance its desirability for potential immigrants.[59] This can be achieved by adopting the right public policies in the domestic context. For example, if it is proven, as it is, that education increases the productivity of the labour force, both national and non-national, then a state must do its best to attract a highly educated labour force from abroad – for example, by rewarding highly educated (both native and alien) workers with a higher income. Otherwise, other states will win this competition and attract the best migrants, thus increasing their power and capabilities in the international system.[60]

From this standpoint, immigration is a positive-sum game: all players gain from the immigration process – not only the immigrants, but also the receiving countries. Even illegal migration responds to the needs of the host countries, as 'the existence and persistence of a black market for immigrants implies that all parties participating in these exchanges benefit from these voluntary transactions'.[61]

The immigration market approach, although still a realist approach, answers the question of whether a state should risk migration in a much more favourable manner than the national security one. However, the principal weakness of realism is that it gives too much emphasis to politics and the capacity of the State to define migratory policies and control migratory flows. Moreover, this approach cannot explain effectively why migration is increasing worldwide.[62]

More promising is the interest-based political economy approach to immigration proposed by Freeman. This is an inside-out, realist approach to international migration which keeps the state firmly at the centre of the international decision-making process and adopts an economic interests approach to the domestic decision-making process. The assumption is that states are still sovereign and can define their entry/exit policy, but in doing so they respond uniquely to organised socio-economic interests.[63] At the socio-economic level, the main problem remains whether 'those who gain from immigration compensate those who lose to produce a net social gain'.[64]

Freeman begins with the traditional realist policy dilemma between allowing immigration when it is in the interests of the State and controlling it when it is not. Then he traces back the interests of the State in some domestic variables and internal dynamics. He identifies in the configuration of internal institutional and interest groups the main independent variables explaining a successful management of migratory issues. In particular, the centralisation of policy-making and capital labour relations is recognised as an important factor in the ability of the state to limit the negative aspects of migration.

Freeman then considers three major types of organised interest groups: economic, ethnic and issue or ideological.[65] Employers are usually the most active in recruiting migrants abroad and lobbying in favour of a relaxed migratory policy. For example, in the USA, the dominant coalition favouring expansive immigration policy is made up of organised business and its affiliated politicians, and liberals supporting immigration for humanitarian and ideological reasons.[66] On the other hand, workers tend to dislike the increase of the labour supply due to immigration, and therefore lobby for more control.[67] However, their success is related to the strength of their organisations. According to Freeman's analysis, labour strength impacts on immigration in three ways. First, organised labour's ability to influence a state's migration policy is related directly to the strength of its trade unions' organisation; second, the increase in the labour supply as a consequence of immigration can be better controlled by a government if organised labour is strong; third, strong trade unions and working-class parties are able to constrain the impulses of the lower classes when confronted with the increase in the labour supply resulting from immigration.[68]

Economic models help to identify the range of coalitions positively or negatively affected by immigration, and, therefore, to project their position in the political debate regarding the implementation of more or less restrictive migratory policies. However, these models are not consensual in hypothesising the societal effect of immigration, and can provide conflicting predictions. The product/output model, for example, predicts the traditional class cleavage between capital and labour based on the consideration that immigration increases the profits of the capital elite and decreases the wages of the working population. On the other hand, in the Heckscher–Ohlin context, immigrants enter into the production process according to their skills, and therefore their impact on labour is limited. In the specific-factors model, immigration is expected to depress the wages of citizens and residents of similar skills, but increase the incomes of other socio-economic actors. This creates sectoral cleavages in which mobile factors tend to gain and specific factors to lose.[69] Introducing fiscal variables, the situation is even further complicated, leading to an array of possible coalitions. It could be possible to hypothesise tensions deriving from perceived competition for public goods, but questions of geographical concentration of groups, especially in a federal system, might produce different outcomes.[70]

Looking at the incentives for interest groups to mobilise politically for or against a certain government's stance on migration, in a political economic context, Freeman identifies four possibilities. In a two-dimensional model, with economic costs (benefits) and political mobilisation on the axes, what is relevant to predict interest mobilisation is the level of concentration of groups (concentrated or diffuse) and the size of costs/benefits (large or small). Client politics is the policy-making modality ensuing from a situation of large economic benefits/costs and concentrated groups. If, however, the socio-economic groups are diffused and economic benefits/costs are large, we get interest-group politics. When economic benefits/costs are small, the mode is entrepreneurial politics if political groups are concentrated, and majoritarian politics with diffuse groups.[71] Despite the many different interest coalitions that immigration may produce, it is clear to Freeman that 'migration is economically advantageous for leading economic sectors. Those for which it is not beneficial can be compensated for their losses, or if not, typically wield limited influence in national politics'.[72]

Some criticisms can be moved to this approach. For example, as Freeman himself recognises,[73] issues of identity and ethnicity cannot be discarded from the analysis of the impact of migration on host societies. Even in stable societies with overtly peaceful social relations, an acquired ethnic diversity can erode societal cohesion and trust, and produce public policies contrary to the interests of leading groups.

However, this does not diminish the importance of Freeman's contribution: his political economy approach to immigration gains merit in emphasising the role of socio-economic interest groups in defining the State's public policy's preferences.[74] Nevertheless, the questions of whether and why migration is increasing in recent times still remains unanswered. Let us see whether a different approach can help to solve the problem, and focus our attention on the second mainstream approach to IPE and its applications to the issues of international migration: liberal institutionalism (or neo-institutionalism).

3.2 Liberal institutionalism and migration

As Hollifield suggests,[75] a liberal institutionalist approach to international migration should propose a number of hypotheses with regard to international migration. First, neo-institutionalists à la Keohane would predict that the increase in migratory flows is the consequence of the formation of coalitions of interests favouring them in the most powerful liberal states. Similar coalitions should coincide with those lobbying for the adoption of anti-protectionist/free trade policies. However, free trade coalitions are much less contentious than coalitions supporting the opening of borders to all immigrants, as the latter no doubt involve more cultural, social and even religious cleavages. Indeed, free trade coalitions are very rarely concerned also with opening borders to foreigners.

Moreover, from the perspective of neo-liberal interdependence, states should be more prone to opening their borders, both to trade and to migration, in the presence of an international regulatory system or institution that can control and regulate similar flows. However, whereas in the field of trade, international institutions were more or less successfully established, in the case of migration no such regime has been set up. Despite this, international migratory flows did not disappear. On the contrary, they continued to increase exponentially during the last decades. This clearly points to the lack of theoretical tools in the liberal institutionalist paradigm to grasp and explain the reality of international migration.

Indeed, the number of scholars offering a neo-institutionalist analysis of the problems relating to migration is limited. They tend to focus on the interplay between institutions and ideas to explain why states accept migration. As detailed below, these differ from the globalisation theorists, who tend to focus more on transnational relations and less on the State, which is no longer considered the only, or even the most relevant, actor in the international system.[76] Hollifield is one of the few addressing international migration from an inside-out neo-liberal institutionalist perspective,[77] which he terms the 'liberal state thesis'.[78] This thesis claims that, irrespective of economic cycles, the play of interests and shifts in public opinion, immigrants and foreigners have acquired rights. Therefore, the capacity of liberal states to control immigration is constrained by laws and institutions.[79] Moreover, it is possible to explain at least partially why migrants move, and, therefore, to explain the increase in migratory flows in the last three decades, as a consequence of what Hollifield terms 'the rise of the rights-based liberalism'.[80] Migrants are attracted in growing numbers to liberal states because the latter attribute to them civil, political and social rights. This does not mean that rights cannot change, but once extended to foreigners they are difficult to withdraw. This, in the opinion of Hollifield, explains why many liberal states, especially in Europe, are not keen to change their national laws on refugees or migration.

How does the author incorporate rights into his analysis of migration in empirical terms? In two ways: first, by analysing how policy changes impacted on migratory flows; second, by studying how the interventions of the judiciary have limited the capacity of the State to control migration.

However, this perspective cannot be fully categorised within the liberal institutional paradigm, as according to Hollifield these rights do not yet derive from international institutions or regimes, but from the nation state. The reason for this is that no organising principle has emerged yet as the basis for international cooperation to regulate migration.[81] However, according to Hollifield, an organising principle can be identified in the rule of law and orderly movement of peoples. Its implementation would require centralisation of authority to overcome collective action problems; and this, in turn, would require a hegemon or a group of hegemonic states, something which remains unlikely to happen. A more likely strategy would be to adopt suasion, through international issue-linking and log-rolling.[82]

The position of Soysal is more positive. According to this scholar, migrants have already acquired rights not only from the State, but also from the international institutional system. In her analysis, post-national membership, deriving from international human rights standards granted on the basis of universalistic notions of personhood, is the ground on which to root migrants' rights of inclusion. This renders national citizenship almost irrelevant.[83]

Indeed, contemporary citizenship is based on two paradoxes that warrant transcending national definitions:

1. the increasing decoupling of rights and identities, the two main components of citizenship;
2. the tendency to claim particularistic rights in the public domain, which is legitimised by a universalistic conception of personhood.[84]

Soysal's insistence on human rights and universalistic conceptions of personhood makes it possible to classify her approach within the liberal institutionalist tradition. Indeed, her analysis does not ground immigrants' claims and mobilisation on identities or narratives, as constructivists would.

More systemic neo-institutionalist analyses of international migration are few, for the very reason that, until recently, there was little demand for international cooperation (or policy) in the area of migration. International migratory regimes are not being established, and therefore liberal institutionalists lack a dependent variable. It is true that there is now some demand for policies to control, manage or stop migration and refugee flows,[85] but this hardly accounts for the development of an international migratory regime and seems more easily accounted for by neo-realist readings of migration as a security issue. The only notable exception is the European Union and the Schengen system.[86]

Following Soysal, Geddes argues that the 'transnational advocacy' of migrants' rights has acquired a significant degree of institutionalisation at the EU level, thanks to the technocratic and bureaucratic insulation of EU institutions. It is the institutional configuration itself of the European Union, especially the European Commission, the European Court of Justice and the European Parliament that allows for a higher degree of inclusion of pro-migrant lobbying activity, as it disengages it from the national level where similar issues do not enjoy the favours of the electorates. All this happens, and is analysed by Geddes, within the context of the emerging EU common framework for migratory and refugee policy.

According to Thielemann, the increasing 'communitarisation' of migratory and refugee policies responds to the increased attention by EU institutions to human rights, as well as to the spillover effects from previous policies and to considerations of efficiency.[87] However, the substantially economic nature of the European Union project and its institutional setting configure a model of inclusion of migrants' rights that privileges economic rights over social and political ones.[88] Moreover, there remain clear impediments to the full protection of migrants' rights by the EU, as the dominance of the common migratory and refugee policy by the securitisation[89] agenda of the member states clearly demonstrates.[90]

From a liberal institutionalist viewpoint, Guiraudon explains the securitisation of EU home affairs and justice as a consequence of the competition of domestic actors to increase their power and enhance their position at the EU level. The transnationalisation game has favoured law and order officials and agencies; that is, those who are in charge of border controls seeking to gain independence from the national institutional constraints.[91] Her main claim is that bureaucrats sitting in interior ministries and other police agencies 'venue shopped' at the international level to escape domestic adversaries (such as the domestic judicial system) and pursue their own agenda on immigration and refugee policy. This led to the securitisation of the EU common approach to home affairs and justice.[92] A similar focus of the role of security agencies and officials is proposed by Huysmans, albeit in a more neo-constructivist fashion.[93]Also intrinsically constructivist is the analysis proposed by Lavenex.[94] She embeds the antagonism between the 'liberal', human rights approach to migration and the 'security' realist perspective into the realm of how ideas are transmitted to the political system through institutions, following Risse.[95]

Concluding the analysis of how mainstream approaches have dealt with international migration, it is fair to claim that neither neo-realists nor liberal institutionalists are in a position to shed light on the reasons why migration has been on the rise in recent decades. More promising in answering this question appears to be the globalisation thesis, to which we now turn.

3.3 The globalisation thesis: An introduction

The bulk of empirical work in international migration has proceeded from the perspective of globalisation.[96] In Chapter 2, the notion of globalisation will be analysed and defined from a number of different IPE perspectives. In this introductory section, it is important to stress that, although the globalisation arguments vary hugely, all globalisation theorists agree that the sovereignty and regulatory power of the State have been weakened by transnationalism, and that politics has been subordinated to economic forces.[97]

Simply put, the globalisation thesis states that there was a process of economic globalisation at work in the late twentieth century, buttressed by transnational social networks and communities. Globalisation has led to the inevitability of migration and a loss of control of borders, to the point that sovereignty and even citizenship itself may be redundant. In this context, the State loses its centrality in the international system, and migration processes are analysed as a consequence of globalisation.

The globalisation thesis was originally proposed by sociologists,[98] but, as further elaborated below, many IPE scholars from non-mainstream perspectives have put forward interesting hypotheses concerning the impact of globalisation on migratory flows to Western countries. A concrete example of how the globalisation thesis has been developed by sociologists in the direction of a political economy interpretation is provided in Saskia Sassen's early interest in migratory flows[99] from developing countries with high levels of Foreign Direct Investment (FDI), Export Processing Zones (EPZs) and high level of growth of GNP (such as South-East Asia and the Caribbean Basin). The author underlines the existence of an enigma in the increase of migratory flows from those kinds of countries. The enigma is that foreign investment and job creation should have acted as a deterrent rather than an inducement to migration. Why did this not happen? Sassen's answer is that we need to specify the links between the occurrence of rapid export-led industrialisation and emigration. The steps to do so are the following:

First, it is necessary to analyse the characteristics of the new industrial growth in less developed countries, and to place it in the context of these countries' economic organisation. Similar characteristics include the development of a world market for these countries' exports which is related to the creation of EPZs through FDI.

Second, we must study the employment effects of these new patterns of growth: they increase the employment rate. Indeed, export-oriented agriculture requires a large supply of low-wage workers at crucial periods in the production cycle. Export-oriented plants tend to be labour intensive and are mostly concentrated in a given area for reasons related to servicing and transportation. Finally, large agglomerations of firms producing for export generate a range of additional jobs, from packaging to construction and operation of airports and harbours.

Third, it is necessary to see how these labour needs are met. This happens through the mobilisation of large numbers of people into wage labour who were previously outside it – in particular, women, which leads to the feminisation of work.

Fourth, it is important to assess the migration impact of all this: does this imply the creation of a pool of potential migrant workers? The answer for Saskia Sassen is, yes, it does. Precisely because of the significant job-creation effect of export-manufacturing and its concentration in few areas, the extent of the mobilisation of new workers into the labour force has been considerable. In areas where the new industrial zones have been developed on a large scale, extensive mobilisation of women into the labour force can contribute to the disruption of traditional work structures in communities of origin. The disruption of traditional work structures resulting from an extremely high incidence of young female migration has further contributed to increase the pool of unemployed. It has stimulated the departure of men and women who may not have planned to leave.

Finally, it is necessary to examine whether the creation of a potential pool of migrants promotes the emergence of emigration as an option for individuals. This happens through the role of foreign investors who create the image of a better life in a foreign country (particularly the USA).

To conclude, for Saskia Sassen, significant levels and concentrations of foreign investment comprise one, and only one, factor contributing to promoting emigration from less developed countries (LDCs) with high levels of growth and integrated in the world economy through:

1 the incorporation of new segments of the population into wage labour and the associated disruption of traditional work structures. Both these phenomena create a supply of migrant workers;
2 the feminisation of the new industrial workforce and its impact on the work opportunities of men, both in the new industrial zones and in the traditional work structures; and
3 the consolidation of objective and ideological links with the highly industrialised countries where most foreign capital originates, links

> that involve both a generalised Westernisation effect and more specific work situations wherein workers find themselves producing goods for people and firms in the highly industrialised countries.

Although Sassen addresses successfully the issue of the increase of migration from less developed countries to Western industrialised ones, her analysis is limited to those countries which are increasingly involved in the globalisation process and are improving their economic situation. It remains to be explained why emigration has also increased in the last decades in places which are increasingly marginalised from the global economy.

To answer this question, the next chapter engages with the debate in IPE about globalisation and its impact on migration.

Chapter 2

The globalisation thesis within the globalisation debate

1 Introduction

The globalisation thesis is not available in a single, universally accepted version. On the contrary, it is the subject of as many debates as approaches in the social sciences. However, as this contribution to the debates addresses the issue of the impact of globalisation on migration from the IPE perspective, the author feels safe enough in reporting only the discussions pertaining to this branch of the academic world.

Before proceeding to the consequences of globalisation for migration, it is important to define what globalisation is from the different IPE perspectives, and to examine what the implications are of the different definitions of the concept on the capacity of the nation state to produce relevant policy-making.

2 A qualitative definition of globalisation

Anthony Giddens, in a lecture entitled 'Globalisation: The state of the debate',[1] referred to the existence of three phases in the development of the globalisation debate. The first phase witnessed the debate between those who believed in the existence of globalisation (so-called 'globalists') and those who did not believe in it ('sceptics'). In the second phase, everyone acknowledged the peculiar characteristics of the phenomenon of globalisation, and the debate moved into the streets, where political activists, commonly referred to as anti-globalists, violently opposed the spread of globalisation, mainly identified with the economic neo-liberalism and political imperialism. In the third phase, the current one, even the anti-globalist discourse has been overcome by a general acceptance of the inevitability of globalisation, and the debate revolves around how to make globalisation also work for the poor. In a few words, the debate moved from the questions: 'Does globalisation exist?' and: 'Is globalisation good?', to: 'How should globalisation be governed?'

Giddens's characterisation is interesting, but is itself globalist within an institutionalist perspective. In fact, there is still no consensus on what globalisation is, nor on whether it is a completely original phenomenon, neither among the different disciplines in social sciences nor, more specifically, among the different approaches in IPE.

Limiting the analysis to IPE perspectives, it is possible to classify the positions adopted by scholars on the subject into three broad groups:[2] those who deny the existence of the phenomenon of globalisation;[3] those who admit it yet tend to provide only a quantitative definition;[4] and those who adopt a qualitative definition.[5]

The school of thought denying globalisation rests on considerations about the historical recurrence of periods of increased international and cross-border interactions. In reality, those who adopt a similar perspective deny the 'originality' of globalisation and its characterisation as a 'new phenomenon'. Sometimes, they may go so far as to deny any 'global', 'globalised' or 'globalising' nature to the current phase of the world economy development. It seems, however, that whether you multiply the number of 'globalisations' taking place in the course of history or even deny its occurrence in the present historical moment, the question of how to define 'globalisation' remains unsolved. Ultimately, the terms of the debate rest on the dichotomy between the 'quantitative' and the 'qualitative' definitions of the phenomenon.

It might even be suggested that the denial of globalisation stems from the failure to identify the distinctive characteristics of the current phase of capitalist development by adopting a quantitative definition of the phenomenon. Indeed, from the quantitative point of view, globalisation is defined as: 'The intensification of economic, political, social, and cultural relations across borders'.[6] However, this definition leaves a number of issues unresolved: on the one hand, the means by which to measure the degree of economic, social and cultural relations across the border, as well as their intensification. On the other hand, it leaves unclear the kinds of relationships existing between the economic, social and political aspects of globalisation; indeed, it does not even specify whether there is any relationship at all. Moreover, by accounting for the phenomenon of globalisation only in quantitative terms, one can hardly succeed in grasping its causes and consequences. This makes it extremely difficult to relate it to other phenomena, such as mass migration from less developed countries. It is therefore necessary to deepen the perspective by adopting a qualitative definition of globalisation.

From the qualitative point of view, globalisation is defined as a process comprising a number of qualitative transformations, which in turn characterise the current phase of capitalist development. In this context, globalisation is identified as a qualitatively new phenomenon, comprising a number of components all of which converge to define globalisation as a process or, as Mittleman suggests, a 'syndrome'.[7] Moreover, these components tend to spill over into each other, without any predetermined single cause/effect relation but in a dialectical way, which makes it possible to identify the direction of the change, if not to react accordingly. The components included in such a qualitative definition of globalisation are represented by: technological transformation; financial transformation; geographical reallocation of production; the process of commodification; the polarisation of wealth; the subordination of politics to economics and the related decline of the nation state; and the emergence of a new global division of labour.[8]

The globalisation thesis on international migration assumes that the State has lost the possibility to control and halt contemporary migratory flows, which are the inevitable consequence of the globalisation process. It is therefore worth analysing the role of the State within globalisation according to the different perspectives in IPE.

2.1 Globalisation and the State

2.1.1 Realist approaches: The globalisation myth and the centrality of the State

Realist understandings of globalisation are characterised by a very sceptical attitude towards the very existence of the phenomenon itself, its relevance for the IPE, or its definition as a new historical phase.[9] The concept of globalisation is, from this point of view, grossly overstated by those who use it either to demonise it as the mother of all evils, or to emphasise it as the panacea of all problems. It is a convenient myth in the hands of politicians or public opinion-makers. In reality, globalisation barely exists, and even where it is possible to identify some new trends in the international political economy, those may be easily explained by making reference to the nation state and the national dimension.[10]

As already made explicit above, this conception relies on a quantitative definition of globalisation, which tends to 'quantify' the extent of globalisation by identifying measures for all the phenomena that are normally included within its scope. This means that, first, it is necessary to define the ideal typical notion of globalisation, identifying all its elements and the modalities by which to measure them. Then, to be able to make a comparison, we must refer to another ideal type: a world economy without globalisation. This also requires the listing of all the components of such a world economy, as well as their measures. Finally, empirical testing is carried out by producing data on the state of the real economy to show whether this is closer to the ideal type of a globalised economy or to that of a non-globalised economy.

This approach is used, for example, by Gilpin, to demonstrate that the relevance of economic globalisation is much overstated, and that the core of the world economy is still the nation state, although now its interests are better served within integrated regional economic areas. First, Gilpin defines globalisation as the increase of integration of the world economy resulting from major changes in trade flows, from the activities of multinational corporations and from developments in international finance.[11] Then, the author demonstrates that this increase has been '... highly uneven, restricted to particular economic sectors and not nearly as extensive as many believe'.[12] In fact, according to Gilpin, the level of economic integration was significantly higher during the gold standard. Even in the late nineteenth century, trade investment and financial flows were greater than they are now, if measured in relative terms. Moreover, although in absolute terms these flows are larger and faster in the twenty-first century, they are confined within the borders of regional economic blocks, dominated by powerful nation states. Even the globalisation of financial markets is limited to short-term and speculative investment. Finally, the most important measure of economic integration and interdependence of different economies, the so-called 'law of one price', according to which economies are perfectly integrated if identical goods and services have the same or nearly equal prices, is not respected around the world.[13]

Furthermore, according to Hirst and Thompson,[14] globalisation is more a myth than anything else. Globalisation does not exist, not even as the 'end' of an ongoing process. On the other hand, regionalisation is increasing, but as a consequence of the desire of the larger and more powerful states to maximise their power. Similar conclusions are reached by contrasting the notion of a 'globalised world economy' with that of an 'internationalised world economy'.[15] An internationalised world economy is, to quote the authors, 'One in which the principal entities remain national economies, or agents that continue to be primarily located in a definite national territory'.[16]

The main characteristics of internationalisation therefore comprise the following:

- national economies remain the principal entities;
- agents continue to be located primarily in a definite national territory;
- there is a clear separation between the national and the international arena;
- there is a quantitative increase in the relation between states.

Consequently, the main actors of an internationalised world economy are multinational companies (MNCs) located in nation states and relying on the national economy as their primary source of earnings, personnel and policy-making.

On the other hand, there is the ideal type of a 'globalised world economy', which is defined as:

> An economy that exists 'above' the national economies and agents, autonomously from those national economies, and that bears down upon those economies and actors .... This would be an economy that escapes 'governance', one typified by unorganised and uncontrollable market forces.[17]

Its main components would therefore be the following:

- economic relations are dis-embedded from the nation states;
- the global economy exists above national economies;
- the global economy is autonomous from national economies and actors;
- the global economy escapes governance;
- the global economy is typified by unorganised and uncontrollable market forces.

In this case, the main actors are transnational corporations (TNCs), actors which are disembodied from any nation state, and would produce and sell genuinely internationally.

Having identified the main components of the two ideal types of world economy to be contrasted, the authors then move to their measurement.[18] The first measure of an integrated global economy is the stock of foreign-owned productive activity. The data proposed by Thompson and Hirst show that the stock of the inward foreign direct investment (FDI) as a percentage of GDP worldwide in 1995 was only 10.1. This, although more than double the 1980 total, does not seem to the authors to be such a dramatic figure as to justify the claim of the death of national economy. In any case, FDI accounts only for what a multinational company is lending to the affiliated company abroad, and not what they are, at the same time, investing in their home country. Therefore, a second measure of the degree of globalisation of the world economy is provided by the assessment of the level of home investment of multinational companies.[19] The main conclusion of this analysis is that multinational companies remain significantly 'home-orientated' in their investment activity, although some of this activity is regionally centred. According to Hirst and Thompson, the data show that between two-thirds and three-quarters of MNCs' aggregate business activity remained home- or regionally centred during the 1990s.[20] These results allow the authors to conclude, 'International companies are still predominantly MNCs, with a clear home base to their operations, and not transnational companies (TNCs), which represent footloose, stateless companies'.[21] A third indicator of the degree of globalisation of the world economy is supplied by the extent of internationalisation in relation to overall national output, measured by the gross product of foreign affiliates as a percentage of national or regional GDP. For developed countries, this increased only from 5.1 per cent in 1982 to 5.4 per cent in 1994, from 6 per cent to 9.1 per cent in developing countries, and from 5.2 per cent to 6 per cent for the world total overall.[22]

Similar conclusions can be reached by analysing the degree of global integration of financial markets, starting from the assumption that the degree of financial integration between different countries relies upon the relationship between national savings and national investments. Indeed, in a completely integrated global financial system, domestic investment would not be fundamentally constrained by domestic savings, and the correlation between investment and savings would disappear.[23]

Therefore, a first measure of the degree of financial globalisation is the correlation (r^2) between savings and investments, which, however, has not declined unambiguously in recent times. A second measure of the importance of domestic resources for domestic investment is the share of inward FDI flows in Gross Domestic Capital Formation (GDCF) for different economies. In this case, the figures also demonstrate the relative unimportance of FDI flows in their contribution to domestic investment.

Another way to look at the globalisation of financial markets is to underline the extent to which financial markets are controllable by national governments. On this subject, the debate is open, but realists remind us that financial markets consist mainly of financial institutions that have a clear national location and are embedded in a national legal framework. Moreover, they raise their assets in national markets and have to use their earnings to meet their obligations to depositors, pensioners and life policy holders. Finally, they must abide by national macroeconomic policy-making, use nationally or regionally defined interest rates, and respect nationally subscribed agreements on the exchange rates.[24] To summarise, financial institutions are embedded in national, political, legal and economic constraints, and therefore are not completely uncontrollable. Hence, the only way to achieve a higher degree of regulation and stabilisation of financial markets lies in major states' willingness to cooperate in order to impose common rules on the system. This is certainly a typical realist recipe.

To conclude, by using figures, realists prove that the 'globalised economy' is a myth, and the fact that the world economy remains sufficiently concentrated in the key national states allows for realist solutions to international problems to be effective. There is, however, a clear trend towards 'regionalisation'. Regionalisation is happening both 'de jure', with the creation of formal regional free trade arrangements, and 'de facto', with the construction of regional economic blocs which do not necessarily coincide with their formal definition.

Focusing on firms' decisions about where to trade and invest, figures show that the 'triad' of the USA, the EU and Japan tends to direct its FDI flows and stock towards a fixed cluster of countries, to form three clearly distinguishable blocs of countries. These country groupings tend to be regionally specific and adjacent to one or the other of the triad members. From the realist perspective, however, regionalisation is simply the demonstration of the economic strength of the larger states, which are able to dominate a number of smaller states within a defined regional area. It does not entail a step towards globalisation; rather, the direction of FDI relationships is first between the triad countries and then between the dominant country and its cluster, but not between the countries within the cluster.[25]

2.1.2 Neo-institutionalist approaches: The transformation of the nation state in the global economy

Whereas the realist perspective may be classified among the 'sceptical' approaches to globalisation, neo-institutionalists are on the opposite side of the spectrum, and have been included in the group of the so-called 'globalists'.[26] Indeed, if for the sceptics globalisation is at best a useful 'myth' which can be used to justify the persistent hegemony of the most powerful nation states, for institutionalists there is no possibility of denying the existence of globalisation or of juxtaposing it with previous historical waves of market integration. It is worth reiterating, however, that despite the fact that neo-institutionalists have been classified among the globalists given their acceptance of the notion of globalisation, in terms of international migration they do not subscribe to the globalisation thesis: as discussed in Chapter 1, this thesis states that the nation state is unable to intervene to stop this new wave of migration as this is the inevitable consequence of globalisation.

To a great extent, realist and neo-institutionalist approaches converge in considering the State still at the centre of the international system. In relation to the globalisation debate, the two mainstream schools proceed from the same definition of globalisation although they reach opposite conclusions. In particular, neo-institutionalists recognise that the process of transnationalisation of the world economy is well advanced, and that this produces a number of transformations both at the national level of governance and at the level of the international system, completely modifying the terms of reference of previously well-established institutional solutions.

However, the definition of globalisation offered by this group of scholars is, again, mainly quantitative. Globalisation is, for Keohane, the intensification of transnational as well as interstate relations;[27] according to David Held, globalisation '... suggests a growing magnitude or intensity of global flows such that states and societies become increasingly enmeshed in worldwide systems and networks of interaction';[28] while for Phil Cerny, globalisation occurs in the interaction between denser economic relations among the states (internationalisation) and denser relations cutting across states (transnationalisation).[29]

Contrary to the sceptics, the evidence produced to substantiate this definition by this group of scholars justifies the emergence of a new phase in the development of the world economy, a phase characterised by the increase in the economic interaction between states as well as by the increase of economic activities which overcome national boundaries to acquire a new dimension lying above the states. This makes it necessary to adopt new forms of governance, which transcend the nation states. Indeed, the global economy appears as a web of interconnected or, better, interdependent activities performed at different institutional levels by actors who are increasingly detached from the national level of governance. Where does this leave the nation state?

Of course, the nation state does not disappear from the picture of the global economy, nor, however, does it remain untouched by the wave of transformations enshrined in this notion of globalisation. The nation state survives, but it undergoes a substantial change, which modifies its role, its position in the international system and even its functions. In particular, the transformation of the State takes place in the following two dimensions:

1. There is a different perception of the role of the State in the economy and of the notion of 'public goods'.
2. There is a re-orientation of how states interact economically with each other, which creates interdependences and international linkages.[30]

As regards the first dimension, given the complex and multi-layered institutional framework which is the consequence of the denser international/ transnational interactions and their relations, it becomes harder to identify which institution should provide which public good; additionally, it becomes harder to define the notion of public good as such.

Taking the four main categories of public goods (regulatory, productive, distributive and re-distributive) one by one, it is possible to identify the effect of globalisation on their provision and to reconsider the overall role of the nation state.[31]

Regulatory public goods are defined as those goods relating to the establishment and application of rules for the operation and interactions of both market and non-market institutions. With the advent of globalisation, the ability of firms, market actors and competing parts of the nation-state apparatus to defend and expand their economic and political reach through activities such as transnational policy networking and regulatory arbitrage has both undermined the control span of the State from without and fragmented it from within.[32] This leads to the necessity of devising new institutional frameworks at the supranational level capable of providing regulatory public goods, which can be enforced outside and above the level of the nation states. Briefly, it enhances the role and functions of international institutions, including international law,[33] and increases the constraints those can impose on the states.

As far as productive and distributive public goods are concerned, the former are defined as the production of goods and services by the State for economies of scale or normative reasons (e.g. production of energy), while the latter are defined as the delivery of goods and services by the State given the collective nature of consumers (e.g. transport). In the case of productive public goods, the increased dimension and relevance of multinational companies brought about the possibility of exploiting private economies of scale, thus eliminating the necessity for the State to provide them. In the case of distributive public goods, it is the individualisation of the consumers through the process of commodification that results in the loss of the raison d'être of the state provision.

Finally, in the case of re-distributive public goods, which are those provided on the basis of a political rationale (e.g. welfare), the impact of globalisation has been dramatic. The power of trade unions as well as the effectiveness of corporatist bargaining has weakened. This was a consequence of international pressures for wage restraint and flexible working practices, and caused a substantial reduction of welfare expenditure.

The new model of state intervention into the economy is no longer the welfare state, but what scholars have termed the 'competition state'.[34] This is a state able to provide a dynamic 'competitive' advantage in the international economy (as opposed to the static notion of 'comparative' advantage), promoting a favourable investment climate to transnational economic actors through the provision of public goods defined as 'immobile factors of capital', such as, for example, human capital, infrastructure, support for new technologies, protection of the environment or maintenance of the standards of life for the middle classes.[35]

The transformation of the State from the domestic-oriented welfare state to the externally orientated 'competition state' leads to the second dimension of the change in the position of the State as a consequence of globalisation: the reorientation in the way it interacts with the international arena and with the other states. The State changes its international role, shifting its priorities from defence and security to business. The 'competition state', both in the developed and in the less developed world, attracts business by:

- shifting its public policy-making from the macro- to the micro-level: e.g. reduction of labour costs;
- pursuing a 'dynamic competitive' advantage and thus rendering its structure more flexible;
- keeping inflation low and the economy stable to attract foreign investment (neo-liberal macroeconomic policies);
- promoting enterprise innovation and profitability at the private and public level.[36]

To sum up, the whole discourse of globalisation is taking place within the not yet well-defined institutional terrains of the competition state and a fragmented international regime whose institutions are still in the making. Of course, the process described so far is an ongoing one, and the end-result is not yet comprehensible. Indeed, the kind of scenario that will prevail at the end of this overall transformation depends on a number of unforecastable factors, including which actors would take the lead in the process.

Regarding this, institutionalists recognise a crucial role as agents of change to political institutions and political agents who act like intermediaries between the international, the transnational and the domestic level in a game which is not simply 'two-level' but multi-level. Indeed, the competition state adds further layers and divisions to the world economy, which increases the complexity and density of network of interdependence and interpenetration. In this context, the process of regionalisation is not interpreted as a barrier to globalisation, but as a moment of this process, institutionalising at the regional level new forms of trans-boundary and supranational governance, which are by no means inconsistent with the institutionalisation of a new international regime.[37]

2.1.3 Transnationalist approaches: The subordination of politics to economics

The transnationalist approach differs from the ones analysed so far because of the emphasis placed on the definition of globalisation as a structural phenomenon, comprising a number of qualitative transformations which define the current phase of capitalist development.[38] In contrast to quantitative definitions of globalisation, this qualitative definition does not need to measure the phenomena included in the process of globalisation, since it is the mere existence of a series of intertwined structural events that defines the 'ontology' of globalisation.

According to Peter Dicken, '[g]lobalisation processes are qualitatively different from internationalisation processes. They involve not merely the geographical extension of economic activity across national boundaries but also, more importantly, the functional integration of such internationally dispersed activities'.[39] For James Mittleman, globalisation is a 'syndrome',[40] composed by a number of events which acquire their meaning by their relation with each other and by their coexistence in a specific historical moment. However, these events are not randomly connected. Their relation is defined within a precise framework, which allows transnationalists to overcome the accusation of 'vagueness' in their definition of the notion of globalisation, often made against them by more mainstream scholars.[41]

Technological transformation is an exogenous component of the qualitative definition of globalisation, and it is the factor which brings about transformation in the financial and productive spheres.[42] This, in turn, triggers related changes in the economic, social and political contexts.

Technological transformation is at the roots of the exceptional developments of financial markets producing what is normally defined as financial globalisation, i.e. the existence of round-the-clock access to financial transactions all over the world. However, this does not mean that the physical location of financial markets loses significance or that financial elites become disentangled from national boundaries. On the contrary, their role and their bargaining power inside the national polity increases as their economic position improves, leading to a shift in the power relations between the different socio-economic groups, whose relevance can hardly be overestimated.[43]

Technological transformation is also the driving force behind the process of transformation of global production and the related global reallocation of production along the lines of the dramatic increase of foreign direct investment and mergers and acquisitions, and the creation of export processing zones. Indeed, the possibility of multinational companies modifying their productive structure to exploit geographically displaced cost-reduction opportunities is greatly improved by the availability of technological progress, allowing for cheap transport costs, distant labour control or economies of scale in specific locations. This restructuring and geographical reallocation of production, in turn, coupled with financial globalisation, spills over into a number of social and political changes affecting all levels of organisation, from local to global.[44]

Among the social consequences of the processes so far described, there is the so-called phenomenon of 'commodification', defined as the inclusion in the market sphere of relations previously left outside its boundaries and regulated by other rules.[45] This certainly happens in the Western industrialised world, where the number of activities submitted to the market rules of supply, demand and price tend to increase and include also those spheres of life previously left outside, such as, for example, the organisation of leisure time. However, the tendency of multinational companies to move abroad, mainly to less developed countries to take advantage of both lower production costs and market opportunities, brings about the expansion of the phenomenon of 'commodification' to cultural enclaves where the market was traditionally a recessive form of organisation of economic relations, with all that means in terms of cultural clashes and related social and political consequences.[46]

Moreover, the process of globalisation, as defined so far, is not neutral in social and wealth terms, but entails new social divisions and challenges, as well as new winners and new losers. Given the innovative nature of the technological tools necessary to grasp the opportunities of globalisation, there is a need for continuous updating of skills and re-qualification. This poses the problem of the polarisation of wealth in both social and geographical terms. Those who are already able to access the educational and vocational systems, and have the economic possibility of remaining in education for longer, if not forever (the so-called 'knowledge society'), will be by far better placed in the global economy. On the contrary, the lower strata of society, as well as the weakest ones, such as the elders or the women, and finally, those living in less developed countries, will be increasingly marginalised by the fast-moving world of new skills necessary to keep pace with globalisation.[47] It follows that the social and geographical wealth gap is doomed to increase, leading to the paradox of 'marginalisation within globalisation'. This is particularly true in the case of the Arab world, where technological integration has been very weak in the previous two decades.[48]

In political terms, the overcoming of national boundaries for the exploitation of global financial and productive opportunities modifies the existing balance of power between national political institutions and an increasingly globalised economic elite. The latter is placed by globalisation in a position to exert credible pressures at the domestic political level by threatening to move its economic activity abroad in exchange for favourable economic policy measures. The credibility of the threat, in turn, is ensured by the possibility of easily moving short- to medium-term capital across the border, as well as displacing production and long-term investment.[49] Whether this leads to a de facto disempowerment of national politics vis-à-vis globalising capital, or if there is still a margin for reaction by national political actors, is still the subject of many debates in both academic and political circles.[50] For some authors,[51] indeed, there is the possibility of the activation of a 'double-movement', Polanyi-style, according to which, after a phase of triumph of liberalism and of subordination of politics to economics, those who are most affected by these developments will react with a counter-movement, and a new social equilibrium will be established that guarantees a new say for the former losers.

The last consideration leads to a further component of the qualitative definition of globalisation. Certainly, globalisation not only produces the conditions for the creation of a transnational capitalist elite, but also creates the premise for the transnationalisation of the working class through the restructuring of the international division of labour and the establishment of a new global division of labour.[52] This might represent the basis for a future reproduction of the class struggle at the transnational level, although, of course, there can be no certainty about the final outcome of this process. How the new global division of labour, which is one of the structural components of globalisation from the transnationalist viewpoint, has impacted on mass migration will be dealt with in the next section.

3 The new global division of labour and the increase of mass migration

As noted above, in the transnationalist perspective of globalisation, technological change represents the engine of a process of transformation, which interests both the productive and the financial structure. Leaving aside the latter, what is particularly relevant to frame the analysis of migratory flows is the geographical reallocation of production. This takes place through the creation of Export Processing Zones in developing countries, through a policy of mergers and acquisitions or through straightforward FDI.[53] As a consequence of production restructuring, the labour structure changes with a substantial reallocation of labour-intensive production in Third World countries. However, this outcome is compounded by the opposite effects of technological development in terms of the increase of distant work, and of the increase of labour mobility, including mass migration and brain drain.

On the one hand, production tends to move to some specialised regions of the globe,[54] where it is possible to exploit the advantages of lower production costs in the form of both lower labour costs and/or lower cost of primary resources. This phenomenon gives rise to the paradox of regionalisation within globalisation, characterised by the creation of economically integrated regions.[55] This further increases the marginalisation of those zones of the globe which are not interested, for reasons too long to analyse here, in the process of geographical displacement of production or by the globalisation of financial markets.[56] On the other hand, however, the populations of those marginalised zones of the globe, whose economic conditions are likely to worsen as a consequence of the process of globalisation, experience an increased incentive to leave their home countries and move to the more developed regions of the world looking for better standards of life. This produces the two interrelated phenomena of the 'brain drain', when skilled or highly educated labour flees the country of origin, and 'mass migration', when unskilled labour migrates.

The ensemble of the above-described dynamics leads to a new global division of labour whose main characteristics comprise the geographical displacement of production alongside regional patterns and the increased use of Third World cheaper labour, and the increase of brain drain and mass migration from the regions left behind by the process of regionalisation within globalisation. One of the outcomes of this new division of labour is an overall decrease of production costs in both Third World and industrialised countries. Indeed, this process not only brings about lower production costs through the reallocation of production abroad or the hiring of immigrants, particularly illegal ones, but it also lowers the cost of domestic labour by putting pressure on organised labour and reducing its bargaining power.[57]

Moreover, mass migration, both legal and illegal, acquires regional patterns, due to historical, geographic, social or cultural reasons. All responses to mass migration, therefore, take the form of regional policies, such as the US or the EU immigration policy. Here, a fundamental paradox arises. The paradox is between the advantages of immigration in terms of reduction of production costs and contribution to the sustainability of the welfare state (particularly given the ageing problem in the more developed world), and the implementation of stricter migration policies at the regional level.[58]

In Europe, for example the ensemble of public policy responses to mass migration both at the national[59] and at the community level has fuelled the debate over the creation of 'Fortress Europe'.[60] The consequences of the adoption of a generally tight approach towards migration from third countries have been an increase of irregular migration and the progressive 'securitisation' of migration.[61] Of course, the main reasons for the adoption of similar responses to mass migration are the traditional concerns over political unrest, social conflict, cultural clashes or religious struggles. This became particularly relevant in the aftermath of the September 11 attacks on the World Trade Center in New York, which sparked a wave not only of securitisation of migration, particularly from Muslim countries, but also of straightforward 'Islamophobia'.[62] However, a further aspect of the issue is represented by the political economy consequences of 'illegal' (as opposed to legal) migration, in terms of cost reduction and decrease of bargaining power of organised labour. There certainly seems to be some evidence that the use of illegal migrant work reduces the wages of legal work and, consequently, the power of organised labour. For example, in Germany, studies have shown that a 1 per cent increase in the share of less-skilled foreign workers in the labour force leads to a 5.9 per cent fall in the wages of blue-collar workers and a 3.5 per cent increase in white-collar wages.[63] In this context, it would be interesting to carry out further investigation of the economic sectors involved in the use and exploitation of illegal immigration and to assess the political economy consequences of similar practices in terms of power shifts between different socio-economic actors.[64]

Moreover, in analysing the dichotomy between legal immigration and illegal immigration, we find that the second is more favourable to the neo-liberal order than the first, because it allows for the internal labour market to be made more flexible, while legal immigrants should be integrated in the existing welfare state provisions system. As Saskia Sassen writes, 'Indeed, those who deal with the real political economy of the city already know this: the rhetoric of the law-and-order Republican mayor here in New York City is surprisingly friendly to illegal immigrants'.[65]

To sum up, the political economy consequences of the increase of mass migration in the context of globalisation are:

- more precarious working conditions in both developed and less developed countries;
- an increase of the power of transnational companies at the international level;
- the reaction of the governments through the constitution of regional governance schemes, such as the EU, where the labour/capital dynamics are reproduced but with a strong reduction of power on the labour side.[66]

4 Conclusion

From the theoretical point of view, the following issues appear particularly relevant:

- the paradox of regionalisation within globalisation and its consequences in terms of the increase of intraregional temporary migration;
- the paradox of marginalisation within globalisation and its consequences in terms of the increase of brain drain and mass migration from marginalised countries;
- the paradox of 'Fortress Europe' and its consequences in terms of illegal migration.

These paradoxes impact on the decision of people to migrate, and on their modalities and motivations for migration.

Egypt is considered here as a paradigmatic case of marginalisation within globalisation, and the MENA area as a clear example of lack of regionalisation, in line with the relevant literature.[67] In the remainder of the book, therefore, we shall look at Egyptian migration so as to verify that:

- Egyptian migration is a consequence of globalisation and therefore is a rather new phenomenon. This will be shown by first looking at the history of Egyptian migration (Chapter 4) and then at the profile of the Egyptian migrant both in theory and in practice (Chapter 7);
- Egypt has been progressively marginalised from the process of globalisation (Chapter 6). This can be demonstrated by exploring the main economic indicators of globalisation:

  1. The level of FDI stock and flows;
  2. The amount of mergers and acquisitions;
  3. The openness of the economy and the production for export.

- The MENA area is not integrated from the economic as well as the political point of view. Economic indicators are analysed here in parallel with the account of the failure to create of an integrated MENA area (Chapter 5).

Before moving to the analysis of the case study of Egypt, however, it is worth deepening our understanding of the concept of 'Fortress Europe', its origins and its relation to the process of European integration and to the issue of securitisation. This will help us in contextualising the debate on illegal migration within the constraints determined by the adoption of strict migratory policies by the EU member states both at the European and at the national level.

Chapter 3

'Fortress Europe'

1 Introduction

In Europe, despite the fact that the implementation of a common migratory policy is still far from being achieved, the outlook of public policy responses to migration from third country nationals (TCNs) has accredited the idea of the creation of the so-called 'Fortress Europe', i.e. an area where internal mobility is promoted while barriers are erected vis-à-vis countries outside the EU.[1] The origins of 'Fortress Europe' have been traced back by scholars to Council Regulation 1612/68, which distinguished between the right to free movement of nationals of Member States and the right to free movement of nationals of third countries.[2] The establishment of freedom of movement only for EU citizens has exacerbated this divide. This was initiated by the Single European Act in 1986 and brought forward by the 'EU citizenship' provisions of the Maastricht Treaty in 1992. Third country nationals' rights of access to the EU were, on the other hand, progressively but steadily restricted. The consequences of the adoption of this extremely tight approach to migration from Third Countries, at both the EU and national level,[3] have been an increase of irregular migration and the progressive 'securitisation' of migration. By 'securitisation', the experts mean the development of migration into a 'security issue', which has to be managed by security agencies such as, for example, Europol.[4]

The chapter will review the developments leading to the creation of Fortress Europe and it will identify the migratory regimes existing within the EU before and after the Amsterdam Treaty. In the conclusion the chapter will give some insights about the explanations proposed to the securitisation of migratory policy.

2 The evolution of 'Fortress Europe'

Scholars of EU integration point out how the process of the Europeanisation of migratory policy is highly correlated with the consensus on the need to adopt more restrictive measures against migration from Third Countries and with a new vision of migration as a security threat.[5] Europeanisation coincided with the creation of 'Fortress Europe' at both the national and the European level. Here is clearly not the place to analyse the development of the migratory policies of all the EU Member states. It is however worth noting that until the 1980s, migration had not been considered a matter to worry about, a security issue, or even a question requiring any special restrictive measure. Equally, until the 1980s, the debate over the adoption of a common European approach to migratory policy had not progressed much.[6]

In the course of the 1950s and 1960s migratory flows from one European country to another were very common, especially from Southern European countries (then mainly countries of emigration) to Northern European ones. These flows were considered by receiving countries merely as a way to obtain more workers in times of need and were therefore often favoured by national legislation.[7] Even the question of the illegal entry of migrants was not particularly controversial. In some European countries, like France, migrants were recruited on site in the original countries and did not need to be regularised in the destination country.[8] Restrictive migratory policies started being adopted by European states in the 1960s and 1970s.[9]

They were mainly related to the need to protect the national labour markets in a period of rising unemployment and economic crisis.[10] Contextually, migratory issues started acquiring relevance at the European level, although still at an embryonic level. Scholars indeed distinguish three phases in the development of a common approach to migratory policy by EU Member States.[11] The first phase covers the period from 1957 to 1974, the second 1974 to 1985, and the third 1985 to 1992.

As already noted, not much was going on in terms of communitarisation of migratory policy in the first phase. Treaty provisions were linking the free movement of people within the EEC to the creation of the internal market (art. 3(1)(c) European Community Treaty (TEC)). Articles 39 to 55 of the TEC established this right only for economic actors (as workers, self-employed persons and providers of services) who were nationals of an EEC country. The regulation of migration of third country nationals remained firmly in the hands of nation states.[12] However, there is some consensus in the literature that 'Fortress Europe' was born in this period.[13] As Ugur puts it: 'Fortress Europe has been with us since 1968 when intra-EU freedom of movement was established by regulation 1612/68'.[14] This distinguished for the first time between the right of free movement of nationals of Member States and the right of free movement of nationals from third countries.

The discrimination between nationals of EEC Member States and those of third countries was confirmed at the Paris summit of 1973. The Paris summit represents a turning point in the evolution of a common EEC approach to migration. On this occasion, the issue of migrant workers from third countries was addressed at the European Community level for the first time.[15] According to Stetter, the creation of Fortress Europe played an important role in this decision by Member States to discuss migratory policy around the same table. One of the reasons he quotes to explain why this happened is that, as the measures ensuring free circulation of member state nationals had already been implemented by 1974, and there were already talks relating to the complete abolition of border controls, this created the need to tackle in a common and restrictive way the question of third country nationals.[16]

Indeed, the second phase of evolution of Fortress Europe is characterised by the fact that although the competence for migratory policy remained largely with the nation states, the creation of the internal market created externalities that demanded some form of co-operation on migratory policies, especially border controls, always strictly at the intergovernmental level.

It was during this period (from 1975) that the first intergovernmental working group on migration, the so called TREVI group, started meeting. It was assigned, right from the start, functions relating to control of borders and security. Its role was to enhance cooperation between law-enforcement agencies in the area of internal security, particularly the fight against terrorism. Its mandate was extended in 1985 to include illegal immigration and organised crime.[17]

However, the institutionalisation of Fortress Europe takes place in the course of the third phase of the evolution of the European migratory policy, between 1985 and 1992.

With the creation of the Single Market and the abolition of internal border control, the question of migrants from countries outside the EC became pressing. In March 1985 the European Commission adopted a communication to the Council on 'Guidelines for a Community Policy on Migration'.[18] The purpose of this Communication was: (1) to update the Commission's existing policy on migrant workers and their families;[19] and (2) to re-launch at the level of the Council and the Parliament a discussion on how best to make progress in this area, especially in view of the fact that the economic and social situation was very different from that of 1974 (when the Commission initiated its original programme).[20] The new economic and social situation faced by the Community was characterised by high unemployment affecting all disadvantaged groups, including migrants, and uncertainty as to the future possibilities of job creation. These circumstances tended to produce an increase in discrimination, racism and xenophobia, aimed at sectors of the migrant population.

This new economic climate led Member States to adopt policies limiting further immigration from third countries and there were attempts to implement measures aimed at voluntary return to the countries of origin. The Commission lamented that these policies had not been coordinated between the Member States, and that a common position had not been developed.[21] In this Communication, the Commission described the situation of the approximately 12 million migrant population within the existing Community, outlined the various sectors to which attention should be given, and pointed to the need for consultation between the Member States and the Commission on migration policies vis-à-vis third countries.[22]

The Communication suggested three areas in which progress could be made:

- community law and related action as regards migrants who are citizens of Member States;
- consultation between Member States and the Commission on national policies, particularly as regards Third Country migrants;
- information for the population of host countries and for migrants.

The Communication was intended to re-open the debate on migration policy and the Commission hoped that all the interested parties (Council, Parliament and migrant groups) would contribute in a positive fashion to the search for solutions to the many problems which the Community faced in this area.[23]

Another important event in this period was the establishment of the intergovernmental *ad hoc* Working Group on Immigration by the Council in 1986. For the first time a supranational body, the Commission, was invited to take part to the meeting of a working group on migratory issues as an observer.

However until 1992 achievements in terms of devising a supranational European migration policy were limited.[24] Fortress Europe, on the other hand, progressed significantly thanks to the establishment of two intergovernmental arrangements: the Schengen Agreement of 1985 for migratory policy and the Dublin Convention of 1990 for asylum and refugees policy, although both entered into force much later on, the Schengen Agreement in 1995 (10 years later) and the Dublin Convention in 1997.[25]

In institutional terms, the Schengen Agreement and the Dublin Convention provided for:

- the creation of external frontiers;
- common rules on carrier liability and punishment of those engaged in illegal migration;
- a system of 'One State Checks' for asylum seekers with the Dublin Convention;
- an Executive Committee to monitor and harmonise policies on 'external frontiers';
- a database on illegal or undesirable migrants (Schengen Information System).[26]

The idea that these two agreements have buttressed the creation of 'Fortress Europe' is widespread in the literature.[27] For example, the 1990 Convention applying the Schengen Agreement of 14 June 1985 directly connects immigration and asylum with terrorism, transnational crime and border control.[28] In general, the Schengen Agreement inserts the regulation of migration within an institutional framework that is devoted to the protection of internal security from external threats.[29]

Signed on the same day as the Commission approved its White Paper on completing the internal market (14 June 1985) by five Member States (Belgium, Germany, France, Luxembourg and the Netherlands), the Schengen Agreement provided for the gradual abolition of checks at their common borders. Indeed, the preamble to the Agreement already contained the commitment by the Member States involved to eliminate all internal border checks at the Community level.[30]

More specifically, according to article 30 of the agreement, the countries signing the Schengen Agreement wished to abolish completely, 'if possible, by 1 January 1990'[31] all checks on both individuals and goods at their common borders. Moreover, the Agreement provided for measures to facilitate checks which were to be applied as from its entry into force. However, it also listed a number of accompanying measures designed to keep the level of security of the new frontier-free area as high as possible.[32] These measures had to be implemented before the opening up of the internal borders.[33]

That this policy responded fully to the attitude of the EU institutions towards migration from third countries is demonstrated by the fact that this list mirrored the programme set out in the Commission's White Paper. According to this, the set of accompanying measures had to include immigration controls, visa and right-of-asylum policies, cooperation between police forces, the combating of drug trafficking, and so on.[34]

As mentioned above, the Schengen agreement could not be implemented immediately. The level of political sensitivity of the issue was such that negotiations between the signatory states went on and on, especially after the collapse of the German Democratic Republic at the end of 1989. Eventually, on 19 June 1990 a Convention applying the Schengen Agreement was signed by the five Member States. This is generally referred to as the Schengen Convention. In the preamble to this Convention it is stated that 'the Treaty establishing the European Communities, supplemented by the Single European Act, provides that the internal market shall comprise an area without internal frontiers' and that 'the aim pursued by the Contracting Parties (Schengen) coincides with that objective, without prejudice to the measures to be taken to implement the provisions of the Treaty'.[35]

Apart from reiterating the commitment to abolishing all checks on individuals at internal borders the Convention also contains all the essential but sufficient accompanying measures to guarantee that internal freedom of movement is associated with security from external threats. These measures relate in particular to:

- surveillance of external frontiers;
- harmonisation of visa policies;
- freedom of movement of aliens;
- criteria for designating the country responsible for processing an application for asylum;
- cooperation between police forces;
- cooperation between the legal authorities in matters covered by criminal law;
- extradition;
- delegation of responsibility for enforcing criminal judgments;
- narcotics;
- firearms and ammunition;
- the Schengen Information System (SIS).[36]

On the other hand, the Convention does not include measures relating to the abolition of checks on luggage, or, in general, on goods, although initially the signatory countries had expressed their intention to intervene in such a matter. The reason is that they finally agreed that the subject fell within the sphere of competence of the Community and that it had been tackled satisfactorily at the Community level.[37]

The Dublin Convention,[38] by limiting the possibility for States to refer refugees to other Member States, was also heavily biased towards reducing the number of applications.[39] This was obtained by making it impossible for a refugee to ask for asylum in more than one member state, thus on the one hand reducing the possibility of being accepted, and, on the other, discouraging potential applicants.

The Convention was signed in Dublin on 15 June 1990. The Dublin Convention was aimed at determining the member state responsible for examining an application for asylum, a matter that is not settled by the Geneva Convention on the status of refugees. The application of this Convention ensured that every asylum-seeker's application would be examined only by a member state, unless a 'safe' non-Member country could be considered as responsible. The Convention set a number of criteria which had to be applied to determine which state would be responsible to file the asylum seeker's application. In 2003 the Dublin Convention was replaced by Council Regulation (EC) No 343/2003 of 18 February 2003 establishing the criteria and mechanisms for determining the member state responsible for examining an asylum application lodged in one of the member states by a Third-Country national.[40]

The restrictive and control-oriented nature of the Dublin Convention and the following regulation of 2003 was strengthened by the adoption of Eurodac which directly links asylum seekers and illegal migrants.[41] Eurodac is a system for the comparison of fingerprints of asylum applicants and certain groups of illegal immigrants, which became operational on 15 January 2003 in the Member States of the European Union and in the third countries bound by the Eurodac Regulation (Norway and Iceland).

The aim of this database is to assist in determining which state is responsible for considering an application for asylum according to the mechanism and criteria set up by the Dublin Convention.

Each participating State could take the fingerprints of every asylum seeker over the age of 14. These fingerprints would be compared with fingerprint data transmitted by other participating states and already stored in the central database. If Eurodac revealed that those fingerprints have already been recorded, the asylum seeker would be sent back to the country where his/her fingerprints were originally recorded.

Eurodac is the very first common Automated Fingerprint Identification System (AFIS) within the European Union.

In institutional terms, Eurodac consists of a Central Unit within the Commission equipped with a fully automated, computerised central database for comparing the fingerprints of asylum applicants and a system for electronic data transmission between participating States and the Central Unit. The Commission submits an annual report to the European Parliament and the Council including information on the management and performance of Eurodac.[42]

The follow up to the Single European Act and the Schengen Agreement was the introduction of a Third Pillar on Justice and Home Affairs by the Treaty on European Union in which migration was explicitly related to security issues.[43]

The Treaty on European Union (or Maastricht Treaty), recognised that some issues relating to immigration and asylum were of 'common interest' although not 'common policies'.[44] These issues were listed in article K1 of the TEU:

1. asylum policy;
2. rules governing the crossing by persons of the external borders of the Member States and the exercise of controls thereon;
3. immigration policy and policy regarding nationals of third countries:
   (a) conditions of entry and movement by nationals of third countries on the territory of Member States;
   (b) conditions of residence by nationals of Third Countries on the territory of Member States, including family reunion and access to employment;
   (c) combatting unauthorised immigration, residence and work by nationals of Third Countries on the territory of Member States;
4. combatting drug addiction in so far as this is not covered by 7 to 9;
5. combatting fraud on an international scale in so far as this is not covered by 7 to 9;
6. judicial cooperation in civil matters;
7. judicial cooperation in criminal matters;
8. customs cooperation;
9. police cooperation for the purposes of preventing and combatting terrorism, unlawful drug trafficking and other serious forms of international crime, including if necessary certain aspects of customs cooperation, in connection with the organisation of a Union-wide system for exchanging information within a European Police Office (Europol).[45]

The content of the Maastricht Treaty provisions on migration and asylum seekers has been judged by the literature to be consistently 'security oriented and restrictive'.[46] Articles K 1–9 of the 1992 TEU constituted the Third pillar on Justice and Home Affairs.[47] Although the Treaty established that one full group (GD1) of the K4 committee were dedicated to asylum, visas and migration,[48] the framework was still highly intergovernmental as it required unanimous decisions by the Council and remained outside the *acquis communautaire*. Indeed not much had been achieved in terms of common policy in the first five years after the establishment of the Justice and Home Affairs Pillar, apart from one joint position on the common definition of a refugee, and five legally binding joint actions, regarding school travel for children of third country nationals, airport transit procedures, a common format for resident permits, burden-sharing for displaced persons and human trafficking.[49] On the other hand, a lot had been realised outside the 'third pillar' in terms of securitisation of the policy: exchange of information; the establishment of a list of countries requiring visas; operationalisation of co-operation between border police, liaison officers, intelligence personnel and magistrates; data exchange through the Schengen Information System (SIS); and technological co-operation in areas such as fingerprinting of asylum-seekers and document fraud.[50]

Overall, scholars believe that the Maastricht Treaty did little to simplify the management of EU migratory policy at the community level and resulted in a 'confused and confusing' approach.[51] However, it increased the level of securitisation of the issue, finally institutionalising Fortress Europe. This happened because, with the lack of a clear supranational structure within which to guarantee scrutiny and accountability of the Member States' migratory regulation, it was possible to elaborate a policy of control which did not include measures protecting TCNs' rights of entry, residence, employment and the like from discrimination. It is true that the Maastricht Treaty substantially increased the level of communitarisation of migration and asylum issues, but the institutionalisation of two different migratory law models for citizens of EU Member States and for TCNs,[52] one liberal (although with some limitations) and the other extremely restrictive, was accompanied by the growth of a 'strong security impulse'.[53] The post-Maastricht EU strategy on immigration revolved around the creation of a buffer zone to keep especially asylum seekers and undocumented migrants outside the EU. This policy was skewed towards control and security,[54] with few if any measures dealing with the rights of TCNs. Equally, the communitarised side of this policy was mainly attributed to the competence of intergovernmental committees whose activities were secretive and who were not accountable to the general public nor to EU institutions. Finally the Maastricht treaty left the future of the common migratory policy unresolved. Overall, the TEU's linking of the internal and external borders of the European Community represented an important step forward in the creation of a 'spill over' effect turning socio economic integration into an 'internal security project'.[55] This gave a clear direction to the future outlook of the EU approach to immigration and asylum policy which was further formalised in the incorporation of the Schengen Agreement in the *acquis communautaire* after the Treaty of Amsterdam (1997), and the Council and Commission action plan on the implementation of the Treaty of Amsterdam in the areas of freedom, security and justice.[56]

In the Treaty of Amsterdam the sections of the Third Pillar relating to immigration, asylum and refugees were partially communitarised.[57] However, this partial form of communitarisation of the Third Pillar has allowed for the final institutionalisation of the security paradigm.[58] It allows the Member States to enforce their restrictive approach to migration flows beyond the borders of the Union covered by the protective umbrella of the EU.[59] Overall, the transfer of migration policy from the Third to the First pillar of the EU, instead of guaranteeing the rights of migrants, especially TCNs, has institutionalised the logic of exclusion characterising the TEU version of the JHA pillar, has deepened the security paradigm and, paradoxically, has ensured that the basic restrictive orientation of the Member States' approaches to extra EU migration continued unhindered.

This happened for a number of reasons.

First of all, the Treaty of Amsterdam communitarised under Title IV (Arts 61-69) of the EC Treaty only contains certain measures in the areas of free movement of persons, checks at external borders and customs cooperation, asylum, immigration and protection for the rights of nationals of non-member countries and judicial cooperation in civil matters.[60]

Moreover, although the provisions regulating Title IV are very different from those regulating the matters still under the Third Pillar in Title VI of the TEU, the Council of the European Union was to continue to play the main role in the following five years after the passing of the Amsterdam Treaty. Even after the five years had passed, the Council was still the main pillar of the policy although it was no longer the only institution involved.[61]

During the first five years the Council could take unanimous decisions on the basis of proposals by the EU Commission or a member state and after consulting the EU Parliament. After the transition period expired, the Council could take decisions only on the basis of proposals by the EU Commission. The Commission, however, would have to consider any request by a member state for a proposal to be put before the Council.

Finally, according to the Amsterdam Treaty, after consulting the European Parliament, the Council could decide by unanimous vote to apply the co-decision procedure and qualified majority voting when adopting measures under Title IV and to modify the clauses relating to the Court of Justice of the European Communities.[62]

Apart from this role as the main decision maker, the Council was consolidated in its role as the co-ordinator between the relevant government departments in the Member States and between these and the European Commission (art 66).[63]

The new Treaty gave the Court of Justice a role to play in the areas of justice and home affairs, in the areas covered by Title IV, whereas previously it had none. However, this is only if it is called upon by a national court, the Council, the Commission or a member state to rule on a question regarding the interpretation of the new title or of acts adopted on its basis. In any event, the Court of Justice does not have jurisdiction to rule on any measure or decision taken pursuant to Article 62(1) relating to the maintenance of law and order and the safeguarding of internal security.

Most importantly, the Member States continue to have the sole responsibility for ensuring internal security, law and order with the prerogative to take foreign policy considerations into account. Freedom of movement or entry of TCNs can be restricted in case of emergency for a maximum of six months by the Council voting by qualified majority on a Commission proposal in the interests of the member state concerned (art 64).[64] The UK and Ireland both eventually managed to secure an opt-out from the application of Title IV.

They also retain the right to exercise controls at their frontiers on persons seeking to enter their territory, in particular citizens of states which are contracting parties to the Agreement on the European Economic Area or to any agreement by which the United Kingdom and/or Ireland is bound, and the right to decide whether or not to let them enter their territory. At the same time, the other Member States may exercise controls on all persons coming from the United Kingdom or Ireland.

Denmark is also not taking part in measures under Title IV except those determining the non-member countries whose nationals must have a visa when crossing the external borders of the Member States and measures introducing a uniform format for visas.[65]

The areas still under Title VI of the TEU ('Provisions on police and judicial cooperation in criminal matters' (Arts 29–42)), and therefore still under an intergovernmental decision making procedure, are extremely relevant and relate to preventing and combating:

- racism and xenophobia;
- terrorism;
- trafficking in persons and offences against children;
- drug trafficking;

- arms trafficking;
- corruption and fraud.[66]

The measures to achieve these objectives all point toward an increase of the level of securitisation of migration and range from closer cooperation between police forces, customs authorities and other competent authorities in the Member States, both directly and through Europol; to closer cooperation between judicial and other competent authorities of the Member States, both directly and through Europol; and approximation, where necessary, of rules on criminal matters in the Member States.[67]

In institutional terms, the Member States have virtually sole responsibility for cooperation in the fields covered by Title VI of the TEU. To coordinate their actions, they inform and consult one another and establish collaboration between their respective government departments or they may decide to use the EU institutions, procedures and mechanisms. However, this is all done on a voluntary basis.

The Treaty of Amsterdam also contained a Protocol integrating the Schengen *acquis* into the framework of the European Union and a Protocol annexed to the Treaty establishing the European Community on asylum for nations of the Member States of the European Union.[68]

It is not difficult to see how these provisions conceal the desire by the Member States not to relinquish too much control over asylum and immigration policy. It is indeed revealing that the integration of the Schengen *acquis* into the Union has not implied any re-definition of its substantially exclusive nature. Moreover, there is a permanence of too many mechanisms that characterise the institutional configuration of the Third Pillar even in title IV of the TEC, for instance, the retention of unanimity, the limitations to the rights of initiative of the EU Commission; the merely consultative role of the EP and the limits imposed to the ECJ's jurisdiction. This made scholars hypothesise that the new Title was somehow instrumental to allowing the Member States to extend the forms of social control, strengthen their regulatory capacities, and reinforce the restrictive nature of Fortress Europe.[69]

As policy towards intra-EU migration was becoming increasingly open and liberal, policy towards TCNs migration had to become more and more restrictive and security oriented. Indeed, freedom of movement within the EU could, in the approach institutionalised at Amsterdam, only be guaranteed by separating the two migration policies (intra-EU and extra-EU) and ensuring that internal freedom would be associated with appropriate measures to control external borders, immigration from Third Countries, asylum, and to prevent and combat crime.

Overall, the Amsterdam Treaty continued the tradition of confused and confusing approaches to immigration and asylum policy at the EU level that had been inaugurated by the Treaty of Maastricht.[70] The continued absence of democratic and judicial control protecting the rights of TCNs, substantiated in the weak role played by the ECJ and the EP on the issue, allowed for the EU Member States to continue exercise substantial decision making powers without, however, the same judicial guarantees that existed before these policies were regulated at the community level. In the shift of the level of regulation from the national to the community level, the scope for the protection of the 'social and political spaces' of migrants from TCNs has diminished.[71] Moreover, this shift did not signify a supranationalisation of the management of the policy, but an institutionalisation of mainly intergovernmental practices which however made the Member States preferences on the issue much more stable.[72] And these preferences were, and continue to be, skewed towards strict control of migration from TCNs without much attention for the rights of the migrants.[73]

There are many more examples of the restrictive and control-oriented nature of the European migration policy. One of the most quoted in the literature[74] is the co-ordination and facilitation of so-called readmission agreements. Such agreements involve reciprocal undertakings by the European Union and third country partners to co-operate over the return of illegal residents to their country of origin or transit.[75] They are a clear example of how the Commission is seeking to integrate migration issues into the Union's overall relations with third countries.

This state of affairs did not change with the following developments of the common approach to migration and asylum issues after Amsterdam. On the contrary, many interventions further accentuated the security oriented nature of Fortress Europe. For example, the Council and the Commission's Action Plan on how best to implement the provisions of the Amsterdam Treaty (1998) explicitly relates the creation of a internal area of freedom of movement to the necessity to control external borders. Indeed it states: 'Freedom loses much of its meaning if it cannot be enjoyed in a secure environment and with the full backing of a system of justice in which all Union citizens and residents can have confidence'.[76]

This connection between internal freedom and protection from external threats was further highlighted by the European Council in Tampere (15-16 October 1999), which set the aim to reconcile the right to move freely throughout the Union with a high degree of protection and legal guarantees for all.[77]

The Seville European Council in June 2002 highlighted the need to develop a common policy in the field of asylum and immigration. It stressed the importance of adopting tangible measures to combat illegal immigration and manage external borders on the basis of two plans adopted in this field during the first half of 2002.

Even more clearly, the Hague European Council of 4–5 November 2004 adopted the Hague programme, which aimed to build upon the results achieved during the Tampere programme. Again, the creation of an internal area of freedom, security and justice had to be achieved by further tightening the controls of the external borders adopting measures such as:

- initiating a debate on the possible creation of a European corps of border guards;
- setting up the Schengen Information System II (or SIS II) and the Visa Information System (VIS);
- establishing the Internal Security Committee;
- introducing the European evidence warrant by 2005;
- setting up a European police record information system.[78]

The Hague programme was translated into a series of concrete measures by the Hague Action Plan, which was approved by the European Council meeting on 16-17 June 2005, updated at the end of 2006.[79]

The analysis of the migratory regime for EU nationals in the next section helps to identify how striking the difference is with the treatment reserved for TCNs.

3 EU immigration models

Scholars of EC law[80] distinguish between three models of Community immigration law: the 'citizen' model, the 'worker' model and the 'alien' model.

The most liberal model is clearly the one reserved for EU citizens. Immigration rules applying to EU citizens are divided into five categories. These are: dependent workers; self-employed persons; service providers and recipients; students; retired persons and other persons.[81]

Dependent workers are allowed to enter and stay in another EU country. They can look for employment and be employed there with no discrimination.[82]

They have the right to family reunion, referring to a substantial extended family. Workers and their families are allowed to remain in the host country after retirement or disability and family members can stay after the death of a worker (or ex-worker).[83]

As far as self-employed persons are concerned, they can enter another EU member state and stay there, they can access professions or any other kind of self-employment without discrimination. They and their families have the right to claim benefits and they are granted rights on retirement, disability or death.[84]

Service providers and recipients are allowed to enter and stay, they can look for and take up employment and professions temporarily and have the right to certain benefits.[85]

The rights reserved to service recipients are also extended to students in private vocational training; students in public vocational training also have rights to enter and stay and cannot be discriminated in education during their study. Rights are also granted to their families.[86]

Pensioners have rights to enter and reside along with their family members.

As far as other persons are concerned, those who have all-risk sickness insurance and income above the level for granting social assistance in the host state can enter and reside in a country.

The distinction between these categories is not as critical for EU nationals as for third country nationals since EU nationals can switch from one category to another and can also belong to more than one category at the same time. Moreover, the formal status of 'citizen' grants them the right to move and reside freely beyond the rights connected to the categories mentioned above. Finally, citizenship and the right to equal treatment entitles persons to equal treatment in benefits even if they do not fall within other categories of migrants.[87]

It has been noted that these provisions entrench the concept of the 'market citizen': the rights of free movement are very liberal for those who can 'pay their way'.[88] Maybe it is an exclusive concept of citizenship, but it certainly grants EU citizens a high degree of freedom of movement and establishment in another EU member state.

Completely different is the immigration model reserved to TCNs before and also after Amsterdam. As already underlined above, before Amsterdam the Member States had full competence to adopt their own migration law. The Council of immigration ministers and the European Council could however define general principles regarding migration for TCNs through 'soft law'. Soft-law means guidelines adopted outside the EU legal system. These guidelines took the form of resolutions proposed by Council Presidencies, not by the Commission without any participation of the European Parliament. The ECJ had no jurisdiction over them; there was no direct impact on Member States, no binding effect as public international law and no enforcement system.[89] However, the principles set out in the resolutions could not be 'relaxed' by the Member States in their national legislation and had to be taken into consideration in any proposal for revising national legislation.[90] In the case of the pre-Amsterdam 'alien' model, the distinction of migrants in categories was very relevant as their treatment was substantially different according to the category into which they fell. There is no doubt however that the treatment of 'aliens' was by far more restrictive than that of Member States' citizens.

According to the workers' resolution adopted in June 1994, as a general rule Member States were to refuse entry to third country nationals for employment purposes. Requests by dependent workers were to be considered only if a job could not be filled by EU nationals or nationals of Third Countries with special agreements with the EU.

Temporary workers could be admitted only if:

- they were specific employees of a specific firm when special qualifications were required; and/or
- there was a temporary manpower shortage which was significantly affecting the operation of the undertaking or the employer itself; and/or
- they were seasonal workers, trainees, frontier workers or intra-corporate transferees being posted as key personnel of a company.[91]

In all these cases they had to fulfil procedural requirements including possession of a work permit and possibly acquisition of a visa or residence permit. The resolution permitted Member States to allow entry to business visitors and to preserve certain existing agreements with third countries.[92]

The self-employment resolution adopted in December 1994 was far more liberal than the workers' resolution.

A third country national could be admitted if:

- they added value through investment, innovation, transfer of technology, job creation; and/or
- they were artists exercising an independent activity of interest.[93]

However, also in this case there were a number of procedural requirements to fulfil, including compliance with national immigration law and provision of detailed information regarding the planned activity.

The students' resolution was passed also in December 1994. It applied only to post-secondary education. Entry was to be limited to the duration of the course. Students could not change their status and look for or take up a job in the host country although they could be allowed to pursue ancillary or short-term employment. Entry and employment of family members were to be regulated by national law.[94]

The 1993 family reunion resolution applied only to third country nationals who were lawfully resident in a member state with the expectation of permanent or long-term residence (although this term was not further specified).[95] The resolution required Member States to allow entry to their territories of the spouses and children of a long-term resident only for the purpose of living together and subject to conditions to be decided by Member States.[96] The Member States could also allow a more liberal approach to family re-unification. For example, family members could be authorised by the Member States to stay on an independent basis and if appropriate be authorised to work after a reasonable period of time following their admission.

Finally, the long-term residents' resolution stated that persons could be admitted as long-term residents after a period specified in national law and after ten years at the latest. This status had to result from a long term or permanent residence permit.[97]

Following Amsterdam, and only on the subjects included in the EU *acquis*, previous soft-law resolutions regarding the immigration of 'aliens' have been substituted by EU legislation. These follow very closely the guidelines which had previously been enacted.

One example is Council Regulation (EC) No 1091/2001 of 28 May 2001 on freedom of movement with a long-stay visa, which extends the provisions of Regulation No 1408/71 on the application of social security schemes to employed persons and their families moving within the Community to third-country nationals legally resident in a member state. The aim is to facilitate free movement within the Union for third-country nationals holding long-stay visas.[98] Another example is Council Directive 2003/86/EC of 22 September 2003 on the right to family reunification. This is aimed at determining the conditions governing family re-unification rights for TCNs legally residing in the Territory of a member state.[99]

Finally, the third model of EU immigration law is the so called 'worker model'.[100] The 'worker' model applies to third countries with special agreements with the EU. The model provides for the application of a more or less liberal immigration regime according to the different country agreements. The most favourable regime is reserved for the countries of the European Economic Area (Norway, Iceland and Liechtenstein) and to the agreement on free movement of persons with Switzerland. In both cases citizens of the contracting countries are granted the full rights of EU free movement law, although not rights of citizenship.[101]

Subject to a less favourable regime are Turkish workers already residing lawfully in the territory of one of the EU Member States. The association agreement with Turkey grants Turkish workers, and their families, rights to employment, education and corollary rights of residence and social security equality.[102] On the other hand, association agreements with Maghreb states give equal treatment in social security and working conditions and remuneration only to nationals of the signatory states.[103]

The European agreements with Central and Eastern European Countries before accession provided for the extension to their citizens of rights to take up and pursue self employment. They were also granted equality in working conditions and access to employment for family members, as well as entry of 'key personnel' of companies.[104] The EEC's Partnership and Cooperation Agreements with former Soviet Republics required the Member States to allow into their territories key personnel of Companies formed in the ex-Soviet States.[105]

Finally, the Lomé convention between the EU and African, Caribbean and Pacific Countries (CAP) called for identical treatment to the Maghreb treaties.[106] Although the provisions of the Lomé Convention could be interpreted as non-binding, the following agreement with ACP countries, the Cotonou Convention of 2000 (revised in 2005), certainly meets the conditions for direct effect.[107] Art. 13 on Migration reaffirmed existing obligations and commitments in international law to ensure respect for human rights and to eliminate all forms of discrimination based particularly on origin, sex, race, language and religion. It also called the parties to consider that the partnership implied, in relation to migration, fair treatment of third country nationals who reside legally on their territories, integration policy aiming at granting them rights and obligations comparable to those of their citizens. With regard to workers of ACP countries legally employed in the territory of an EU member state, the Convention asked for treatment free from any discrimination based on nationality, as regards working conditions, remuneration and dismissal, relative to its own nationals.[108]

4 Conclusion

There seems to be little doubt in the literature that, since regulation 1612/68 the process of communitarisation of European migratory policies has been accompanied by a growing consensus on the need to restrict entry of TCNs into the territories of the Member States and by a progressive securitisation of the issue.[109] The reasons why this happened have been traced in different events by different authors. Guiraudon explains the securitisation of the EU Home and Justice Affairs as a consequence of the competition of domestic actors to increase their power and enhance their position at the EU level. The transnationalisation game favoured law and order officials and agencies; that is, those who are in charge of border controls seeking to gain independence from the national institutional constraints.[110] Bureaucrats sitting in interior ministries and other police agencies 'venue shopped' at the international level to escape domestic adversaries (such as the domestic judicial system) and pursued their own agenda in immigration and refugee policy. This led to the securitisation of the EU common approach to home and justice affairs.[111] A similar focus of the role of security agencies and officials is proposed by Huysmans. Lavenex[112] embeds the antagonism between the 'liberal', human rights approach to migration and the 'security' realist perspective into the realm of how ideas are transmitted to the political system through institutions.[113] According to Kostakoupolous [114] the *communitarisation* of migration and asylum offers states the opportunity to expand the logic of control and law enforcement beyond the borders of the nation state and impose their security agenda even outside the European Union. Therefore, the communitarisation of migratory policy responds to the interests of the nation states to strengthen their restrictive and security oriented approach to migration, not to grant more rights to TCNs.

Overall the future outlook of the EU common migratory regime seems to leave little hope of a more liberal and openminded approach to the entry and establishment of 'aliens'. However, as further elaborated in the next chapters of this book, this might even worsen the security challenges posed by migration to developed Western countries. Indeed, the imposition of strict border controls in a climate of rising migratory pressures, inevitably following from the process of globalisation, produces, as its only consequence, an increase in the number of undocumented migrants. This, in turn, can and does lead to a sort of self-selection process of the incoming migrants favouring those that have fewer problems in undergoing an illegal migratory process and, possibly in being introduced in the underground or straightforwardly illegal sectors of the economies of the receiving countries.

With this in mind we turn now to the dynamics of migration from the Middle Eastern and Northern African countries to the EU.

Chapter 4

Migration in practice

Egyptians did not emigrate!

1 Introduction

In 1936, a famous study on population in Egypt stated: 'Egyptians have the reputation of preferring their own soil. Few ever leave except to study or travel; and they always return … Egyptians do not emigrate.'[1] Is this statement still true nowadays? Do Egyptians emigrate now? What are the dynamics of Egyptian migration? Answering these questions is not straightforward. Surveys and data-sets on the topic are very rare; although they would be very welcome their implementation is not an easy task.

This chapter provides a brief and necessarily incomplete overview of the developments of the Egyptian government's attitude towards migration, from the immediate aftermath of the revolution in 1952 to recent times. It also provides some data on migratory flows outside Egypt, relying on both Egyptian official sources (CAPMAS/Egyptian Ministry of Manpower and Emigration) and the existing literature.

2 The policy of the Egyptian government

The Egyptian labour migration policy in modern times was inaugurated with the government's official sponsorship of migration of school teachers to Iraq in the 1930s. After the 1952 revolution, this sponsorship was extended to other Arab countries.[2] In the 1960s, the main concern of Egyptian migration policy related to immigration. This did not stop the government from imposing strong political controls on emigration, mainly through exit visa requirements.

The first attempt to promote emigration openly took place in 1960. Young Egyptians were encouraged to pursue additional education abroad. This policy brought the number[3] of emigration requests to an official figure of around 28,000 in 1969, compared with a total of around 15,000 for the previous six years combined.[4] However, the Egyptian government's official policy vis-à-vis emigration was ambivalent, and this continued to be the case throughout the Nasserian era. Only Sadat adopted an unambiguous open door policy, abolishing the exit visa requirement and including labour emigration in the economic development strategy.[5] However, the Egyptian government changed its official stance and policy on emigration completely from the 1950s through to the 1980s.[6] Dessouki[7] speaks of three phases in the development of Egyptian migration policy. The first, between the 1950s and 1967, was characterised by the imposition of limits on exit and exit visa requirements; the second, in the late 1960s, witnessed a relaxation of the government's attitude; and the third, under Sadat, launched an open promotion of migration.

Since the 1960s, the Egyptian government had made increasing efforts to attract foreign currency, and this included remittances from emigrants. In the late 1960s, the government eased conditions consistently for potential emigrants. It agreed to grant six months' unpaid vacation to every citizen wishing to leave Egypt to look for work. These citizens would be permitted to return to their previous employment if they were unable to find a job abroad. However, some categories of workers, such as engineers, doctors and technicians, could be asked to serve a number of years after the termination of their studies in governmental offices. Moreover, emigration was allowed only after receiving an exit visa issued by the Ministry of Interior, and this implied a complicated procedure. New legislation encouraging both temporary and permanent emigration was not passed until 1970. In 1971, the Constitution (Art. 52) recognised for the first time in Egyptian history the citizen's right to emigrate.[8] Then in 1971, the government issued Law 73, which gave public sector employees the right to retain their jobs for one year after emigration.[9]

In 1974, the exit visa was replaced by a traveller's visa. Additionally, the procedures to issue passports were facilitated. It became possible for Egyptian embassies abroad to renew passports for expatriated Egyptians without having to apply to the Interior Ministry. Furthermore, the travel restrictions on passports, which could have been imposed in the 1960s, were abolished; Egyptians were allowed to hold dual nationality; and emigrants' incomes were exempted from tax. Finally, the emigrants could retain the right to their previous job for two years after their expatriation.[10] Subsequently, in 1981, Presidential Decree no. 574 established the Ministry of State for Emigration Affairs. The role of the new ministry was to provide services to Egyptians willing to migrate abroad. The ministry was also in charge of drafting an Egyptian migration strategy aimed at favouring the economic development of Egypt.[11]

The first comprehensive migration law appeared in 1983, and is still in force today: no. 111, 'Emigration and sponsoring Egyptians abroad'.[12] It consists of five chapters. The first chapter contains general provisions to be applied to all migrants and the first article establishes the right for Egyptians to emigrate, both permanently and temporarily. Egyptians are entitled to keep their Egyptian nationality according to the Egyptian nationality law. As long as they remain Egyptian nationals, they enjoy Egyptian constitutional or legal rights. The State should sponsor Egyptians abroad through the Ministry of Emigration Affairs and the Ministry of Foreign Affairs, and should do its best to strengthen their ties with Egypt (Arts 2 and 3). Article 4 set up a Supreme Committee for Emigration, headed by the Minister concerned with Emigration Affairs. It was composed of the representatives of various ministries, chosen from among high-ranking officials. This committee was responsible for establishing professional centres to train potential migrants, especially in the fields of agriculture and industry; organising specialised courses aiming at potential migrants; providing Egyptians abroad with the necessary cultural, media and national materials to maintain their ties with their homeland; sponsoring the Arabic language among migrants' children; and supporting religion. The committee was also responsible for identifying the benefits to be attributed to migrants, before, during and after their departure. Art. 6 states the obligation for temporary potential migrants to be registered in a record kept in the ministry concerned with Emigration Affairs. The original aim was to allocate emigration opportunities according to fields of specialisation and capacities, as well as according to the priorities identified by the Minister of Emigration Affairs and by the law (Art. 7).

Chapter 2 of Law 111 regulates permanent emigration. A permanent migrant is defined as an Egyptian who stays abroad permanently after having received the status of foreign national or a permanent residence permit; an Egyptian who stays abroad for at least ten years; or one who obtains an immigration permit from one of the countries of destination (Art. 8). The law (Art. 9) states that potential permanent migrants must request and obtain a 'permanent emigration permit' issued by the Ministry of Interior, and her/his data have to be recorded. Egyptians migrating abroad or born of Egyptian permanent migrants may have dual nationality (Arts 10/11). The status of permanent migrant may be lost if the person does not travel to the country of destination within six months, or if the person returns to Egypt for more than one continuous year. Losing the status of permanent migrant also entails losing all the advantages attached to it (Art. 12).

The provisions of Chapter 3 refer to temporary migration. A temporary migrant is one who works abroad for one continuous year (Art. 13). The status of temporary migrant is lost if the citizen returns home and remains for more than six continuous months, or if the citizen returns to work in Egypt. The loss of the temporary migrant status leads to the loss of all advantages acquired (Art. 14).

Chapter 4 lists the rights and the various advantages attributed to migrants by the Egyptian government. These range from exemption from taxes and fees for bank deposits and other financial facilities (Art. 15) to the right to be reappointed to their previous position in the public sector if permanent migrants return to Egypt within two years. A person whose emigration duration exceeds these two years may be reappointed, if he/she meets the conditions required for filling the post (Art. 16).

Finally, Chapter 5 contains transitional provisions. In general, in the 1970s and 1980s, Egypt's policy-makers allowed for free emigration to Arab countries, despite the shortage of professionals in several sectors at home.[13]

From the early 1990s to the time of writing, a new phase in Egyptian migration has begun. Many of those who had been migrating in the Gulf area have returned to Egypt, and the number of contracts granted to new migrants from Egypt has declined steadily. However, permanent migration to more developed countries has increased substantially.[14] The responsibility for both migration and Egyptians abroad was attributed to the Egyptian Ministry of Manpower and Emigration by Presidential Decree no. 31 in 1996. In 1997, resolution no. 2000 established the Higher Committee for Migration (HCM). The HCM includes all the authorities concerned with migration, and is headed by the Minister of Manpower and Emigration.[15]

3 Egypt's migration dynamics

Historically, Egypt has been a land of immigrants, not of emigrants.[16] This was true even when the standards of life were very low. According to Cleland,[17] in 1927, the number of Egyptians registered outside Egypt was 21,565; of these, 18,383 were living in neighbouring Sudan. Moreover, just before the 1952 revolution, the great majority of Egyptians were hardly living at a level above subsistence, but this did not produce pressures to leave the country in search of better living conditions.[18] Certainly, this was the case until very recently. Scholars[19] have since identified five phases in the evolution of the Egyptian migratory flows after the 1952 revolution (Table 4.1).

Table 4.1 Phases of Egyptian migration

Phase 1: Before 1974 ***The early phase of migration***	Very limited migration, mostly highly skilled or politically determined
Phase 2: 1974–1984 ***The expansion phase***	Expansion of temporary migration in the Arab oil-producing countries
Phase 3: 1984–1988 ***The contraction phase***	Contraction of migration to the Arab world
Phase 4: 1988–1992 ***The deterioration phase***	Significant flow of return migrants from the Gulf area to Egypt
Phase 5: 1992 onwards ***The recent phase***	Significant increase of permanent migration to the more developed world

The first wave of international migration in Egypt after the revolution was provoked by a number of contextual economic, political and social events. However, emigration was limited to a small number of students and professionals. Almost all those who emigrated at that time belonged to the upper class. They were either the highly educated Egyptians or the capitalists, fleeing Nasser's nationalisation and property-seizing measures. Emigration was a consequence of the revolution and of the disruption of Egyptian social construction. In this context, those who had occupied a privileged position before 1952 were marginalised and prosecuted, and decided to leave the country. [20] Most of them headed to Canada and the USA.[21] During the 1960s, therefore, migration from Egypt existed, but was never substantial in scale and scope.

It was during the 1970s that Egyptian emigration became a sizeable phenomenon.[22] According to Sell,[23] 1973 marked a watershed in contemporary Egyptian migration due to a number of shocks hitting migration dynamics. First, the new war with Israel caused internal dislocations of people, including the movement of civilians to and from the canal area as well as the military mobilisation itself. Moreover, the open door policy and the end of previous restrictions facilitated emigration.[24] Finally, and most importantly, the first oil shock stimulated migration to the wealthy members of OPEC, which were experiencing sudden job shortages. In 1975, there were an estimated 1.6 million migrant workers in the labour-importing countries of Bahrain, Kuwait, Libya, Oman, Qatar, Saudi Arabia and the United Arab Emirates, of which 1.1 million were of Arab origin.[25]

The number of Egyptians abroad was estimated by the Central Agency for Public Mobilization and Statistics (CAPMAS) to be about 70,000 in 1970. In 1976, according to that year's census, that figure had already reached 1.4 million.[26] These migrants were unskilled or semi-skilled. They left Egypt heading to the oil-rich countries of the Gulf or Libya, first after the 1973 boom in oil prices, and again after the second increase in oil prices in 1979. Moreover, emigration within the Arab region was meant to be temporary, and most Egyptians intended to return to their homeland once their economic situation had improved and they could lead a better life in Egypt. Egyptians had started emigrating.[27]

It is not an easy task to reconstruct Egyptian migration dynamics in the course of the 1980s and 1990s, due to a shortage of data.[28] Zohry and Harrell-Bond identify a third phase of development, between 1984 and 1988, which, according to them, witnessed a contraction in the number of Egyptian migrants. The contraction had commenced in 1983, with the reduction of oil revenues induced by the beginning of the Iran–Iraq war. Then, from the second half of the 1980s, they claim, the fall in the number of Egyptian migrants was hastened by the Iran–Iraq war, the fall of oil prices, the declining demand for construction workers in Arab countries, and the policy of replacing foreign labour with nationals in the Arab Gulf States.[29] The situation then deteriorated further in the period between 1988 and 1992, which was characterised by a significant return flow from the Gulf area to Egypt.

Contrary to Zohry and Harrel-Bond,[30] Zahlan[31] believes that, rather than talking about a reduction in the aggregate levels of migration, it is more appropriate to refer to a redistribution of labour across the region in the 1980s/early 1990s.[32] This was the consequence of the fall of oil prices and the recession. To substantiate this hypothesis, Zahlan notes that the amount of remittances in the major labour-exporting countries of the Middle East increased instead of decreasing.[33] The single most important outcome of this redistribution of labour was the emergence of Iraq as the largest importer of migrants, especially from Egypt. Iraq was indeed heavily involved in war with Iran. Therefore, it needed to import manpower to substitute those in the military as well as to support its war economy. According to Zahlan, at least 1.25 million Egyptians were working in Iraq during the 1980s, about one in every three Egyptian migrants.[34] Moreover, Egyptian migration to Iraq offset the decreased demand of Arab workers in the area, who tended to be substituted by the lesser-paid and less politically controversial Asian workforce. Also, Jordan increased its demand for unskilled Egyptian workers during this period thanks to the construction boom brought about by the increase in remittances of highly skilled Jordanian migrants to Gulf countries. This redistribution of immigrants was the consequence of many factors. Obviously, the level of wages and of wage differentials played a major role. However, one should not underestimate the importance of political alliances and their changes in the unstable area of the Middle East. This clearly determined which migrants were welcome where and when.

However, a certain contraction of temporary migration in the Arab world cannot be denied. Zohry and Harrell-Bond[35] indicate that, taking 1988 as a benchmark, the number of contracts granted to new Egyptian migrants halved in 1989. In 1990, it further decreased to 43 per cent of the base year. The decline is to be explained by the reduction in the number of contracts with Jordan, Iraq, Yemen, Saudi Arabia and other Arab Gulf countries. Moreover, data from the Egyptian Ministry of Manpower and Emigration show that Egyptian migration to Arab countries declined by one-third from 1984 to 1990 (from 3,157,139 to 2,083,262; see Table 4.2 below).

Of course, the first Gulf War fundamentally altered migration patterns in the region. As a result of the war, about two million people, including more than two-thirds of Kuwait's citizens and more than a million foreign workers, were displaced from Kuwait, Iraq and Saudi Arabia.[36] By the end of the war, virtually all Egyptian immigrants in Iraq and Kuwait were forced back to Egypt or were displaced to other countries in the region.[37]

According to ILO figures, the number of Egyptians abroad fell from 1,964,000 in 1989 to 1,541,000 in 1991, with a contraction of around 21.5 per cent.[38] This leads to the final phase in the development of Egyptian migration, to which we turn our attention in the next section.[39]

4 Egyptian migration today

The most distinctive characteristic of the recent phase of development of Egyptian migration (1992 onwards) is the increase of permanent migration to more developed countries, especially to Europe. Table 4.2 below shows that the number of permanent migrants to developed countries increased from 1990 to 1998 on average by 83 per cent, with an increase of migration to Europe of around 125 per cent (from 225,251 to 506,028 migrants). Temporary migration to Arab countries also increased, but by only 68 per cent.

In terms of absolute numbers, Egyptian official statistics are in disagreement. According to the Egyptian Ministry of Manpower and Emigration, as shown in Table 4.2, the total number of Egyptians abroad was almost five million in 1998, of which 3,500,000 were temporary migrants, mainly in Arab countries, and approximately 1,400,000 were in developed countries.

Table 4.3, issued by the Egyptian Ministry of Manpower and Emigration, reports the number of Egyptian emigrants in 1998 by country of residence. Here, the total number of migrants is just over five million, with 500,000 in Europe and almost 800,000 in the Americas.

Table 4.2 Egyptians abroad: Permanent and temporary migration

	1982	*1983*	*1984*	*1990*	*1995*	*1998*
Temporary Migration						
Arab countries	2,946,120	3,206,169	3,157,139	2,083,262	2,129,050	3,511,859
African countries	600	2,411	75,358	952	–	2,545
Asian countries	–	284	635	601	–	6,073
Total	**2,946,720**	**3,208,864**	**3,233,132**	**2,084,815**	**2,129,050**	**3,520,477**
Permanent Migration						
Australia	50,000	42,718	45,735	32,423	75,000	80,350
European countries	155,775	100,998	155,503	225,251	400,068	506,028
American countries	260,440	195,111	444,438	485,545	396,000	780,841
Total	**466,215**	**338,827**	**645,676**	**743,219**	**871,068**	**1,367,219**
Total Temporary and Permanent Migration	**3,412,935**	**3,547,691**	**3,878,808**	**2,828,034**	**3,000,118**	**4,887,696**

Source: Egyptian Ministry of Manpower and Emigration, Emigration Sector, as reported by CARIM 2008; updated: 7 February 2005.

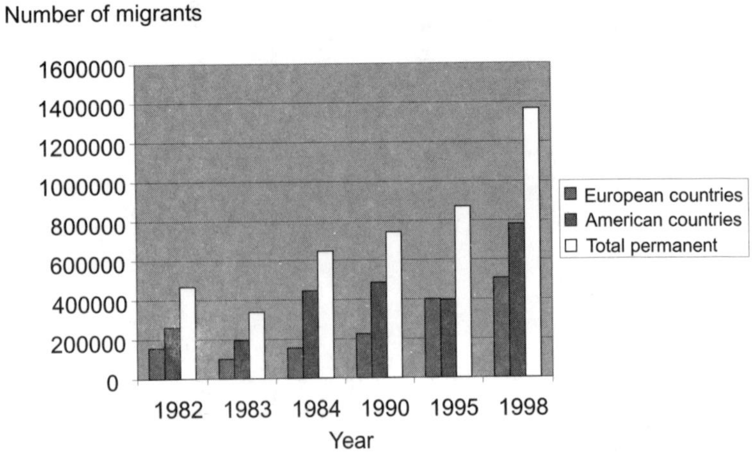

Figure 4.1 Egyptians abroad, permanently, in USA/Europe 1992–1998.

Source: Adapted the author on data by the Egyptian Ministry for Manpower and Emigration as reported by CARIM 2008.

Table 4.3 Approximate number of Egyptians abroad by country of residence, 1998

Host Country	*Number*
Arab Countries	**3,781,859**
Algeria	2,100
Bahrain	6,000
Iraq	150,000
Jordan	500,000
Kuwait	250,000
Lebanon	300,000
Libya	950,000
Mauritania	159
Morocco	800
Oman	40,000
Qatar	20,000
Saudi Arabia	1,350,000
Sudan	2,000
Syria	10,000
Tunisia	500
United Arabs Emirates	160,000
Yemen	40,300
African countries	**1,278**
Benin	46
Burundi	8

Host Country	*Number*
Central African Republic	30
Congo	–
Côte d'Ivoire	101
Djibouti	160
Eritrea	–
Ethiopia	60
Ghana	62
Guinea	100
Madagascar	9
Mali	43
Nigeria	350
Senegal	90
Sierra Leone	–
Tanzania	39
Uganda	180
American countries	**780,841**
Argentina	40
Bolivia	40
Brazil	4,600
Canada	141,000
Chile	20
Colombia	20
Cuba	–
Ecuador	10
El Salvador	–
Guatemala	5
Mexico	40
Panama	7
Peru	7
United States	635,000
Uruguay	20
Venezuela	12
Other countries	
Australia	80,350
Bangladesh	22
Burma	1
China	45
Hong Kong	20
India	32
Indonesia	100
Iran	35
Israel	750
Japan	1,000
Malaysia	300
Nepal	–

Source: Egyptian Ministry for Manpower and Emigration, as reported by CARIM 2008.

Table 4.4 Egyptian emigrants by country of residence, 2000

Country of Residence	*Numbers*
Temporary Migration[1]	
Bahrain	4,000
Iraq	65,629
Jordan	226,850
Kuwait	190,550
Lebanon	12,500
Libya	332,600
Oman	15,000
Qatar	25,000
Saudi Arabia	923,600
United Arabs Emirates	95,000
Yemen	22,000
Total	**1,912,729**
Permanent Migration[2]	
Australia	70,000
Austria	14,000
Canada	110,000
England	35,000
France	36,000
Germany	25,000
Greece	60,000
Holland	40,000
Italy	90,000
Spain	12,000
Switzerland	14,000
United States	318,000
Total	**824,000**
Combined totals	**2,736,729**

Source:
1 CAPMAS 2001, as reported by CARIM; updated 20 January 2005.
2 CAPMAS 2000, as reported by CARIM; updated 20 January 2005.

The numbers are substantially different for the Egyptian Office of Statistics (Central Agency for Public Mobilisation and Statistics, CAPMAS).[40] In 2000, according to CAPMAS estimates,[41] the total number of Egyptians abroad was about 2.7 million (see Table 4.4). They comprised about 4 per cent of the total population of Egypt, and about 1.5 per cent of total migrants worldwide (estimated total is 175 million).[42] Egyptian migration scholars most often refer to CAPMAS figures to identify the number of Egyptians abroad,[43] although the figures quoted by the Egyptian Ministry of Manpower and Emigration are likely to be closer to the truth.[44]

However, all statistics seem to agree on the proportions of temporary and permanent migration. More or less two-thirds of Egyptian migration is temporary, while one-third is permanent, in both CAPMAS and Egyptian Ministry of Manpower and Emigration figures. Temporary migration is mainly labour migration to oil-rich Arab countries. According to CAPMAS, in 2001, Saudi Arabia absorbed about 50 per cent of Egyptian temporary migration, followed by Libya (17 per cent), Jordan (12 per cent) and Kuwait (10 per cent); see Table 4.5.

Table 4.5 Egyptian migrants (temporary) in Arab countries, 2001

Receiving Country	*Number of Migrants*	*%*
Bahrain	4,000	0.2
Iraq	65,629	3.5
Jordan	226,850	11.9
Kuwait	190,550	10.0
Lebanon	1,255	0.1
Libya	332,600	17.5
Oman	15,000	0.8
Qatar	25,000	1.3
Saudi Arabia	923,600	48.6
United Arabs Emirates	95,000	5.0
Yemen	22,000	1.2
Total	**1,901,484**	**100**

Source: CAPMAS (2001) as reported by CARIM 2008; updated 7 February 2005.

The figures from the Egyptian Ministry of Manpower and Emigration include other Arab countries and show a different total number of temporary migrants (3,781,859). However, Saudi Arabia, Libya and Jordan still absorb the highest number of Egyptian temporary migrants (see Table 4.6).

As far as permanent migration to developed countries is concerned, the figures of CAPMAS and of the Egyptian Ministry of Manpower and Emigration diverge again (see Table 4.7).

According to the CAPMAS estimates, in 2000, permanent Egyptian emigrants were headed mainly to the USA, Canada, Australia and Western European countries. The USA was the first destination of permanent migration from Egypt, Egyptian migrants to the USA comprised about 40 per cent of the total Egyptian permanent migration.[45] The total number of permanent migrants to developed countries was estimated by CAPMAS to be 824,000. The Egyptian Ministry of Manpower and Emigration proposes a higher figure of emigrants to the same developed countries in 1998, a figure of over 1,300,000 migrants. Moreover, according to the ministry's

Table 4.6 Egyptian migrants (temporary) in Arab countries, 1998

Receiving Countries	*Number of migrants*	%
Algeria	2,100	0.1
Bahrain	6,000	0.2
Iraq	150,000	4.0
Jordan	500,000	13.2
Kuwait	250,000	6.6
Lebanon	300,000	7.9
Libya	950,000	25.1
Mauritania	159	0.0
Morocco	800	0.0
Oman	40,000	1.1
Qatar	20,000	0.5
Saudi Arabia	1,350,000	35.7
Sudan	2,000	0.1
Syria	10,000	0.3
Tunisia	500	0.0
United Arab Emirates	160,000	4.2
Yemen	40,300	1.1
Arab Countries	3,781,859	100

Source: Egyptian Ministry for Manpower and Emigration, Emigration Sector, as reported by CARIM 2008.

Table 4.7 Egyptian permanent migration

Receiving countries	*CAPMAS 2000*	*Egyptian Ministry of Manpower and Emigration 1998*
Australia	70,000	80,350
Austria	14,000	18,000
Canada	110,000	141,000
England	35,000	74,764
France	36,000	70,000
Germany	25,000	40,265
Greece	60,000	50,000
Holland	40,000	20,000
Italy	90,000	210,000
Spain	12,000	1,000
Switzerland	14,000	12,000
United States	318,000	635,000
Total	**824,000**	**1,352,379**

Source: Adapted by the author.

Table 4.8 Stock of foreign population by nationality – Italy, 1996–2005

	1996	*1997*	*1998*	*1999*	*2000*	*2001*	*2002*	*2003*	*2004*	*2005*
Albania	66.6	72.6	87.6	133.0	146.3	159.3	171.6	240.4	316.7	348.8
Morocco	115.0	122.2	128.3	155.9	162.3	167.9	170.7	231.0	294.9	319.5
Romania	26.9	28.8	33.8	61.2	70.0	83.0	94.8	244.4	248.8	297.6
China	31.6	35.3	41.2	56.7	60.1	62.1	64.0	105.0	111.7	127.8
Ukraine	1.3	1.9	3.1	6.5	9.1	12.6	14.8	117.2	93.4	107.1
Philippines	56.2	57.3	59.1	67.4	65.1	67.7	65.6	76.1	82.6	89.7
Tunisia	40.0	41.4	41.1	46.8	46.0	53.4	51.1	62.7	78.2	83.6
Serbia and Montenegro	33.0	31.7	36.1	41.2	40.2	39.3	40.2	46.8	58.2	64.1
Ecuador	4.3	4.7	4.9	10.5	11.2	12.3	12.3	48.3	53.2	62.0
India	19.1	20.5	22.0	27.6	30.0	32.5	34.3	49.2	54.3	61.8
Poland	23.2	22.9	23.3	29.5	30.4	32.9	35.0	64.9	50.8	60.8
Peru	21.9	23.0	23.6	29.1	30.1	31.7	31.3	48.8	53.4	59.3
Egypt	23.5	23.6	23.8	34.0	32.4	31.8	31.1	47.1	52.9	58.9
Senegal	31.5	32.0	31.4	40.9	39.2	37.8	37.0	49.7	53.9	57.1
Sri Lanka	23.7	24.8	27.4	32.0	33.8	38.8	35.7	43.0	45.6	50.5
Other countries	468.1	480.1	504.1	568.4	573.7	585.2	613.8	753.0	753.5	822.0
Total	**986.0**	**1022.9**	**1090.8**	**1340.7**	**1379.7**	**1448.4**	**1503.3**	**2227.6**	**2402.2**	**2670.5**

Source: OECD 2008.

estimates, the first choice of country of emigration for Egyptians is still the USA, but the number of emigrants is 635,000, whereas for CAPMAS it is only 318,000.

The figures referring to migration to Europe also diverge between the two sources (around 326,000 for CAPMAS and around 500,000 for the Egyptian Ministry of Manpower and Emigration). Moreover, there is also a huge discrepancy here between the numbers of Egyptian emigrants to Italy provided by the two official agencies: the statistical office lists 90,000 and the ministry 210,000 (Table 4.7). This difference could be attributed to undocumented migrants, although there is no way to ascertain this. The issue is further complicated if we consider the numbers indicated by official Italian sources to the OECD. The OECD reports only 32,400 residence permits held by Egyptians in Italy in 2000 (Table 4.8).

What cannot be denied, however, is that the European country experiencing the highest inflow of Egyptian migration is Italy. In terms of trends, the number of residence permits held by Egyptians in Italy has increased substantially in the last decades, from 7,000 in 1985[46] to 58,900 in 2005 (see Figure 4.2).

Other countries of destination in the EU for Egyptian migrants are England, France, Germany, Greece and Holland. A smaller number of Egyptians reside in Austria and Spain.

The majority of Egyptians entering the EU are undocumented.[47]

In the next section we will elaborate on the main smuggling routes to Southern European countries from the MENA area.

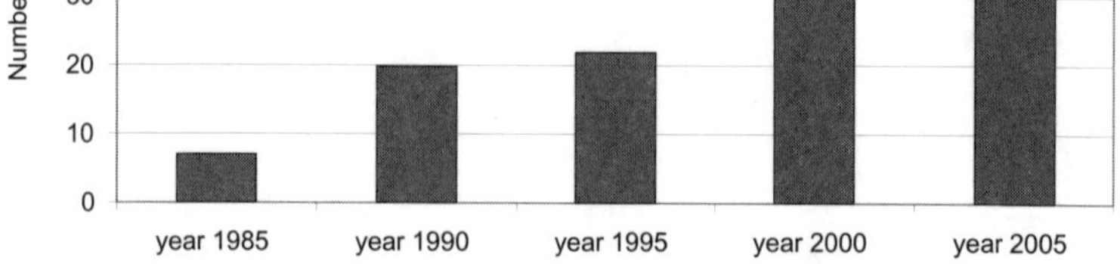

Figure 4.2 Residence permits to Egyptians in Italy, 1985–2005
Source: OECD 2008.

5 Mapping the routes

The phenomenon of illegal migration is particularly worrying in the relations between Europe and its Mediterranean counterparts. Smuggling illegal immigrants into Europe has become a profitable business.

There are several favourite routes in: via boat from Albania, Tunisia or Morocco into southern Europe; via Libya through the desert route from sub-Saharan Africa; from Sarajevo airport via Croatia and Slovenia into Italy and Austria; or overland starting from Istanbul and often ending up in Germany.

5.1 The Spanish route

Spain is a magnet for migrants from Northern and Sub-Saharan Africa. A Moroccan Arabic word is often used to describe the effort to get into Spain: *hareq*, 'to cross the Mediterranean illegally in a small boat'. Its root means 'to burn', perhaps as in to burn a Moroccan identity card so as not to be deportable, to give up the past.[48]

The fastest illegal route from Northern Africa to Europe is the nine-mile sea journey in small boats from northern Morocco to Spain. Spain also

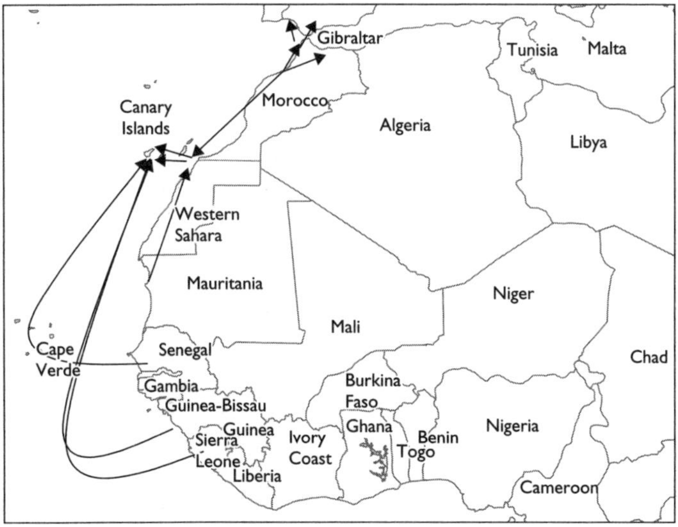

Figure 4.3 The Spanish route

Source: Delegacion del Gobierno para la Inmigracion y Extranjeria, adapted by the author.

has two enclaves on the Moroccan coast, Ceuta and Melilla, and both are ringed with fences to keep out migrants. Finally, the Spanish route includes the smuggling route leading from Northern and Sub-Saharan Africa to the Canary Islands. The Canary Islands, 70 miles off Morocco's southwestern coast, have been drawing boatloads of illegal migrants since 1995. They became a more popular destination after 2002, when monitoring at the Strait of Gibraltar was increased.[49]

In the last years, both the Canary and the Gibraltar routes experienced the highest number of boat passages and casualties ever. According to the Delegación del Gobierno para la Extranjería y la Inmigración, in 1999 there were just 3,569 total intercepted migrants, of which 875 were stopped in the Canary Islands. One-third of these migrants were women who, in many cases, arrived at an advanced stage of pregnancy. At the end of December 2000, the number of immigrants who were caught on board small boats trying to enter Spain by sea was already around 15,000 (14,893). Of these, 2,387 were captured on the Canary route. These immigrants reached the Spanish shore, with more than 780 boats intercepted in the Strait of Gibraltar or in the Canary Islands. Between January and September 2001, Spanish officials apprehended 13,000 migrants; this included 8,500 Moroccans. In 2002, Spanish police intercepted 1,000 boats and arrested 16,504 people.[50] In 2004, 15,675 illegal migrants travelled on 740 boats and 300 migrants were intercepted in a single day in early September 2005. In the first nine months of 2006 more than 26,000 Africans arrived in Spain, half from Senegal, usually coming in groups of 50 to 60 in open fishing boats after paying smugglers 400 to 500 Euros each.[51]

These figures, however, do not include those who made it without being caught or those who legally entered the country at the border with a three-month tourist visa and enough money to stay. Nor are those people included who disappeared or lost their lives in the many shipwrecks (see Table 4.9).[52] Spanish officials estimate that 200 people die every year trying to reach Spain across the Strait of Gibraltar.[53]

Table 4.9 Casualties on the Spanish route

	1999	*2000*
Shipwrecks	30	54
Disappeared	23	47
Recuperated corpses	29	55
Rescued people	387	1,037

Source: Delegación del Gobierno para la Extranjería.

Between 28 January and 8 February 2003, ships from five European nations began patrolling the Mediterranean to prevent migrant smuggling, the first time EU members have cooperated in this way. Under Operation Ulysses, Spanish, British, French, Italian and Portuguese police, customs and navy ships are patrolling from Algeçiras, Spain to Sicily. The EU launched its first joint border patrols in August 2006, aimed at stopping African migrants from reaching the Canary Islands. The EU said that the patrols would have both enforcement and humanitarian faces, aimed at combating smuggling and saving lives.[54]

Although small boats are the most common means to reach Spain, there are also other ways, just as risky, to try and make it to Spain from Northern Africa. Many immigrants, especially young men or teenagers, who do not have enough money to pay for the services of organised crime, cross the Strait of Gibraltar or reach the Canary Islands hiding in the backs of trucks travelling to Spain by ferry. This system, which led Spanish authorities to control vehicles from North Africa more strictly, allows immigrants to get to central and northern areas of the peninsula. Sometimes, however, the entry by trucks is also controlled by the mafia.[55]

Alternatively, immigrants may clandestinely board transport or mercantile ships; these ships are sometimes intercepted by the coastal patrols and the sailors detained.

Spain has received over four million immigrants since 2000, adding 10 per cent to its population. In 2005, Spain granted legal status to 700,000 foreigners in an effort to reduce illegal immigration and the underground economy.[56]

Indeed, in December 2004, Spain had an estimated 1.2 million unauthorized migrants. The majority of them come from the Maghreb, around 38 per cent of the total, and from Latin America (25 per cent). Three of the smaller groups are sub-Saharans (12 per cent), Chinese (8 per cent) and Eastern Europeans (8 per cent).[57]

Spain has 44.3 million residents, including four million foreigners. They include 505,000 Moroccans, 492,000 Ecuadorians, 314,000 Romanians, 269,000 Colombians and 225,000 Britons. The number of foreigners in Spain rose from 1.6 per cent of the population in 1998 to 9 per cent in 2005. Between 1998 and 2002, some 100,000 Moroccans arrived in Spain. Spain returns unauthorized Moroccans under a bilateral agreement, but most sub-Saharan Africans who arrive in Spain are given expulsion orders and released. Most travel to mainland Spain and disappear into the underground economy. Critics allege that enforcement is concentrated on Moroccans and Eastern Europeans (23,400 Moroccans were deported in 2002, followed by 18,900 Romanians) and that the Spanish government goes easy on Latin Americans because they are easier to integrate. Latin Americans usually arrive in Spain with tourist visas, and then often work illegally in cities.[58]

Spain has recently signed labour recruitment agreements with Romania, Poland, Ecuador, Morocco[59] and Bulgaria. There are three categories of foreign workers: those with contracts for a year or more, seasonal workers with contracts for less than nine months work in Spain, and young people aged 18 to 35 who can be employed in Spain for up to 18 months. The agreements are reciprocal, and permit Spaniards to work in these countries on the same basis. The foreign workers participate in Spanish social security and health systems on the same basis as domestic workers.[60]

However, as of September 2005, only 352,500 migrants had become members of the social security system; 34 per cent were domestic helpers, 19 per cent were in construction and 14 per cent in agriculture.[61]

A EUROSTAT survey shows that the reasons why so many Moroccan immigrants decide to use the Spanish route are, of course, easily traced to the physical proximity of the two countries.[62] Added to this, people from the Maghreb also believe that entering Spain, even if clandestinely, is much easier than entering other European countries.

5.2 *The Libyan route*

If Moroccans mainly use the Spanish route, Egyptians pass through Tunisia and Libya to Italy.[63] This happens thanks to the ability of Colonel Qaddafi, the unassailable authoritarian leader of Libya, to accredit himself as the paladin of pan-African unity, and thanks also to his open-minded policy towards immigration.[64]

At the borders of the desert of Niger, where the Sahara unfolds to the end of the horizon, Dirkou, once an abandoned village without any major attractions, is now a thriving town where money circulates in abundance and those who are smart enough can find their fortune. This is just the last outpost on the way that leads to Tripoli from Agadez in Niger, through the desert, but it has now become the symbol of the underground thread linking sub-Saharan Africa to northern Africa and, ideally, to Europe. Dirkou is the last sub-Saharan stop on one of the continent's greatest, and possibly most dangerous, smuggling routes: Africans travel hundreds of miles through desert to arrive there and board Libyan trucks that take them across the remaining expanses of the Sahara into North Africa. There the migrants stay to work, or they save up the money to jump to Europe and even America, where some may end up in New York working in restaurants and grocery stores.[65]

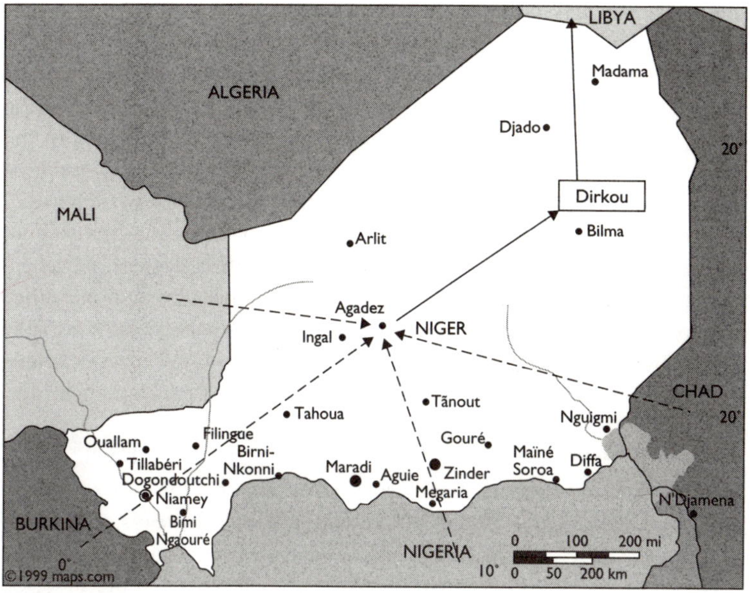

Figure 4.4 The Agadez-Dirkou route to Libya
Source: Adapted by the author from *The New York Times*, various issues.

This smuggling route was discovered after, in October 2000, Libyans killed or hurt thousands of African expatriates, lynching a Chadian diplomat and burning down the Niger Embassy. This outburst of violence was a revenge for the alleged rape of a Libyan girl by a Nigerian immigrant. Thereafter, in a sudden reversal of the exodus, tens of thousands of Africans were herded into buses and trucks, and then dumped in the desert south of Libya or expelled by plane to Nigeria and Ghana. Yet after less than two months, Africans were flocking again to Dirkou on their way to Libya. The surprisingly quick resumption of the exodus has been related to the worsening of the standards of life in sub-Saharan Africa in recent years. Civil wars, diseases and authoritarian regimes are plaguing the continent and even traditional regional powers like the Ivory Coast and South Africa have been breaking down politically or economically. Ordinary Africans are now finding it hard to survive, much less to have hope of improving their condition, with the consequence of a dangerous brain drain to the West. However, the desert of Dirkou witnesses the exodus of the lowest strata of African society, namely, young African men with little or no education.

Some of them border on criminality; others are engaged outright in smuggling products like heroin, or just ordinary people looking for a chance to improve their lives.

Before making it there, migrants entering Niger pass through Agadez, about 560 kilometres southwest, which, like Timbuktu in neighboring Mali, has served for centuries as a gateway between black Africa to the south and Arab Africa to the north. In Agadez, the smuggling system is highly organised. Middlemen from the subregion direct their countrymen to one of the dealers in the Agadez-Dirkou route. At the bus station, dealers hand the middlemen $3 for each passenger they receive. Travellers with passports are charged $15 for a one-way ticket to Dirkou. Since however, around 80 per cent of the passengers lack papers, most also pay what may be called a corruption surcharge of $7 to bribe the authorities at the four security checkpoints dotting the desert between Agadez and Dirkou.[66]

Migrants are loaded like cattle onto open-air trucks filled with goods, without any guarantees that they will arrive safely at the other edge of the desert. The cargo is normally composed of Guineans, Nigerians, Ghanaians, Cameroonians, and Congolese, as well as Nigerois, who stay in Libya as long as it is necessary to collect enough money to be smuggled to Europe or to the United States. Along the way, some get lost, some die, some get arrested – for much of the smuggling of migrants goes along with the smuggling of a number of other products, especially drugs.[67]

Many migrants sail for Italy from Libya in the summer months. Sicily is the Italian region most interested by the landing of illegal migrants coming from Libya. In the last few years the Libyan route seems to have overtaken the Turkish and the Sarajevo ones in popularity. Indeed, figures show that in 2003 the number of migrants arriving in Sicily (6,286) was by far higher than the number of those arriving in Calabria (177) and Puglia (81), which are normally the final stops of the Balkan routes (see Table 4.10).[68]

Table 4.10 Number of migrants landing on the shores of Italy (2001–2003, as at 15 June of each year)

	Sicily	*Calabria*	*Puglia*	*Total*
2001	1,334	1,038	5,236	7,608
2002	6,886	1,442	2,174	11,042
2003	6,286	177	81	6,544

Source: Panorama, Li manda Gheddafi, 16 June 2003.

Egyptians can enter neighbouring Libya easily, without even needing a passport. Frequent buses connect Alexandria and Tripoli at a very low fare (around 150 Lev).[69] Once arrived in Libya, Egyptians are smuggled by organised crime to Lampedusa in Sicily (Figure 4.5). On average, a smuggler charges 2,000 US dollars per migrant for a journey and the promise of a job.[70] The illegal trip by sea to Italy frequently ends in capture and deportation by the Italian authorities.[71] However, it is reported[72] that if a migrant is repatriated but does not reveal his/her identity, smugglers will try again and again until they are successful.

Sometimes, Egyptians cannot reach the 'promised land', and they drown at sea. On June 2008, for example, a boat with 150 Egyptians on board sank close to Lampedusa. Only one person survived.[73] An alternative is to take the air route to Europe. Zohry[74] reports that being smuggled by plane to Europe can cost between 6,700 and 9,500 Euros. As it is so expensive, the air route is chosen mainly by wealthy migrants, whereas young and poor Egyptians still risk their lives at sea. To avoid fatalities in the migration process, the Egyptian Ministry for Manpower and Emigration offers many services to Egyptians wishing to migrate. Among them is the possibility to obtain a work contract certified by the ministry itself before going abroad. However, migration without a job contract, as further clarified in this book, is still very common.[75]

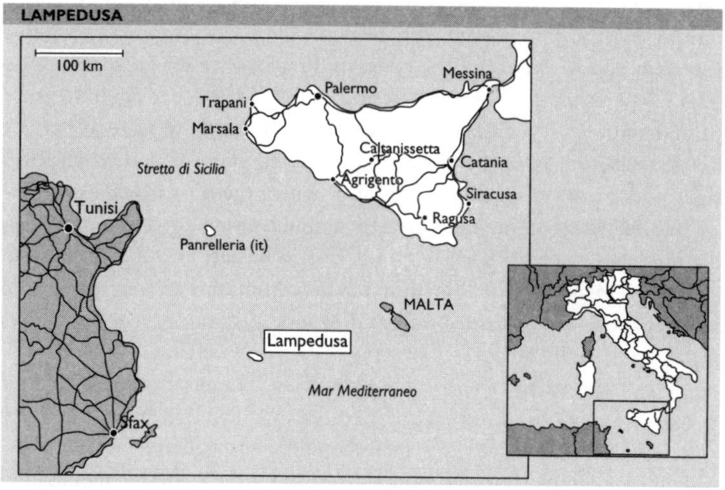

Figure 4.5 Lampedusa

5.3 The Turkish route

A report published by *The New York Times*,[76] described the Laleli quarter of Istanbul as a place to buy false passports and visas for prices that range from several hundred to several thousand dollars. An Iranian passport, for example, goes for $250 with the original photograph in it, or $350 with the migrant's own photo inserted and a forged official Iranian stamp applied to it. Western passports are far more desirable and expensive – a Danish one costs $9,000 and an American one $14,000 – but the Iranian document can prove extremely useful. In fact, the migrants gathering in Istanbul are likely to use their Iranian passports for visa-free travel to Bosnia from which illegal access to Europe is easily available.[77]

People choosing this route to Europe are normally from northern Iraq, northern Africa and Central Asia. Many of the migrants seeking entry to Western Europe are in Turkey legally, arriving by plane, by boat or by land, but they need to be smuggled from Turkey into countries that deny them visas. Istanbul thus becomes a waiting room before migrants jump to Europe through illegal means. From here, migrants can either move to Sarajevo to try the Balkan routes, or sail to Albania and reach Europe through the Italian coast, mainly Lecce and Bari, but also, more rarely, through the French coast. Some of them remain stuck in Turkey and live a life of misery and humiliation, unable to go back to their own countries of origins nor to proceed in the journey of hope to Europe.[78]

A major human disaster in February 2001 showed the entire world the appalling conditions in which migrants sailing from Turkey are brought to Europe. A cargo ship packed with more than 900 Kurdish migrants, mostly from Iraq, ran aground off the coast of France after the crew abandoned ship. The journey to Europe cost the Kurds $4,200 per adult to get to Europe, with $1,700 charged per child, of whom there were about 300. It lasted seven days in the most intolerable conditions, during which the migrants were not even allowed to know where the boat would arrive.[79]

The smuggling of migrants from Istanbul is dominated by Turkish and Albanian gangs, composed of about five to twenty members. However, the involvement of the North African community is huge, not only amongst those trying to be smuggled in, but also amongst those actively participating to the business. Charging between $1,000 and $4,000 to move people to Western Europe from Turkey, those organisations quickly build up large amounts of cash that are invested in stolen luxury cars, property, restaurants and illegal activities, including drug smuggling.[80]

Many immigrants borrow money from the same criminal organisations to be able to pay crime gangs to move them. This is actually how migrants add themselves to the number of the new-slaves, tied to the criminal groups by the debts they made to be smuggled in. Indeed, dealing in human beings is a business that, though very profitable, implies few risks on the side of the organised criminal groups, for penalties are much lighter than for other criminal activities like drug smuggling. It is true that Turkey has recently added extra border posts at its frontiers, increased the number of border guards, tightened inspections in various Aegean ports, started sharing intelligence on human smuggling with other countries including Italy and Bosnia, and begun new training for guards. However, this is far from representing a substantial policy against traffickers and smugglers and it is very much dictated by Turkey's will to please the EU in view of its eventual entry.[81]

Turkish authorities apprehended 47,518 migrants in 1999, and 40,245 in the first six months of 2000. In 1997 the number of illegal immigrants captured in Turkey was only 28,439. However, thousands more are never caught.[82]

5.4 The Sarajevo route

For many migrants coming from the Middle East, Northern Africa and Central Asia, Sarajevo is the last stop before Europe. Indeed, the Balkan

Figure 4.6 The smuggling route from Turkey to the EU
Source: Adapted by the author from *The Guardian*, various issues.

routes are well established. Chinese migrants come via Belgrade,[83] migrants and asylum seekers from the Middle East, Bangladesh and Sri Lanka via Sarajevo, where Bosnian authorities tend to favor fellow Muslims. In Bosnia the largest immigrant groups come from Iran, with Turkish Kurds and Chinese next on the list. Arrivals of smaller groups of Sri-Lankan, Bangladeshi, Afghan, Egyptian, Pakistani, Iraqi, Macedonian and Yugoslavian nationals have been also reported.[84]

According to information from the Bosnian authorities and international agencies, more than 5,000 individuals migrate to Bosnia each month with the intention of continuing towards Western Europe. Many of them come from Istanbul, by truck or even by plane. Turkish airlines fly regularly from Istanbul, charged with young men with no luggage, claiming to be tourists, for tourists in Bosnia do not need visas. The numbers speak for themselves. It is estimated that in 2000, 50,000 migrants entered Bosnia through the two main airports; 28,000 are unaccounted for and assumed to now be in Europe.[85]

From Sarajevo, three overland routes sneak them into Italy and Austria via Croatia, Slovenia and Hungary. There are 400 crossing points out of Bosnia and only four of them are controlled. Croatia and Bosnia, who recently signed a readmission agreement, share 1,200 miles of largely un-patrolled mountainous border. In the first eight months of 2000, the number of irregular migrants caught crossing into Croatia was 11,500, 40 per cent more than in the same period in 1999. Romanians, Turks and Iranians topped the list of nationalities, with 3,640, 2,500 and 2,470 respectively. However, given the thriving trade of Iranian and Turkish passports in Istanbul, it is an easy guess that many nationalities were disguised.[86]

Alternative routes lead through Albania or Croatia to cross the Adriatic from Vlore or Split in small boats. It is estimated that more than 130 drowned in 2000.[87]

The International Organisation for Migration calculated the trade in migrants is worth upwards of £70 million a year in Bosnia alone.[88]

This is not all. In Bosnia the traffic in illegal migrants conceals a second, more venal trade in humans: the trade in sex slaves which lures women and young girls to Bosnia mainly from Eastern Europe and former Soviet republics with the promise of jobs as au pairs or waitresses in the EU.[89] However, in Bosnia prosecutions have been almost non-existent for both crimes; detection is hindered by those willing to help the people-smugglers and these are mainly represented by the corrupted elite of the country. Evidence exists too that the smuggling business is part of a sophisticated international network that supplies forged documents as well. The shocking reality of Bosnia today, international officials say, is this. Only a few years after the Dayton Peace Agreement was signed to bring a genocidal war to an end, a country that has received unprecedented military and economic aid from the international community has turned, not into a model Balkan democracy, but into one of Europe's main hubs for smuggling people.[90]

5.5 *Egypt as a transit country*

Egypt is also a primary transit country. According to the International Office for Migration (IOM), there has been a noticeable increase in the number of illegal migrants using Egypt as a transit station to nearby countries such as Israel.[91] Israel estimates that 2,800 people have entered the country illegally through its border with Egypt in recent years. Most are believed to be refugees from the Darfur region of Sudan.[92] Egypt is also used by Chinese workers and Eastern European women to enter Israel via the Sinai. Moreover, the Suez Canal has been used recently to carry illegal migrants from Sri Lanka or Bangladesh to Europe (Table 4.11).[93]

Table 4.11 Primary smuggling routes from and through the Middle East

Origins	*Areas of Transit*	*Destinations*
Iraq	Turkey	Europe, Indonesia, Australia
OPT	Lebanon, Turkey	Southern Europe
Jordan, Egypt	Tunisia, Southern Libya	Southern Italy
China, Eastern Europe	Egypt	Israel
Turkey	Jordan	Israel
Sub-Saharan Africa	Libya	Egypt
Syria, Turkey, Iran, Iraq	Lebanon	Europe (esp. Cyprus, Greece, Italy)
Somalia	Yemen	GCC
Pakistan, Afghanistan, Iran, Yemen		GCC
Nigeria, Senegal	Egypt	Lebanon, S.Arabia, Western Europe

Source: IOM 2005.

6 Conclusion

To sum up, Egypt is increasingly becoming a source of both legal and illegal migration to the EU, especially to Italy. Although the numbers are not yet comparable with those of other national groups, such as Turks or Moroccans, the trend is clearly positive and the numbers are increasing.

What remains to be ascertained is why this is happening. This is the subject of the following chapters.

Chapter 5

Why do Egyptians migrate now?

The lack of integration of the MENA region

1 Introduction

Despite the various definitions and approaches to globalisation,[1] scholars of International Political Economy from different traditions agree that the current phase of capitalist development is characterised by a marked process of regionalisation into three distinct blocks, the so-called 'triad'.[2] For realists, the 'triadisation' of the world economy is the consequence of the increased hegemonic position of the USA in the Americas, of the EU (in particular the UK, Germany and France) in Europe, and of Japan in the Asian region. Neo-institutionalists agree on the triadisation thesis, but maintain that this is just a step towards a truly globalised economy in which international institutions would contribute to the creation and government of an interdependent global economy. Finally, transnationalists underline how, inevitably, the creation of macro-regions in some areas of the world produces, as a consequence, the marginalisation of other areas where regionalisation has not taken place. This, in turn, contributes to the increase of permanent migration to industrialised countries.[3]

The MENA area is a clear example of lack of regionalisation. Despite a number of attempts to create an integrated economic and even political region, the literature unanimously portrays such attempts as a failure.[4] This chapter assesses the state of regional integration in the MENA area and in the Arab world. For the sake of this analysis, it is important to make clear, following the International Monetary Fund (IMF), that the MENA region comprises a group of countries bound together by their geographical location, close historical and cultural ties, and common economic challenges. These are: Algeria, Bahrain, Egypt, the Islamic Republic of Iran, Jordan, Kuwait, Lebanon, Libya, Morocco, Oman, Qatar, Saudi Arabia, the Syrian Arab Republic, Tunisia, the United Arab Emirates and Yemen. Moreover, to account for fundamental differences in economic structure, countries within the region are divided into oil-exporting countries and other MENA countries, which are traditionally referred to as non-oil MENA countries (Egypt, Jordan, Lebanon, Morocco, Syria, Tunisia and Yemen).[5] The oil-exporting MENA countries are further divided into the members of the Gulf Cooperation Council (GCC) (Bahrain, Kuwait, Oman, Qatar, Saudi Arabia and United Arab Emirates) and other MENA oil-exporters (Algeria, Iran and Libya).[6]

2 The institutional steps towards more economic integration in the MENA region

The paradox of regionalisation within globalisation is one of the pillars of the qualitative, transnationalist approach to the impact of globalisation on migration. This entails that those regions experiencing a high degree of integration into the global economy tend also to increase their level of economic and, to a certain extent, political regional integration. The Middle East and Northern Africa are a clear example of the opposite.[7] Leaving aside a more detailed analysis of the theoretical aspects of the concept of integration,[8] and of the political and institutional dimension of Arab integration (or, better, 'disintegration'[9]), what mainly concerns this contribution is the degree of economic integration, or lack of it.[10]

Since the creation of the Arab League in 1945, there have been numerous attempts to realise economic integration in the Arab world. In 1953, the Arab League promoted a multilateral trading agreement among Arab countries. This included provisions to exempt Arab agricultural commodities from tariff barriers, and reduced tariffs on some industrial goods. In 1956, Egypt, Iraq, Jordan, Kuwait and Syria signed the Arab Economic Unity Agreement, which aimed at providing full economic union. The Arab Common Market was established in 1964 by the same countries, excluding Kuwait. The objective was to eliminate all tariff and non-tariff barriers within ten years. However, there is no doubt in the literature that all these and numerous other attempts to promote integration have failed.[11]

A new wave of integration programmes for the Arab world succeeded the oil booms in the 1970s. Owen[12] reports that the main purpose of these programmes was redistributive; that is, to transfer some of the resources accumulated by the wealthy oil-exporters to the poorer countries in the region. To this aim, the Kuwait and Abu Dhabi Funds for Arab Economic Development were established in 1973. In 1974, similar national funds were created in Saudi Arabia and Iraq. A number of regional institutions were established between 1968 and 1976 with the aim of providing balance of payments support or financing for projects. These were: the Arab Fund for Economic and Social Development, created in 1968; the Arab Bank for Economic Development in Africa, in 1973; the Islamic Development Bank, the Arab–African Technical Assistance Fund, the Arab–African Oil Assistance Fund, and the Special Fund for Arab Non-oil-exporting Countries, all in 1974; and the Arab Monetary Fund in 1976. In a similar context, more than multilateral economic integration in the MENA area, it is appropriate to talk about transfers from rich to poor states.[13]

Scholars refer to two stages in Arab attempts to create a multilateral framework for greater regional economic integration.[14] The first, relating to the creation of a free trade area, goes back to the ratification of the Treaty for Joint Defence and Economic Cooperation by the ministers of Egypt, Jordan, Lebanon, Syria, Saudi Arabia and (North) Yemen in 1950. This focused on tariff reductions and on measures to facilitate the free movement of people and capital. Along the same lines, in 1953, the Convention for Facilitating Trade and Regulating Transit was signed by the members of the Arab League. This provided for an agreement to abolish tariffs on agricultural products and minerals. Despite these efforts, however, the elimination of existing barriers to the trade in manufactured goods was not successful in the face of the protectionist attitude of states like Iraq, or the insistence of countries like Saudi Arabia and Yemen on imposing duties on imported goods.[15] In the second phase, dating back to the end of the 1950s, Arab countries attempted to create a common market, on the model of the European one.

The crisis of the Suez Canal had facilitated an Arab rapprochement, and in 1958, the Arab League's Economic Council achieved an agreement in principle that was followed in 1962 by the joint declaration of Egypt, Jordan, Morocco, Syria and Kuwait to commit to engage in a process of unification of both economic policies and economic legislation. In August 1964, the five states signed a treaty to establish the Arab Common Market, starting from 1 January 1965. The treaty provided for the progressive abolition of all duties and quantitative restrictions by January 1974. Eventually, Kuwait failed to ratify the Treaty. However, the other four states also had great difficulty in respecting their pledge to reduce tariffs and restrictions. The number of products that were supposed to be exempted from tariff reduction for each of the member states was very long; also, the abolition of quantitative restrictions did not prove an easy task. Finally, the countries in question failed to agree on a common external tariff, and in 1971, the whole idea of an Arab common market was simply abandoned for a much lighter putative free trade area.[16]

A very detailed analysis of the impact of both multilateral and bilateral agreements between the Arab states from 1951 to 1960 on regional trade has been carried out by Diab. His conclusions are pretty grim.[17] Additionally, Yusif Sayigh notes that inter-Arab trade during the 1950s and 1960s never became more than a tenth of the Arab total,[18] and this remains the case today.[19] In the literature,[20] two reasons are commonly provided as to why this happened. The first is the lack of political will, and the second the lack of economic differentiation among the countries attempting to integrate, which did not facilitate trade.

Indeed, apart from Kuwait, which withdrew even before ratifying the common market, the other members produced roughly the same range of agricultural and manufactured goods. However, Owen adds two important qualifications to this explanation.[21] First, the model adopted by the Arab regimes to promote development resembled very closely the Soviet approach of Import-Substituting Industrialisation (ISI). This is the production of a relatively simple range of previously imported manufactured goods for sale in a protected local market. This choice proved especially detrimental to economic growth, as well as to intraregional trade. Indeed, if exports receive low priority, foreign exchange is scarce and almost completely used for essential imports of capital goods and raw materials. However, as periodic balance-of-payments crises led to reduced convertibility for local currencies and an increasing number of controls, foreign exchange became almost non-existent, making it increasingly difficult to produce goods even for the local market, let alone for the regional one. At the same time, there was a serious shortage of skills in the management of the newly nationalised industries, which made it difficult for the countries concerned to market their goods abroad. These were not the conditions most conducive to success in the creation of a regional free trade area.

This was especially true in the case of Egypt, with the Nasser regime, while both Lebanon, with its small, more export-oriented economy, and the oil-exporting Gulf countries followed an opposite development model, which proved more successful.[22] Also, in the rest of the MENA area, namely, in the Maghreb and the Mashreq, attempts to create Arab common markets during the 1960s collapsed. The reason was, again, the unwillingness by the countries involved to limit control over their economic policies or to allow access to their domestic markets. The attempts to establish the Maghreb Union started with the Permanent Consultative Council set up in Tunis in 1966, whose task was to promote greater regional integration. Despite the efforts put into creating a North African market, the project foundered because of the decision of individual states to pursue growth through import substitution-led industrialisation. In the case of Algeria, the difficulty was even greater given the existence of state trading organisations with monopolies over the import of many strategic foreign products.[23]

The second reason adduced by Owen to explain the failure of the MENA economic integration projects is related to the gap between commercial treaties and economic reality. Essentially, the whole idea of increasing trade between Arab countries through institutional devices such as a free trade area or common market was a way to conceal the grim situation of real trade flows. The oil price increase in the 1970s had made a substantial impact on intraregional capital and labour flows, but had a much less pronounced effect on trade. However, these developments were hardly governed by centralised Arab institutions. Regarding migration, apart from the facilities provided by the Egyptian government (and described in the previous chapter), for its emigrants in Iraq at the beginning of the 1980s, Arab migration was largely uncontrolled and unregulated.[24] Also, capital flows were mostly unplanned, unpredictable, and subject to the political interests of the separate states.[25]

The ineffectiveness of the Arab economic institutional arrangements was evidenced also by the creation of smaller sub-regional groupings such as the Gulf Cooperation Council (GCC), the Maghreb Union, and the short-lived Arab Cooperation Council created in the late 1980s among Egypt, Iraq, Jordan and Yemen. The only body which would survive the 1980s was the GCC, providing for a genuine common market, with a common external tariff and common internal laws and regulations. The Gulf countries indeed were the only ones which were actually trading substantially among themselves. For the rest of the area, the situation was not good.

In the course of the 1980s, the proportion of intra-Arab to total Arab trade, though growing, remained small, particularly if compared with other regions of the non-European world. Of total Arab exports, only 5.2 per cent in 1980 and 6.6 per cent in 1984 were sent to another Arab country. However, the absolute values involved were declining as a result of the falling price of oil. Thus, inter-Arab exports were worth $8.4 billion in 1984, whereas their value had been $12 billion in 1980. Besides, as pointed out above, much of the already limited amount of intra-Arab trade was taking place among the Gulf oil-producers themselves.[26]

Many factors served to contribute to the lack of regionalisation of Arab economies during the 1980s. One of the most important was the debt crisis that hit a number of Arab countries as a result of falling oil prices. Of course, this was most severe in non-oil-producing countries, especially Egypt and Jordan, whose economies were supported by remittances from migrants in the Gulf and by Arab aid.[27] The economic stabilisation programmes which followed the debt crisis did not help to give incentives to intraregional trade. Moreover, the first Iraq war further reduced the level of communication in the area, increasing political divisions in particular among the Gulf States and their western Arab neighbours, as well as among the GCC states themselves. As a result, any attempt to Arab economic cooperation was nullified, and economic interactions in the zone curtailed.

Overall, the record of Arab economic integration in the 1980s was even worse than that of the 1970s.[28] The reasons are easily identified by the scholars in the reduction of the revenues of oil-producing countries. The unprecedented affluence following oil price increases in the 1970s had allowed oil countries to be more pro-active in financing the needs of poorer Arab countries, and had increased their needs of Arab workers. In this context, institutional economic integration was viewed more sympathetically.[29] However, as revenues decreased in the 1980s, the prospects of economic integration also suffered.

In the 1990s, two new economic organisations in the Middle East and North Africa emerged. The first was a plan for a Euro-Mediterranean free trade area put forward by the European Union (EU). The second, more general scheme was unveiled in Barcelona in November 1995. This included three 'baskets': economic, security and cultural. The economic basket was meant to establish a Euro-Mediterranean free trade area in manufactured goods no later than 2010. Signatories included the members of the EU, as well as Turkey, Israel, Cyprus, Malta, the Arab States of Mauritania, Morocco, Tunisia, Egypt, Jordan, Syria, Lebanon and the Palestinian National Authority (PNA).[30] Born with the Barcelona declaration of 1995, the Euro-Mediterranean Partnership (EMP) seemed to have set in motion a crucial dialogue between the southern Mediterranean countries and the European economic, political and cultural sphere. Although never without its contradictions and spill-backs, the process had achieved sizeable results, particularly in terms of economic integration and political cooperation, and much could be hoped for the future as far as the more complex cultural and political dimension was concerned.

However, the events of September 11 marked a watershed in the relations between the Muslim and the non-Muslim world. In this context, the question of how these events impacted on further developments in the process of Euro-Mediterranean Partnership becomes unavoidable. How did Euro-Mediterranean relations change after September 11? Is further marginalisation of the southern Mediterranean a necessary consequence of September 11? Many scholars have attempted to answer precisely these kinds of questions.[31]

The most controversial effect of September 11 on the Euro-Med process was securitisation.[32] It is certainly difficult to deny that the terrorist threat from Muslim fundamentalism has reshaped the EU attitude towards Muslim citizens in a much more security-oriented fashion. The foreign policy consequences of such a development are universally appreciated, and are represented by the tendency to move the political discourse from low politics to high politics, or to make socio-economic cooperation dependent on the adoption of measures designed to curb the security threats. However, there is a much less obvious risk that this situation poses for the democratisation of southern Mediterranean countries: that domestic governments can justify and legitimise their stepping back from the respect of basic democratic principles or even human rights as a fight against a vital threat. This is very clear cut in the case of the isolation of human rights organisations in Egypt.[33] Other scholars underline how the focus on security seriously undermines previous efforts to reinforce the dialogue between civilisations and the cultural cooperation enshrined in the third basket of the EMP.[34] Additionally, the development of the European Security and Defence Policy is perceived, after September 11, as a potential threat for Muslim countries, although some political elites welcome it as a positive alternative to the American military might.[35]

To be sure, the roots of the uneasiness in relations with the Islamic world predate the events of 2001. A main obstacle to Euro-Mediterranean Partnership was, and still is, the Palestinian question.[36] This poses broader questions about the role of Israel in the EMP and, even more controversial, the possibility of its admittance as a full member of the EU in the not-so-distant future.[37] However, the very fact that the Arab region, far from benefiting from the general trend towards regionalisation, appears increasingly unable to pursue a successful regional integration exercise, not even from the economic viewpoint, does not help in stabilising its international position.[38]

To conclude, there is no doubt that the impact of September 11 on the Southern Mediterranean has been to increase its marginalisation; and there is no doubt that the road ahead for economic integration of the MENA area is opaque and full of uncertainties.

3 Actual economic integration in the MENA region

3.1 Intraregional trade integration

The Arab world has experimented with a variety of mechanisms to promote trade integration, from free trade areas to customs unions and common markets. Despite this, or maybe as a consequence of the failure to identify a successful economic institutional arrangement at the regional level, the most striking feature of trade patterns in the Middle East is how limited is the level of intraregional trade in the area: the percentage share of intraregional imports and exports in the Middle East is only a fraction of the percentages of regional trade with other parts of the world. IMF figures relating to the period from 1998 to 2007 show that the region is importing and exporting mostly from and to industrial countries, and the share of intraregional trade is just one tenth of the total (Table 5.1). Additionally, although the share of exports/imports to developing countries has increased, intraregional share of total exports (Figure 5.1) and imports (Figure 5.2) within the Middle East has hardly changed in the last ten years, remaining around 10 per cent.

What is remarkable, as shown by the data, is the increase of imports to the Middle East from other developing countries, whose share increased by 18.1 per cent. This was led by an increase of the share of imports from Asia (+9.6 per cent). Indeed, imports from China in 2007 were ten times more than in 1998 (Figure 5.3). The increase of imports from Asia and China, therefore, crowded out the potential for intraregional integration providing the region with cheap goods produced by less developed countries.

Data on the percentage share of exports to the Arab world (members of the Arab Monetary Fund, which includes all MENA countries plus Mauritania, Somalia and Sudan) over total exports provide a similar picture. Excluding the cases of Iraq, Jordan, Syria and Lebanon, which are under

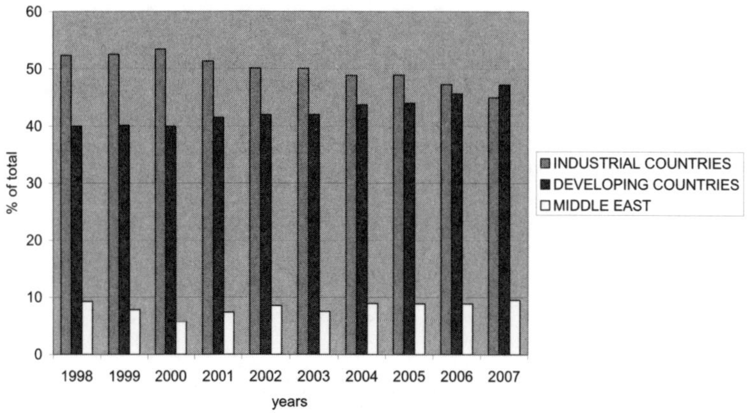

Figure 5.1 Share of exports from the Middle East to other areas, 1998–2007
Source: Adapted by the author on IMF data, available at http://www.imf.org/external/data.htm, accessed 4 September 2008.

Table 5.1 Intraregional Middle Eastern exports and imports as a share of total exports and imports, 1998–2007

% of world exports/ imports	*Exports* *1998*	*1999*	*2000*	*2001*	*2002*	*2003*	*2004*	*2005*	*2006*	*2007*	*Imports* *1998*	*1999*	*2000*	*2001*	*2002*	*2003*	*2004*	*2005*	*2006*	*2007*
Industrial countries	52.4	52.6	53.5	51.4	50.1	50.1	48.9	48.9	47.3	45	64.3	61.6	61.2	60	59.5	56.1	51.6	51.1	48.4	47.4
United states	12.7	13	13.6	14.3	13.95	13.8	12.7	12.1	11.4	10.9	12.9	12.2	12.3	11.4	10.7	9.4	8.4	9.17	9.51	9.17
Developing countries	40	40.1	39.9	41.5	41.99	42	43.7	44	45.7	47.2	32.1	34.8	34.4	36.7	37.5	40.4	46.1	46.4	49	50.2
Asia	23.5	26.8	27.7	27.6	26.84	27.8	27.5	29.2	29.8	30.4	15.5	17.3	16.7	17	17.7	19.5	21.7	21.8	23.5	25.1
Middle east	9.26	7.83	5.79	7.38	8.563	7.52	8.9	8.87	8.86	9.53	7.8	9.08	8.54	10.1	10.4	10	11.2	12.5	13.4	12.9
European union	23.5	22.7	21.3	19.1	18.93	18.9	20.4	19.7	18.6	18	38.9	37.9	37.5	36.5	36.9	36.6	34.9	34.1	31.2	30.2
Exporting ctys	7.12	6.45	4.74	5.95	6.858	5.95	6.25	6.19	6.15	6.65	6.93	8.32	7.74	8.32	8.58	8.38	8.36	9.46	10.1	9.51
Non-oil develop. ctys	32.9	33.7	35.2	35.6	35.14	36.1	37.5	37.9	39.5	40.6	25.2	26.5	26.7	28.4	28.9	32.1	37.7	36.9	38.8	40.7

Source: Adapted by the author on IMF data, available at: http://www.imf.org/external/data.htm, accessed 4 September 2008.

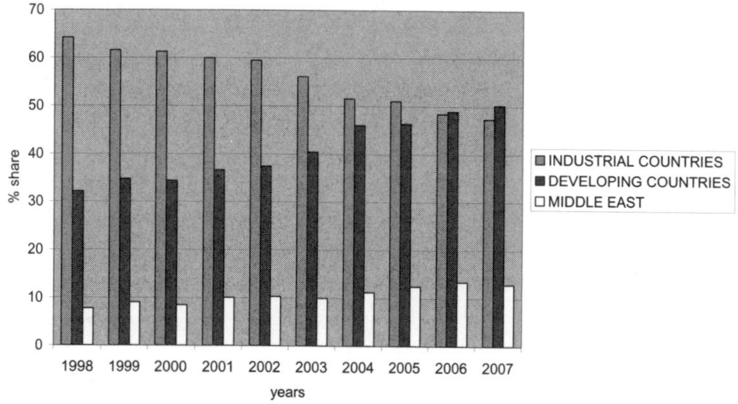

Figure 5.2 Share of imports to the Middle East from other areas, 1998–2007
Source: Adapted by the author on IMF data, available at http://www.imf.org/external/data.htm, accessed 4 September 2008.

political constraints limiting trade with the rest of the world, the average share of intraregional exports between 1991 and 2001 ranges from 1.9 per cent for Algeria to 12.5 per cent for Egypt and Oman (Table 5.2). It might

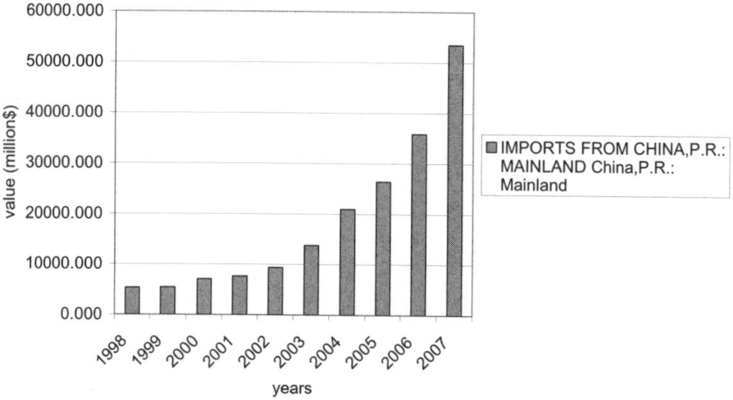

Figure 5.3 Imports from China to the Middle East (US$ millions), 1998–2007
Source: Adapted by the author on IMF data, available at: http://www.imf.org/external/data.htm, accessed 4 September 2008.

Table 5.2 Percentage share of exports from Arab countries by destination, 1991–2001

To	*From Algeria*	*Bahrain*	*Egypt*	*Emirates*	*Iraq*	*Jordan*	*Kuwait*	*Lebanon*	*Libya*	*Morocco*	*Oman*	*Qatar*	*S. Arabia*	*Syria*	*Tunisia*	*Yemen*	*Avg*	*Partial Avg*
Total Islamic Countries	5.5	17.3	15.0	12.5	50.8	44.2	11.7	54.1	10.5	9.5	15.3	8.7	14.9	26.1	10.9	12.2	19.9	12.0
of which Arab (AMF Members)	1.9	11.6	12.5	7.0	49.0	36.1	4.1	50.1	5.3	6.4	12.5	6.0	9.3	20.2	8.4	9.8	15.6	7.9
of which Non-AMF Arab and Non-Arab -Islamic	3.5	5.7	2.5	5.5	1.7	8.1	7.6	4.0	5.2	3.1	2.8	2.7	5.6	5.9	2.5	2.3	4.3	4.1
Total Industrial Countries	84.5	19.0	48.5	40.9	42.3	9.5	43.4	36.5	84.4	68.2	31.2	60.3	54.5	56.5	80.1	30.5	49.4	53.8
of which EEC Members	64.4	5.3	35.4	5.0	22.9	4.7	14.0	19.5	79.4	57.1	1.6	2.1	18.3	53.1	78.7	10.3	29.5	31.0
Total Developing Countries	6.2	20.6	7.1	18.7	2.6	15.6	32.5	2.1	0.8	7.7	34.3	25.0	23.0	0.7	2.8	38.6	14.9	18.1
Total Socialist Countries	1.5	0.6	3.0	0.5	1.4	2.9	1.0	3.7	1.0	1.3	11.5	2.0	0.8	2.8	1.4	16.6	3.2	3.4
Total rest of world	2.4	42.6	26.3	27.4	2.9	27.8	11.5	3.6	3.4	13.2	7.6	4.0	6.9	13.9	4.8	2.2	12.5	12.7
Total	100.0	100.0	100.0	100.0	100.0	100.0	100.0	100.0	100.0	100.0	100.0	100.0	100.0	100.0	100.0	100.0	100.0	100.0

Source: Adapted by the author on data from the AMF, available at: http://www.amf.org.ae/pages/page.aspx, accessed 4 September 2008.

Table 5.3 Ratio of total inter-Arab trade to total external trade

Country	*1994*	*1995*	*1996*	*1997*	*1998*	*1999*	*2000*	*2001*	*2002*	*2003*	*2004*
Jordan	27.06	29.91	27.92	28.40	24.14	24.50	25.52	28.88	29.64	22.27	31.48
Emirates	4.63	5.33	4.69	4.44	5.54	5.83	5.12	5.70	6.26	6.49	7.94
Bahrain	12.89	11.48	10.24	11.02	12.25	11.36	8.37	10.26	11.03	11.50	10.37
Tunisia	6.53	7.34	7.55	6.13	5.77	6.26	7.63	7.47	7.56	7.27	6.63
Algeria	3.62	2.82	2.14	2.71	2.15	2.11	1.57	2.03	3.07	2.96	3.04
Saudi Arabia	7.89	8.39	8.89	9.31	10.06	9.15	7.31	8.36	9.18	10.04	10.81
Sudan	29.33	27.21	27.48	28.00	30.73	27.73	17.84	18.39	27.59	25.96	18.86
Syria	15.32	14.97	12.79	16.86	3.60	14.31	13.73	12.59	17.76	17.45	22.33
Somalia	23.95	33.58	31.86	38.33	41.55	41.32	32.87	44.16	54.40	44.52	42.72
Iraq	62.29	68.65	57.27	22.61	8.63	5.77	5.38	9.22	14.90	9.63	9.22
Oman	20.41	18.67	17.21	19.66	24.93	22.23	18.17	18.99	20.73	17.65	23.19
Qatar	12.15	8.57	10.15	10.41	9.67	11.21	8.65	6.87	9.27	7.13	8.39
Kuwait	6.19	6.09	5.98	6.45	7.99	7.24	5.67	6.72	7.37	7.49	6.71
Lebanon	13.02	18.22	14.72	12.39	11.99	12.38	15.76	14.46	16.08	17.92	20.37
Libya	6.15	7.41	6.16	7.36	8.06	7.91	5.70	6.62	6.51	5.08	4.84
Egypt	6.61	5.67	5.60	6.35	6.98	6.99	8.81	8.02	8.30	10.06	9.27
Morocco	9.72	7.43	7.77	7.97	5.82	6.52	8.96	8.99	8.52	6.89	6.85
Mauritania	3.00	2.88	3.62	7.26	4.65	2.72	3.68	5.82	6.38	4.71	4.70
Yemen	7.56	8.68	13.56	14.95	21.93	20.54	17.75	19.80	26.20	26.10	20.01
Total	8.42	8.59	8.27	8.58	8.76	8.71	7.73	8.54	9.79	9.28	9.99

Source: Arab Monetary Fund 2008, available at: http://www.amf.org.ae/pages/page.aspx, accessed 4 September 2008.

be worth noting that the total average share of exports from the area to industrial countries was almost 50 per cent.

Overall, the ratio of inter-Arab trade to total external trade for all Arab countries that were members of the AMF between 1994 and 2004 was never above 10 per cent (see Table 5.3).

In terms of trade openness of Middle Eastern economies, the IMF uses as a measure the ratio of imports plus exports over GDP. Figure 5.4 shows that, in the period between 1980 and 2000, overall MENA countries had a much lower openness to trade than East Asia. The only exception was, for reasons detailed above, the members of the Gulf Cooperation Council (GCC).

Another measure of trade integration often used in the literature [39] is the average level of import tariffs applied to non-agricultural and non-fuel products. Figures from UNCTAD show that, apart from Lebanon and Algeria, non-oil-producing countries are ranked very low in terms of import tariffs (Table 5.4). Indeed, Morocco was ranked 119 of 121 countries, with an average import tariff for the most favourable nation of 23.49 per cent; Tunisia was at 118, with an average of 22.45 per cent, and Sudan at 115, with 18.21 per cent. Unfortunately, no data were available for Egypt and the other MENA countries for the year 2006.[40]

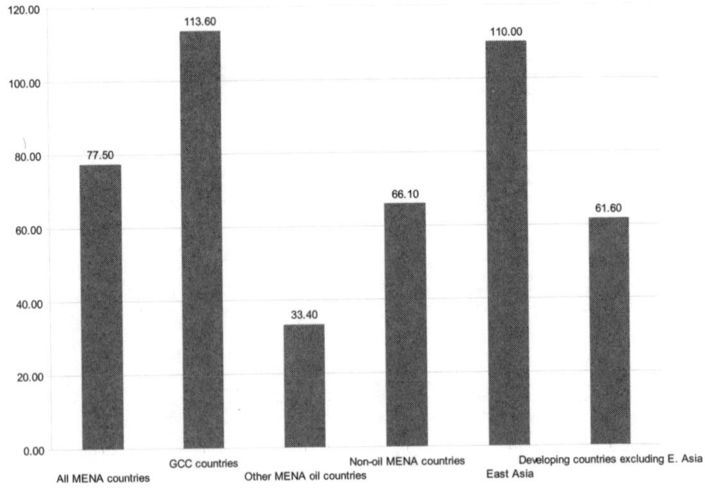

Figure 5.4 Trade openness of MENA countries, 1980–2000

Source: Adapted by the author from IMF data, available at http://www.imf.org/external/data.htm, accessed 4 September 2008.

Table 5.4 Average applied import tariff on non-agricultural and non-fuel products in percentage and rank

Indicator	*Most favourable nation*	
Year	*2006*	
Market	%	*rank*
Libyan Arab Jamahiriya	0	1
Lebanon	4.24	21
Kuwait	4.85	24
Saudi Arabia	4.85	25
United Arab Emirates	4.86	26
Bahrain	4.87	27
Oman	4.87	28
Qatar	4.87	29
Israel	4.99	30
Brunei Darussalam	5.33	31
Yemen	6.1	35
Jordan	10.25	78
Algeria	18.18	114
Sudan	18.21	115
Tunisia	22.45	118
Morocco	23.49	119

Source: Adapted by the author on data in UNCTAD 2008.

Note: 'Rank' refers to where a particular country is relative to the 121 in the sample.

The economic literature on trade integration in the MENA area is pretty scarce.[41] Economists, however, point to the existence of a mismatch between what economic theory would predict, and the present level of trade integration in the MENA area, even within the existing trade blocs (such as the Gulf Cooperation Council and the Arab Maghreb Union).[42] Some authors have explored the possibility of an increase in trade and monetary integration in Africa as a consequence of the introduction of the euro.[43] They all seem to be very negative about the prospects for further intraregional trade integration in Africa and in the Middle East.

Fazio, however, starting from the consideration of a level of integration in the MENA region below average, presents a more positive view of the future of the area after the establishment of the Euro-Mediterranean Partnership and the adoption of the euro. However, using a gravity model specification to identify the emergence of trade blocs along different geographical directions, he concludes that, within the Euro-Mediterranean Partnership, EU trade remains clearly dominant. Moreover, North European trade still dominates trade within the EU; Southern Mediterranean trade is still below average; and the integration between the EU and the Southern Mediterranean, despite the introduction of the euro, is still very limited.[44]

3.2 Inter-Arab aid capital flows

Aid capital flows dynamics in the MENA region do not configure a pattern of integration either. On the contrary, they are highly influenced by external factors, such as the prices of oil in the 1970s and, *a contrario*, in the 1980s, or geo-political strategies of extra-regional actors, as in the 1990s and 2000s.[45] Reference is made here mainly to intraregional transfers of Official Development Assistance funds, which represent the bulk of intraregional capital flows together with remittances.[46]

Analysing the data on real flows of net Official Development Assistance (ODA) to the Arab region provided by the OECD, it is possible to observe a huge variation over the years (Figure 5.5). Starting from small figures at the beginning of the 1970s, total aid flows to Arab countries peaked in 1977, reaching a maximum of nearly $16 billion.[47] However, this aid was mainly coming from other Arab countries and represented a way to redistribute resources from the booming oil-rich countries to the others. By contrast, in the 1980s, these transfers of money fell considerably and collapsed after the oil price crash of 1986 to $6.7 billion in 1989.

ODA flows to the MENA region increased again during the Gulf War of 1990–91, this time thanks to the financial intervention of the USA and other Western countries (Figure 5.5). Egypt was the main recipient of these

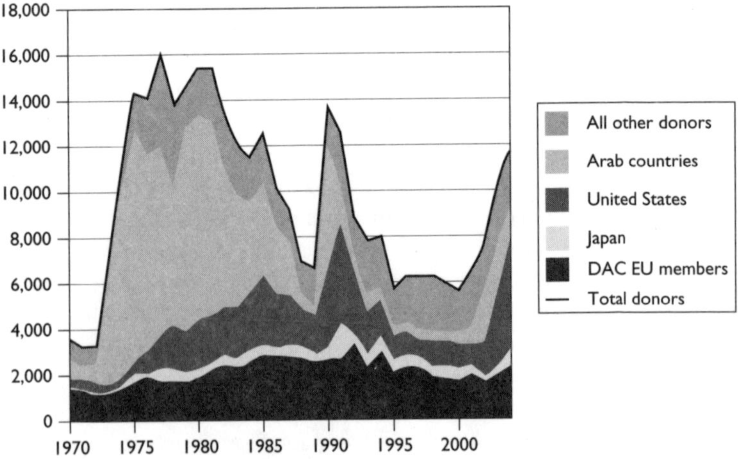

Figure 5.5 Real flows of net ODA to the Arab region (US$ millions)
Source: OECD, as quoted by UN 2007.

additional funds. After the first Iraq war, foreign aid declined sharply, falling to a low of $5.7 billion in 1995. However, both the outbreak of the second intifada in Palestine in the autumn of 2000 and the second war in Iraq in 2003 prompted a surge in the amount of money sent to the region. In 2004, the volume of aid money received by Arab countries had neared $12 billion, an amount which is nevertheless below the transfers of the 1970s and early 1980s.[48]

The main donor country in inter-Arab aid has been, and still is, Saudi Arabia. Data from the 2005 Arab Unified Economic Report (AUER) of the Arab Monetary Fund[49] reported in Table 5.5 show that Saudi Arabia provided more than 67 per cent of total Arab donations in the period between 1970 and 2004. The United Nations Economic and Social Commission for Western Asia (ESCWA) reports that, in the period between 2000 and 2004, Saudi Arabia accounted for 78 per cent of total Arab aid donation.[50] In 2004, the total amount of net ODA given by Saudi Arabia was estimated at $1,734 million, and it represented 47 per cent of total non-DAC donors.[51] Aid provided by Saudi Arabia is not disbursed multilaterally through international institutions, but bilaterally through the government or the Saudi Fund for Development (Saudi Fund). It is normally given through soft loans, which are directly extended to the governments of the receiving countries. According to the UN,[52] between 1975 and 2005, the Saudi Fund provided aid totalling $6.83 billion to 71 countries. These funds were allocated to infrastructure and energy projects (50 per cent); to social projects, including health and education (21 per cent); and to productive sectors, mainly agriculture and industry. The fund's commitments in 2005 amounted to $214 million, mainly allocated to Algeria, Ivory Coast, Ethiopia, Lebanon, Morocco and Turkey. The Arab Monetary Fund reports a figure of US$7,636.9 million in loans extended by the Saudi Fund from its establishment until 2004 (Table 5.6).

The other important Arab donors are Kuwait and the United Arab Emirates, with respectively around 15 per cent and around 10 per cent of total Arab aid in the period between 1970 and 2004 (Table 5.5). Official Development Assistance from Kuwait reached $209 million in 2004.[53] This money is managed by the Kuwait Fund for Arab Economic Development (Kuwait Fund), which is in charge of both bilateral and multilateral donations. The Kuwait Fund extended loans for US$13,014.4 million from its establishment until 2004 (Table 5.6). Most of this money was distributed to other Arab countries. The projects financed were mainly transport, communication and energy infrastructural projects. The fund also provided financing to agriculture and industry, technical assistance and financial studies.[54] In 2004, the Kuwait Fund loan commitments amounted to $372

Table 5.5 Nominal aid flows from Arab sources, 1970–2004 (US$ millions)

	Total Arab	*GCC*	*United Arab Emirates*	*Saudi Arabia*	*Oman*	*Qatar*	*Kuwait*	*Other Arab*	*Algeria*	*Iraq*	*Libyan Arab Jamahiriya*
1970–1974	7696	6611	923	4013	—	279	1396	1085	73	453	559
1975–1979	31870	29130	4857	18515	—	1076	4682	2740	449	1577	714
1980–1984	32741	30450	2768	21503	6	692	5481	2291	354	1091	846
1985–1989	15515	14831	272	12253	198	28	2080	684	262	–76	498
1990–1994	13429	13190	1957	8698	189	44	2302	239	45	76	118
1995–1999	6811	6811	482	4359	77	187	1706	—	—	—	—
2000–2004	15776	15776	1471	12339	73	392	1501				
2000	3227	3227	376	2505	24	94	228	—	—	—	—
2001	3265	3265	398	2455	24	129	259	—	—	—	—
2002	3888	3888	558	2674	6	73	577	—	—	—	—
2003	2982	2982	130	2803	10	23	16	—	—	—	—
2004	2414	2414	9	1902	9	73	421	—	—	—	—
1970–2004	139614	132575	14201	94019	616	3090	20649	7039	1183	3121	2735
Percentage	100.00	94.96	10.17	67.34	0.44	2.21	14.79	5.04	0.85	2.24	1.96

Source: UN 2007, from data in the Arab Unified Economic Report (AUER) 2005.

Table 5.6 Arab-based national, regional and multilateral ODA (US$ millions)

	Total aid extended since creation	*To Arab region*	*To Africa*	*To Asia*	*To Latin America*	*To other countries*	*Share of each institution*
Regional Arab institutions							
Arab fund (AFESD)	15923.4	15923.4	0	0	0	0	21.98
Arab Monetary Fund	4293	4293	0	0	0	0	5.93
Sub-total	20216.4	20216.4	0	0	0	0	27.91
National institutions for ODA							
Abu Dhabi fund	3316.8	2595.6	147	567	0	7.2	4.58
Saudi fund	7636.9	3674.7	1440.6	2367.8	59.9	93.9	10.54
Kuwait fund	13014.4	6965.1	2280.5	3196	302.5	270.3	17.97
Sub-total	23968.1	13235.4	3868.1	6130.8	362.4	371.4	33.09
Share of each beneficiary region	100	55.22	16.14	25.58	1.51	1.55	
Non-exclusively Arab institutions							
Islamic bank	20528.3	10049.2	2014.6	8422.7	17.5	24.3	28.34
Arab Bank for the Development of Africa	2348	9.6	2338.4	0	0	0	3.24
OPEC fund	5371	955.3	2173.7	1547.4	641	53.6	7.42
Sub-total	28247.3	11014.1	6526.7	9970.1	658.5	77.9	39.00
Share of each beneficiary region	100	38.99	23.11	35.30	2.33	0.28	
Total Arab and associated funds	72431.8	44465.9	10394.8	16101	1020.9	449.3	100.00
Total share of each beneficiary region	100	61.39	14.35	22.23	1.41		0.62

Source: UN 2007, from data in the Arab Unified Economic Report (AUER) 2005.

million, destined for Bahrain, Bangladesh, China, Egypt and Mauritania. The countries allocated the highest amount of aid were Afghanistan, Bahrain and Palestine.[55]

Figure 5.6 below shows that the other Gulf countries, members of the GCC, contributed to total Arab donations considerably in the 1970s and in the 1980s, but now their role is negligible.

Although the total sum disbursed by Arab countries to the Arab region is considerable, around US$45 thousand million until 2004 according to the AUER figures, the highest volume of aid to Arab countries comes from non-Arab sources (Table 5.7). Disaggregating the data relating to gross ODA for the year 2003–2004 by main donors per country, it emerges that the Arab countries are among the top five donors only in Syria, Egypt and Morocco. Indeed, in the period between 1970 and 2004, Syria received 84 per cent of its total aid from Arab countries (Table 5.8). However, Morocco received the majority of aid from the EU, as did the other Maghreb countries. On the other hand, the USA financed mainly Egypt and Iraq, distributing 38 and 48 per cent of total ODA respectively during 1970–2004 (Table 5.8). Finally, multilateral organisations, under the label 'Other donors' in Table 5.8, provided aid mainly to countries in conflict, especially Palestine, where they extended 50 per cent of total aid.

As far as the allocation of total Arab countries aid to other Arab countries is concerned, Figure 5.7 shows the geographical distribution for the period 1970–2004. Based on OECD data, Syria received 24 per cent of total Arab aid in the period, Egypt 22 per cent, and Jordan 16 per cent. These were followed by Morocco (8 per cent), Yemen (6 per cent), and Sudan (5 per cent).

Based on the above analysis of aid distribution, it is possible to draw the following conclusions. First, aid from Arab countries follows patterns which

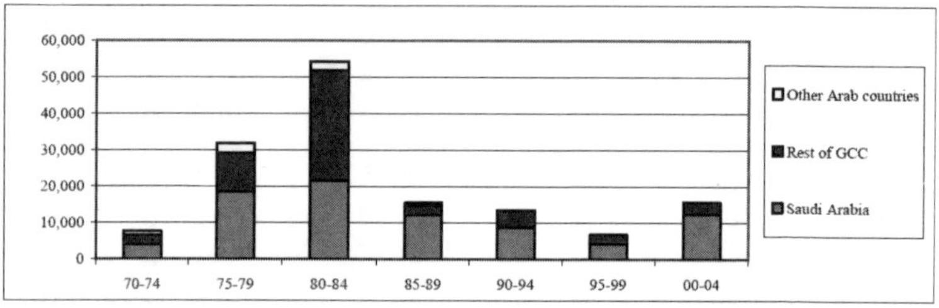

Figure 5.6 Amount of Arab aid donations, annual averages, 1970–2004 (US$ millions)

Source: UN 2007, from the Arab Unified Economic Report 2005.
Note: Data include donations to non-Arab countries.

Table 5.7 Top five donors of gross ODA, 2003–2004, averages (US$ millions)

Algeria		*Bahrain*		*Comoros*		*Djibouti*		*Egypt*		*Iraq*	
France	165	Arab Countries	95.6	France	13.9	France	25	United States	767	United States	2286
EC	72	France	0.93	IDA	5.9	IDA	20	EC	160	Japan	333
Spain	26	Japan	0.23	EC	4	Japan	8	France	149	United Kingdom	228
Italy	25	UNTA	0.17	UNTA	1.8	EC	7	Germany	134	Netherlands	107
Germany	11	Germany	0.06	UNICEF	0.7	United States	5	Arab Countries	104	EC	99
Jordan		*Lebanon*		*Libyan Arab Jamahiriya*		*Mauritania*		*Morocco*		*Oman*	
United States	666	EC	61	France	2.6	Japan	54	France	302	Arab Countries	62.2
UNRWA	89	France	55	Germany	2.58	EC	51	EC	184	Belgium	6.3
Japan	72	UNRWA	54	Italy	1.73	IDA	49	Japan	89	Japan	4
Germany	71	United States	29	Turkey	0.77	France	48	Arab countries	82	France	0.8
EC	59	Japan	14	UNHCR	0.7	United states	19	Germany	75	UNTA	0.8
Palestine		*Somalia*		*Sudan*		*Syrian Arab Republic*		*Tunisia*		*Yemen*	
UNRWA	268	EC	38	United States	277	EC	70	France	167	IDA	91
United States	234	Norway	37	EC	158	Arab countries	48	Japan	110	Germany	34
EC	184	United States	33	United Kingdom	75	Japan	31	EC	104	United States	33
Norway	54	Netherlands	15	Norway	45	UNRWA	28	Germany	46	Japan	30
Sweden	37	Italy	12	Germany	32	France	23	Italy	41	Netherlands	29

Source: UN 2007, from OECD data.

Table 5.8 Cumulative net ODA to selected Arab countries by major donors, 1970–2004

	United States (Millions of $)	*(%)*	*DAC members of the EU (Millions of $)*	*(%)*	*Japan (Millions of $)*	*(%)*	*Arab donors (Millions of $)*	*(%)*	*Other donors[a] (Millions of $)*	*(%)*	*All donors (Millions of $)*
Algeria	(19)	(0)	8123	71	114	1	829	7	2353	21	11401
Bahrain	0	0	47	1	19	0	3944	97	64	2	4074
Comoros	12	1	1067	51	60	3	241	11	732	35	2112
Djibouti	98	2	2328	59	169	4	687	17	689	17	3971
Egypt	38489	38	17606	17	4957	5	30128	30	9802	10	100982
Iraq	5308	48	2255	20	1186	11	296	3	2048	18	11092
Jordan	5248	17	3185	10	1868	6	17842	56	3605	11	31748
Lebanon	703	8	1727	21	55	1	3508	42	2296	28	8289
Libyan Arab Jamahiriya	0	0	355	53	6	1	3	0	304	46	668
Mauritania	462	5	2729	27	441	4	2661	26	3889	38	10182
Morocco	1820	6	11375	40	1193	4	9356	33	4753	17	28497
Oman	247	6	88	2	130	3	3657	87	104	2	4227
Palestine	1135	12	1926	21	254	3	1576	17	4471	48	9362
Somalia	2647	17	4694	30	181	1	2556	17	5324	35	15402
Sudan	3400	13	7013	26	811	3	6389	24	9368	35	26981
Syrian Arab Republic	547	2	1584	5	1157	3	27968	84	2050	6	33307
Tunisia	677	5	7406	55	793	6	1323	10	3340	25	13539
Yemen	971	5	3339	18	839	4	9028	48	4663	25	18840

Source: UN 2007, from OECD data.

Notes: Percentages in the table represent the share of various donors to total aid for each of the respective recipient countries. Kuwait, Qatar, Saudi Arabia and United Arab Emirates are major Arab donors and were therefore excluded from the table.
'Other donors' includes multilateral organisations.

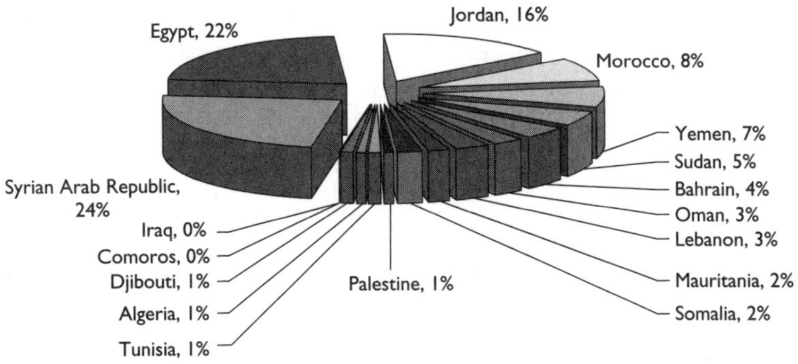

Figure 5.7 Distribution of aid to Arab countries from Arab donors, 1970–2004 (%)

Source: Adapted by the author on data from the OECD, available at: http://www.oecd.org/statsportal/0,3352,en_2825_293564_1_1_1_1_1,00.html, accessed 4 September 2008.

Note: Kuwait, Libyan Arab Jamahiriya, Qatar, Saudi Arabia and United Arab Emirates did not receive significant amounts of development aid during the period under consideration, and were consequently excluded from the figure.

are heavily influenced by geo-political considerations. Second, despite the revival of Arab contributions to the Arab region in the wake of the second Iraq war, the amount of money distributed is considerably less than in the 1970s and 1980s (Table 5.5, Figures 5.5 and 5.6). Moreover, the bulk of funds attributed to Less Developed Arab countries does not come from wealthier Arab neighbours, but from the USA, the EU or multilateral organisations. Finally, those MENA countries that rely heavily on aid, such as Egypt, are receiving it mainly from countries outside the region (in the case of Egypt, the USA). All this does not encourage a vision of the MENA region as an integrated one, as far as the redistribution of aid capital flows is concerned.

4 Conclusion

Analysis of the attempts at regional economic integration, as well as of the data presented in this chapter, leads to the conclusion that the integration of the MENA region is an oxymoron. Whereas other regions of the globe, most notably the three identified in the literature as the 'triad' – namely, Europe, the Americas and South Eastern Asia – have achieved high and increasing levels of economic and institutional integration, the Arab countries are still fundamentally divided between oil-exporting and labour-intensive countries, as well as, within the first group, between the wealthy members of the GCC and the other, less affluent oil-exporting countries. Not even the solidarity among the Muslim 'Ummah' seems to have provided a stable path to integration. Indeed, aid capital flows within the region are mainly determined by geopolitical considerations, and do not come exclusively, or even predominantly, from other Arab countries. It seems possible to conclude that the MENA region is notably lacking in economic and political integration in the era of globalisation. The MENA region is therefore a clear example of the paradox of lack of regionalisation within globalisation.

In the next chapter, attention turns to Egypt to verify to what extent this country can be identified as a clear example of the paradox of marginalisation within globalisation.

Chapter 6

Why do Egyptians migrate now?

The marginalisation of Egypt

1 Introduction

What is important to assess now, is whether Egypt has been excluded or marginalised in the process of globalisation. To be sure, the qualitative definition of globalisation adopted here would require a holistic approach to the marginalisation of the country. However, given the importance of economic regionalisation or marginalisation in assessing the phenomenon of mass migration within the new global division of labour, the analysis here will be mainly economic in scope.[1]

The main economic indicators of the integration of a country's economy into globalisation are Foreign Direct Investment stock and inflows, the number of mergers and acquisitions, and the relative openness of the economy, measured by the ratio of the sum of exports and imports over GDP, used as a proxy of production for exports.[2] These indicators are assessed below with reference to the case of Egypt, together with other indicators that can provide a broader picture of the degree of the country's integration in the global economy. Before undertaking such an empirical analysis, it is worth asking to what extent the Egyptian economy is open to foreign investment.

2 The steps towards an open and stable economy

Egypt is considered in the literature as the 'mother of Arab liberalisations'.[3] The liberalisation and privatisation programme was inaugurated in 1974, with the *infitah*, the open door policy, by Sadat. In 1974, the Egyptian government adopted Law no. 43, 'On Arab and Foreign Investment and Free Zones' (the 'Old Egyptian Investment Law'). The aim was to entice foreigners to invest in Egypt both in association with Egyptians or alone.

This law was reformed in 1989 with the passing of Investment Law no. 230. After the adoption of the *infitah*, the restructuring of the Egyptian economy and the privatisation programme peaked formally in 1987, with the passing by Parliament of a bill allowing for a number of sales of public-owned properties. Then on 11 May 1997, a new law cancelling all previous regulations relating to foreign investment was approved. This was the Law of Investment Guarantees and Incentives, and its executive regulations were issued by the Prime Minister's Decree no. 2108. On 1 October 1999, the new Commercial Code, replacing the old 1883 version, came into force.

The aim of the Egyptian government in this process of opening the economy was to boost foreign investment.[4] It was a strategy based on an alliance between the State and international capital. Although the Egyptian bourgeoisie favoured and supported the open door policy and the liberalisation process, they would have opted for a soft approach which could allow the Egyptian upper class to control and define it.[5]

Despite the existence of a clear consensus on free market economy and the implementation of the liberalisation process, foreign direct investments made only a limited appearance in Egypt.[6] Instead, much of the activity to date has been in one-off acquisitions, such as the sale for US$1.6 billion of the Bank of Alexandria, which took place in October 2006, or the private equity deal that transferred the family-owned Amoun Pharmaceutical into US hands for US$450 million.[7]

The process of stabilisation of the Egyptian economy was facilitated by external aid, disbursed especially during the first Iraq war in 1990/91. During this period, Egypt received about $3.9 billion, while the USA and the Gulf states cancelled some $12.9 billion worth of debts, substantially reducing debt-servicing burdens.[8] This should have enticed foreign capital, but the level of FDI did not increase significantly.[9] Not even the substantial programme of macroeconomic adjustments carried out by the Egyptian government in the course of the 1990s helped to attract more FDI. Such a programme, agreed with the IMF, was part of a broader package starting in May 1991 for the cancellation of half of the Egyptian public debt. This had to be effected gradually: 15 per cent between May 1991 and October 1992; another 15 per cent with the implementation of the second agreement (November 1992 to April 1993); and the rest in the period between May 1993 and November 1994. In turn, the IMF conditioned its offer of credit[10] (60 per cent of Egyptian contribution to the fund) to the gradual implementation of structural macroeconomic reforms according to the guidelines of the IMF and the World Bank (Table 6.1).[11]

Table 6.1 Egypt: History of lending arrangements with the IMF, 1 May 1984 to 30 June 2008 (in thousands of SDRs)

Facility	*Date of arrangement*	*Date of expiration or cancellation*	*Amount agreed*	*Amount drawn*	*Amount outstanding*
Standby arrangement	Oct 11, 1996	Sep 30, 1998	271,400	0	0
Extended fund facility	Sep 20, 1993	Sep 19, 1996	400,000	0	0
Standby arrangement	May 17, 1991	May 31, 1993	234,400	147,200	0
Standby arrangement	May 15, 1987	Nov 30, 1988	250,000	116,000	0
Total			1,155,800	263,200	0

Source: IMF 2008.

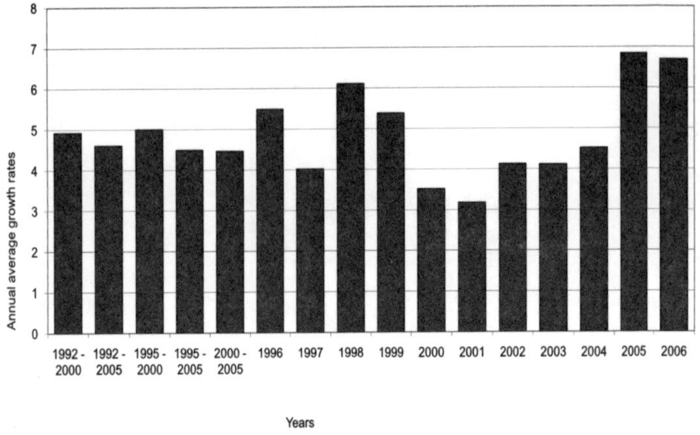

Figure 6.1 Egypt: Annual average growth rates of real GDP, 1990s–2000s
Source: Adapted by the author on UNCTAD data, available at: http://www.unctad.org/Templates/Page.asp?intItemID=1584&lang=1, accessed 5 September 2008.

The implementation of liberalisations and structural reforms, the stabilisation programmes which were part of the conditionality of IMF loans, debt relief and grants, especially from the USA, seem to have been successful in helping Egypt improve its macroeconomic performance. During the 1990s, the annual average increases of real GDP were around 5 per cent, and growth continued to be sustained throughout the second half of the decade (5 per cent) and the first half of the 2000s (4.5 per cent) (Figure 6.1).

Additionally, the level of foreign reserves (Figure 6.2), the size of the external debt (Figure 6.3) and the fiscal balance (Figure 6.4) improved in the course of the 1990s. Data from the IMF show that the amount of total reserves minus gold in Egypt increased almost seven times between 1990 and 1998, levelling out from 2000 (Figure 6.2). The Egyptian current account also improved drastically in the first half of the 1990s, recording substantial surpluses, while remaining balanced in the second half of the decade (Figure 6.3). Finally, cash deficits as a percentage of GDP were very contained in the course of the 1990s, and there were even some surpluses; however, these deteriorated in the 2000s (Figure 6.4).

As a consequence of macroeconomic stability, inflation decreased drastically. The GDP deflator moved from almost 20 per cent in 1992 to almost nothing in 1999 (Figure 6.5).

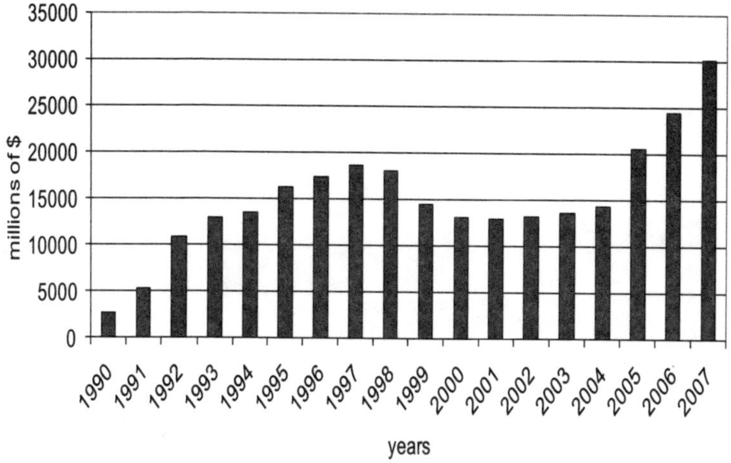

Figure 6.2 Egypt: Total reserves minus gold, 1990–2007

Source: Adapted by the author on IMFdata, available at: http://www.imfstatistics.org/imf/, accessed 5 September 2008.

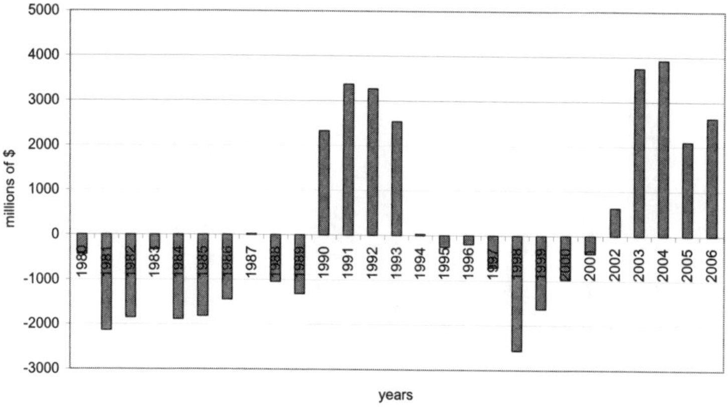

Figure 6.3 Egypt: Current account, balance of payments 1980–2006

Source: Adapted by the author on UNCTAD data, available at: http://www.unctad.org/Templates/Page.asp?intItemID=1584&lang=1, accessed 5 September 2008.

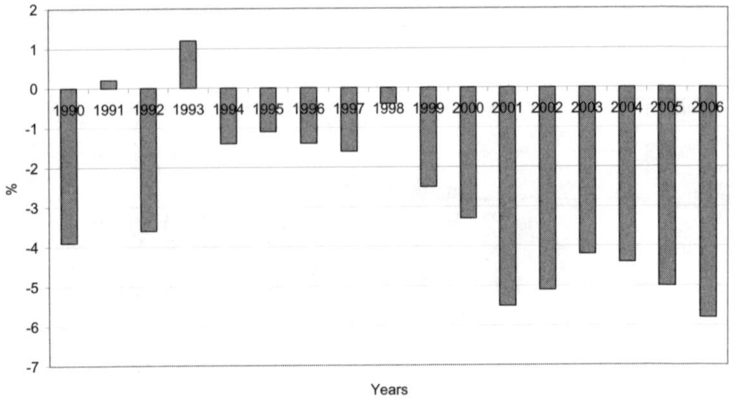

Figure 6.4 Egypt: Cash surplus/deficit (percentage of GDP), 1990–2006

Source: Adapted by the author on World Bank data, available at: http://go.worldbank.org/SI5SSGAVZ0, accessed 5 September 2008.

This enabled the exchange rate to be pegged to the dollar, with all foreign exchange transactions taking place within a ±3 per cent range around the central rate announced by the Central Bank of Egypt (Figure 6.6).[12]

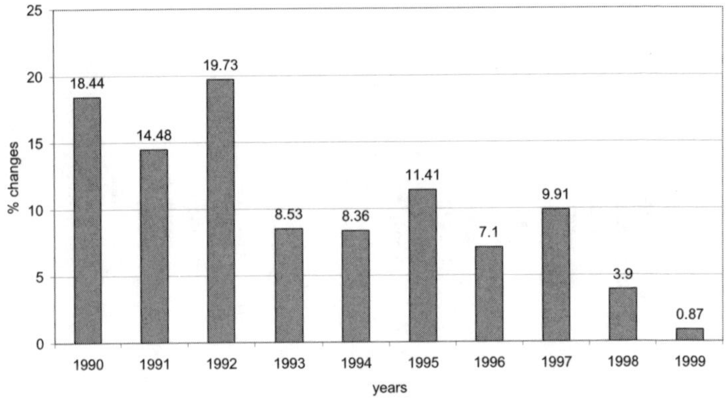

Figure 6.5 Egypt: Inflation, GDP deflator (annual percentage), 1990–1999

Source: Adapted by the author on World Bank data, available at http://go.worldbank.org/SI5SSGAVZ0 , accessed 5 September 2008.

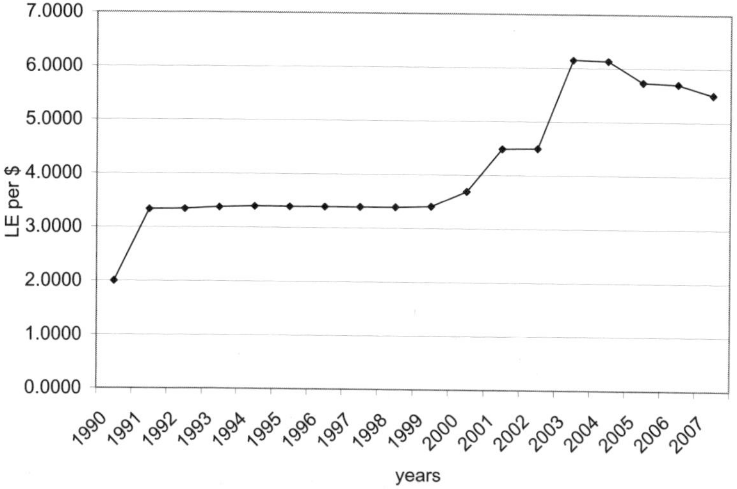

Figure 6.6 Egyptian pound (LE) exchange rate in US$, 1990–2007
Source: Adapted by the author on IMF International Financial Statistics data, available at: http://www.imfstatistics.org/imf/, accessed 5 September 2008.

However, neither the relative macroeconomic stability experienced by Egypt in the course of the 1990s, nor the substantial programme of privatisation, nor its commitment to economic reform and structural adjustment has helped Egypt in attracting Foreign Direct Investment and enticing foreign business to invest in the country.[13]

3. The marginalisation of Egypt

3.1 Economic marginalisation

Looking at the patterns of world stock of FDI, the paradoxes of regionalisation within globalisation, and marginalisation within globalisation emerge clearly. Despite the dramatic increase of world FDI stock since 1980, it is worth noting that the largest share continues to be held by developed nations (stable around 70 per cent for the whole period) – see Figure 6.7 and Table 6.2.

As far as developing countries are concerned, Asia is clearly the region with the highest stock of FDI (16 per cent in 2006, of which 14 per cent belonged to South, East and South-East Asia, see Figure 6.8 and Table 6.2).

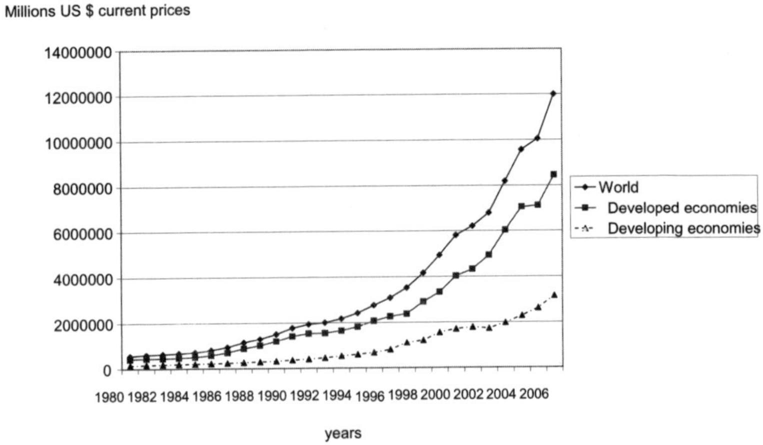

Figure 6.7 Stock of FDI: Developed and developing countries

Source: Adapted by the author on UNCTAD data, available at: http://www.unctad.org/Templates/Page.asp?intItemID=1584&lang=1, accessed 5 September 2008.

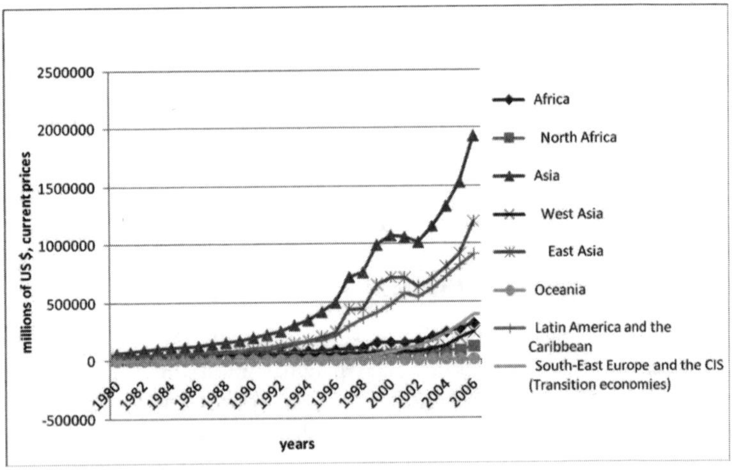

Figure 6.8 Stock of FDI: Developing countries

Source: Adapted by the author on UNCTAD data, available at: http://www.unctad.org/Templates/Page.asp?intItemID=1584&lang=1, accessed 5 September 2008.

Table 6.2 Flows and stock of FDI, 1980 and 2006

Year	*1980*				*2006*			
Flow	*Flow*	%	*Stock*	%	*Flow*	%	*Stock*	%
Economy								
World	55262.45	100	551221.4	100	1305852	100	11998838	100
Developed economies	47574.75	86.08874	410865.1	74.53721	857498.7	65.6658	8453853	70.4556
Developing economies	7664.105	13.86856	140356.3	25.46278	379070.5	29.0286	3155856	26.30134
Africa	400.352	0.724456	39836.41	7.226934	35544.22	2.72192	315127.9	2.62632
North Africa	152.37	0.275721	10790.93	1.95764	23323.56	1.78608	115795.8	0.965059
Algeria	348.67	0.630935	1525.17	0.276689	1795.4	0.13749	10150.6	0.084597
Egypt	548.29	0.992157	2260.38	0.410068	10042.8	0.76906	38925	0.324406
Libyan Arab Jamahiriya	−1089.34	−1.971212	1855.425	0.336602	1734	0.13279	3755.36	0.031298
Morocco	89.42	0.16181	1780.387	0.32299	2898.2	0.22194	29794.62	0.248313
Sudan	8.85	0.016014	28.96001	0.005254	3541.36	0.27119	11391.24	0.094936
Tunisia	246.48	0.446017	3340.61	0.606038	3311.8	0.25361	21779	0.181509
Latin America and the Caribbean	6482.817	11.73096	35059.14	6.360264	83753.37	6.4137	908574.5	7.572188
Asia and Oceania	780.9355	1.413139	65460.76	11.87558	259772.9	19.893	1932153	16.10284
Asia	662.6821	1.199154	64262.13	11.65813	259433.5	19.867	1926949	16.05946
West Asia	−3246.6	−5.874875	14463.24	2.623854	59902	4.5872	242603.1	2.021889
Bahrain	−418.04	−0.756463	60.742	0.01102	2914.894	0.22322	11402	0.095026
Iran, Islamic Republic of	80.91	0.14641	2962.22	0.537392	901.076	0.069	4543.368	0.037865
Iraq	1.53	0.002769	−52.3	−0.009488	271.76	0.02081	1051.131	0.00876
Jordan	33.83	0.061217	1006.175	0.182536	3120.592	0.23897	16349.4	0.136258
Kuwait	0.83	0.001502	30.37	0.00551	109.579	0.00839	778	0.006484
Lebanon	−12.16	−0.022004	20.04	0.003636	2793.84	0.21395	18290.79	0.152438
Oman	98.44	0.178132	482.7967	0.087587	951.8856	0.07289	3881.404	0.032348
Palestinian Territory	0	0	—	NA	37.8	0.00289	1111.4	0.009263
Qatar	10.84	0.019615	82.99	0.015056	1785.8	0.13675	7593.275	0.063283
Saudi Arabia	−3192.31	−5.776635	−5139.352	−0.932357	18293	1.40085	51828	0.431942
Syrian Arab Republic	−0.04	−7.24E-05	5560.091	1.008686	600	0.04595	9039	0.075332

Table 6.2 Flows and stock of FDI, 1980 and 2006 (continued)

Year	*1980*				*2006*			
Flow	*Flow*	%	*Stock*	%	*Flow*	%	*Stock*	%
Economy								
Turkey	18	0.032572	8845	1.604618	20120	1.54076	79075	0.659022
United Arab Emirates	97.64	0.176684	409.23	0.074241	8386.476	0.64222	37098.27	0.309182
Yemen	33.93	0.061398	195.24	0.03542	–384.7	–0.02946	562.1	0.004685
South, East and South-East Asia	3909.282	7.07403	49798.89	9.034281	199531.5	15.2798	1684346	14.03757
East Asia	949.7014	1.718529	28782.06	5.221507	125774.3	9.63159	1191291	9.928389
China	57	0.103144	1074	0.19484	69468	5.31975	292559	2.438228
Oceania	118.2534	0.213985	1198.627	0.217449	339.4009	0.02599	5204.305	0.043373
South-East Europe and the CIS	23.60006	0.042705	0.00009	1.63E-08	69282.67	5.30555	389129.6	3.243061

Source: Adapted by the author on UNCTAD data, available at: http://www.unctad.org/Templates/Page.asp?intItemID=1584&lang=1, accessed 5 September 2008.

The second largest share of FDI stock is in Latin America and the Caribbean, with 7.6 per cent in 2006, higher than the 6.3 per cent of 1980. The third largest share belongs to Eastern Europe and the ex-Soviet Union countries, with 3.2 per cent in 2006, increasing from 0 per cent in 1980. The MENA region (more or less Northern Africa plus West Asia in Table 6.2) together with Africa as a whole comprise the two regions (if we exclude Oceania) experiencing a decrease in the total share of FDI stock from 1980. In particular, MENA countries received less than 3 per cent in 2006, decreasing from their 4.6 per cent of 1980 (Table 6.2).

Briefly, the developing regions increasing their total share of FDI stock are the ones belonging to the 'triad' (Europe, the Americas and South-East Asia), whereas those who are experiencing a progressive marginalisation from the world economy and present a declining share of their stock of FDI are Sub-Saharan Africa and the MENA region (Figure 6.9).

As far as Egypt is concerned, Figures 6.10 and 6.11 show the dynamics of FDI flows. Allowing for yearly fluctuations, the pattern of FDI inflows shows a clear declining trend from the 1980s to the 1990s, reaching very low levels at the beginning of the 2000s (Figure 6.10). In absolute terms, in the first years of the twenty-first century, the level of FDI was below even that of remittances, with a low of US$237.4 million in 2003 (Table 6.3).

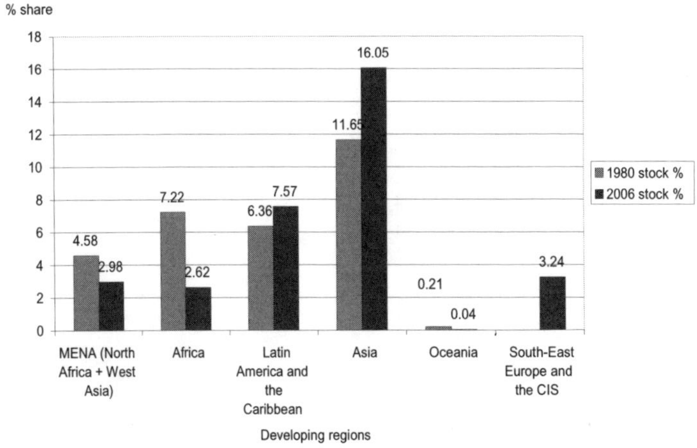

Figure 6.9 Percentage share of total FDI stock, 1980 and 2006

Source: Adapted by the author on UNCTAD data, available at: http://www.unctad.org/Templates/Page.asp?intItemID=1584&lang=1, accessed 5 September 2008.

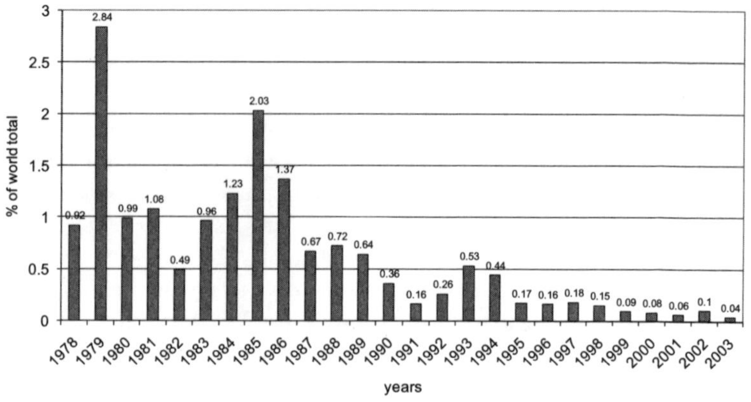

Figure 6.10 Egypt: Average percentage share of world total FDI stock, 1978–2003

Source: Adapted by the author on UNCTAD data, available at: http://www.unctad.org/Templates/Page.asp?intItemID=1584&lang=1, accessed 5 September 2008.

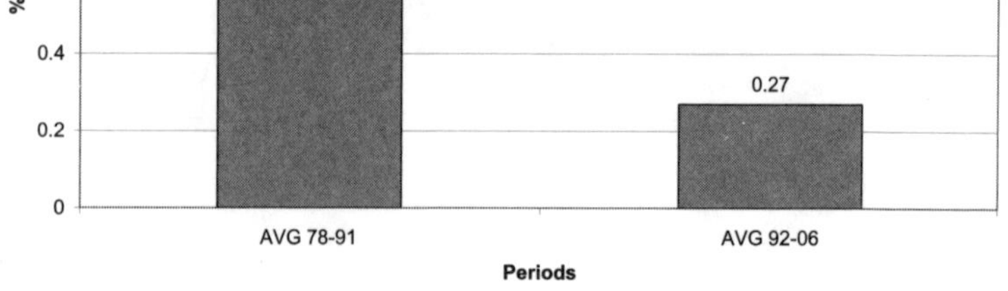

Figure 6.11 Egypt: Average percentage share of world total FDI, 1978–2006

Source: Adapted by the author on UNCTAD data, available at: http://www.unctad.org/Templates/Page.asp?intItemID=1584&lang=1, accessed 5 September 2008.

Table 6.3 Egypt: Comparison between remittances/FDI inflows, 1999–2006 (US$ millions at current prices)

	1999	*2000*	*2001*	*2002*	*2003*
Remittances	3235.3	2852	2911.4	2893.1	2960.9
FDI inflows	1065.3	1235.4	509.9	646.9	237.4
	2004	*2005*	*2006*	*2007*	
Remittances	3340.7	5017.3	5329.5	4330	
FDI inflows	2157.4	5375.6	10042.8	3863	

Source: UNCTAD 2007; World Bank 2008

Overall, the average of the percentage of inflows to Egypt over the world total for the period 1978–1991 is 1.03 per cent, whereas an average for the period 1992–2006 is only 0.27 per cent (Figure 6.11).

The situation is very similar as far as the stock of FDI is concerned. The average share of inward stock of FDI in the period between 1994 and 2006 in the country was only 61.5 per cent of the average of the period between 1980 and 1993 (Figure 6.12).

In the case of Egypt, not only is the level of FDI limited, but Western portfolio investment in company shares quoted on regional stock markets is also minimal, if not negative. Net portfolio investment in Egypt in the

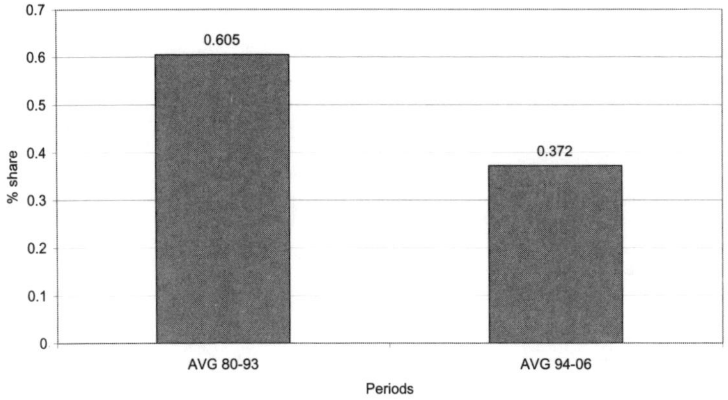

Figure 6.12 Egypt: Average percentage share of world total FDI stock, 1980–2006
Source: Adapted by the author on UNCTAD data, available at: http://www.unctad.org/Templates/Page.asp?intItemID=1584&lang=1, accessed 5 September 2008.

fiscal year 2001/2002 amounted to $45.3 million, and the first three quarters of the FY 2002/2003 saw a net outflow of $206 million.[14]

In terms of mergers and acquisitions, the percentage share of sales over world total is negligible in Egypt (0.1 per cent in 2006) (Table 6.4).

Table 6.4 Mergers and acquisitions (sales) by country and region, 2006 (US$ millions)

Economy	*2006*	%
World	880456.7	
Developed economies	727954.9	82.67924
Europe	451287.8	51.2561
European Union	432143.7	49.08177
Developing economies	127371.8	14.46656
Africa	17569.07	1.995449
North Africa	6319.408	0.717742
Algeria	18.26	0.002074
Egypt	1218.89	0.138438
Libyan Arab Jamahiriya	0.51	5.79E-05
Morocco	618.301	0.070225
Sudan	2138.018	0.242831
Tunisia	2325.429	0.264116
Latin America and the Caribean	37562.38	4.266238
Asia	71579.47	8.129811
West Asia	17856.64	2.028111
Abu Dhabi	0	0
Bahrain	0	0
Iran, Islamic Republic of	0	0
Iraq	0	0
Jordan	566.344	0.064324
Kuwait	12.86	0.001461
Lebanon	0	0
Oman	0	0
Qatar	0	0
Saudi Arabia	20.997	0.002385
Syrian Arab Republic	1157.781	0.131498
Turkey	15303.07	1.738083
United Arab Emirates	79.934	0.009079
Yemen	715.652	0.081282
South, East and South-East Asia	53722.83	6.101701
East Asia	28271.39	3.210992
China	6723.76	0.763667
Oceania	660.888	0.075062
South-East Europe and the CIS (Transition economies)	25129.99	2.8542

Source: Adapted by the author on UNCTAD data, available at: http://www.unctad.org/Templates/Page.asp?intItemID=1584&lang=1, accessed 5 September 2008.

Finally, in the 1990s, trade as a share of purchasing power parity GDP fell in most countries in the Middle East, and in the region as a whole. The figures refer to the sum of exports and imports divided by PPP GDP. This index is usually regarded as a measure of openness of the economy. The table shows that very few countries in the region opened up in the period considered, while the majority underwent a closure of their economies. Egypt remains stable, with a very low percentage of trade over PPP GDP moving from 8.9 per cent in 1990 to 9.1 per cent in 1999 (Table 6.5).

Although the value of exports has increased recently, Egypt's economy relies heavily on tourism, remittances from Egyptians living abroad, revenues from the Suez Canal, and oil (Table 6.6).

According to the data of the Egyptian Ministry for Foreign Trade in 2002/2003, the main sources of foreign exchange in Egypt were exports, tourism and travel receipts, oil revenues, remittances and Suez Canal duties. FDI inflows and official transfers represented only 3 per cent each of the total amount of foreign currency received (Figure 6.13).

UNCTAD data suggest that 50 per cent of Egypt's GDP in 2006 was generated by the services sector (Figure 6.14), with tourism as the most important voice (Figure 6.15).

Table 6.5 Trade as a percentage PPP GDP for Middle Eastern countries, 1990–1999

	1990	*1999*
Algeria	19.9	14.3
Bahrain	128.3	76.5*
Egypt	8.9	9.1
Iran	15.4	8.4
Israel	45.9	52.4
Jordan	34.2	29.4
Lebanon	45.1	30.9*
Morocco	15.9	18.6
Saudi Arabia	45.9	36
Syria	22	10.4
Tunisia	28.4	25.5
Turkey	13	16.2
UAE	85.3	106.7
Yemen	25.9	34.1
Middle East	23.5	16.8

* 1998

Source: World Bank, (2001), The Little Data Book, Washington DC: World Bank

Table 6.6 Egypt: Sources of foreign currency inflows, 1993/94–2002/03 (US$ millions)

	Petroleum exports	*Suez Canal duties*	*Travel and tourism receipts*	*Official transfers*	*FDI inflows*	*Exports*	*Remittances**
1993–94	1772.1	1990.3	1779.3	813.6	1320.8	3337.3	4866.11
1994–95	2176	2058.4	2298.9	918.6	782.7	4957	4325.41
1995–96	2226	1884.7	3009.1	723.6	626.9	4608.5	3522.2
1996–97	2578	1848.9	3646.3	889.6	769.7	5345.4	3690.87
1997–98	1728.4	1776.4	2940.5	882.6	1103.9	5128.4	3873.02
1998–99	999.7	1771	3235.1	1096.7	710.6	4445.1	3465.9
1999–00	2272.9	1780.8	4313.8	932.4	1656.1	6387.7	3711
2000–01	2632.4	1842.5	4316.9	769.3	509.4	7078.2	2926.4
2001–02	2381	1819.8	3422.8	1143.6	428.2	7120.8	2907.87
2002–03	3160.8	2236.2	3796.4	663.6	700.6	8205.2	2689.25

Source: *Egyptian Ministry of Foreign Trade Bulletin, various issues*

* (at constant prices 1999/2000)

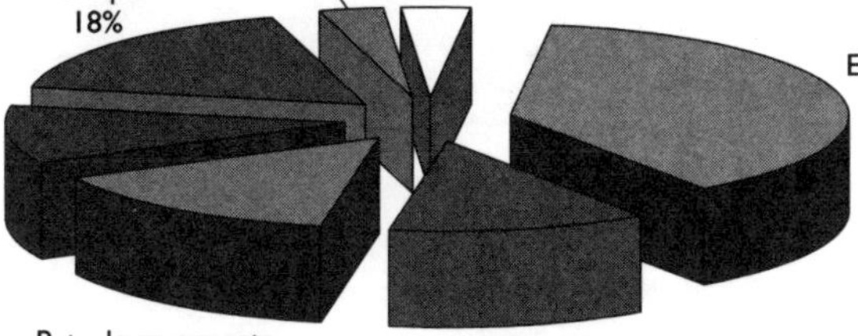

Figure 6.13 Egypt: Foreign exchange inflows, 2002–2003
Source: *Egyptian Ministry of Foreign Trade Bulletin*, various issues

In the decade between 1993 and 2003, remittances from workers abroad represented 4.5 per cent of GDP (Figure 6.16).

The importance of workers' remittances for the Egyptian economy is clearly shown in Figure 6.17.[15] From the beginning of the 1990s, workers' remittances have surpassed official development assistance and official aid (Figure 6.17).

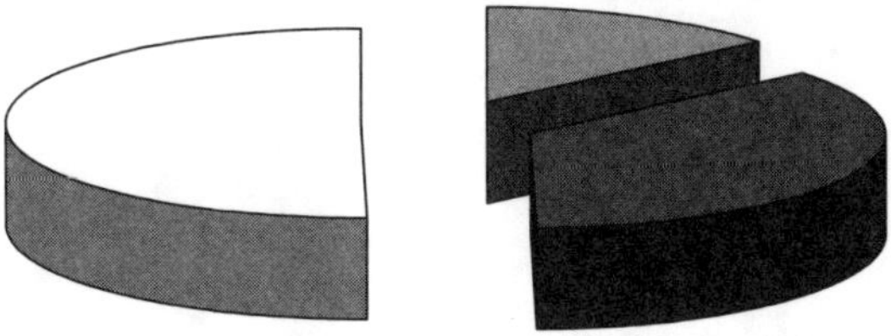

Figure 6.14 Egypt: Economic structure, 2006
Source: Adapted by the author on UNCTAD data, available at: http://www.unctad.org/Templates/Page.asp?intItemID=1584&lang=1, accessed 5 September 2008.

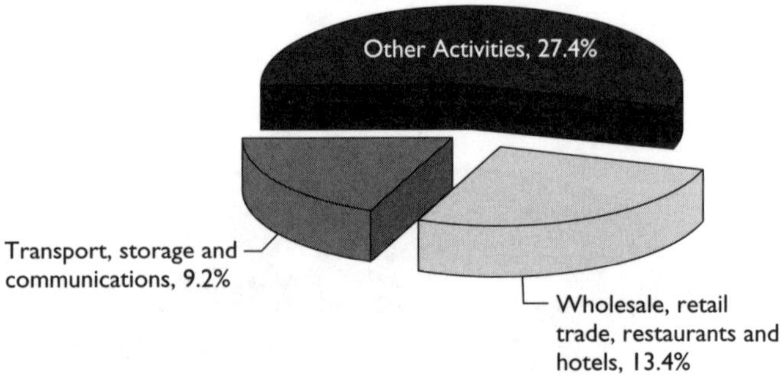

Figure 6.15 Egypt: Economic structure, composition of services, 2006
Source: Adapted by the author on UNCTAD data, available at: http://www.unctad.org/Templates/Page.asp?intItemID=1584&lang=1, accessed 5 September 2008.

Moreover, the percentage of remittances coming from permanent migrants living in developed countries is higher than from temporary migrants living in Arab countries. In 2001/2002, according to the data of the Central Bank of Egypt, the share of remittances from developed countries was 50 per cent, while that of remittances from Arab countries was 47 per cent (Figure 6.18).

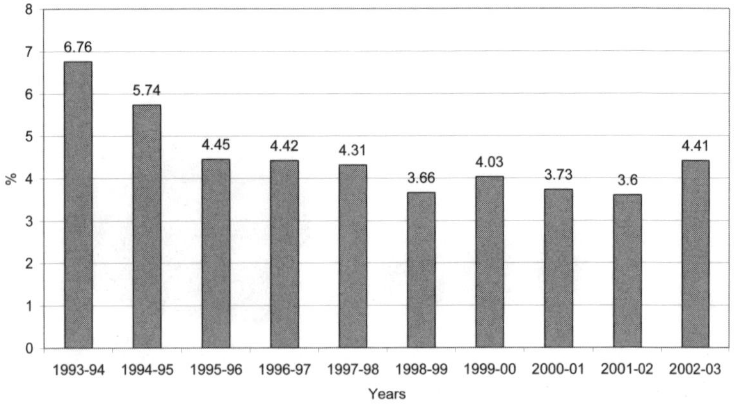

Figure 6.16 Egypt: Remittances as a percentage of GDP
Source: Nassar 2005.

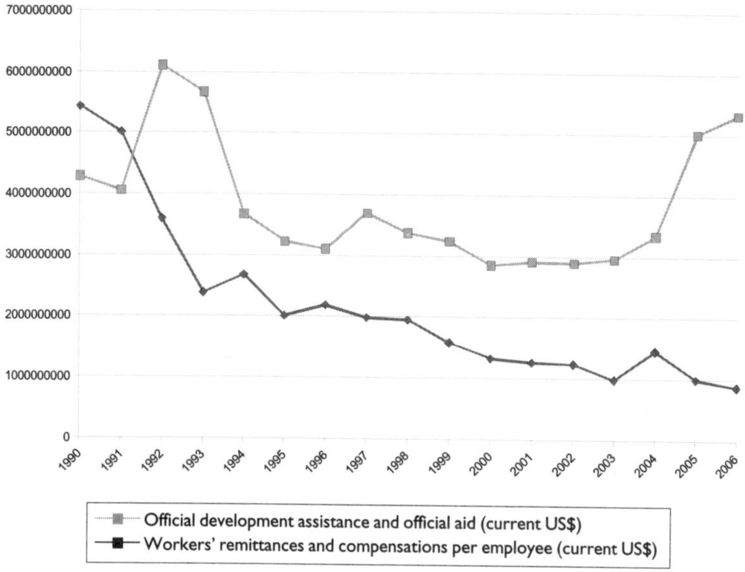

Figure 6.17 Egypt: Official Development Aid and remittances, 1990–2006
Source: Adapted by the author on World Bank data, available at: http://go.worldbank.org/SI5SSGAVZ0, accessed 5 September 2008.

Finally, the majority of remittances come from the USA (US$955.9 million) and not from Arab countries, which indicates the growing importance of permanent migration to developed countries (Table 6.7).

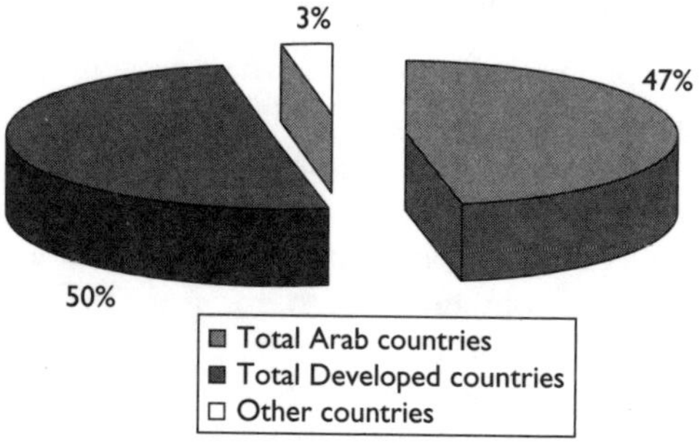

Figure 6.18 Egypt: Share of remittances by region of origin, 2001/2002
Source: Adapted by the author on Central Bank of Egypt data, available at: http://www.cbe.org.eg/Monthly Statstical Bulletin.htm, accessed 5 September 2008.

Table 6.7 Remittances by country of origin, fiscal year 2001/2002 (US$ millions)

Developed countries	
United States	955.9
Switzerland	119.9
United Kingdom	116
Germany	89.1
France	47.3
Italy	32.4
Netherlands	12
Japan	8.6
Canada	5.9
Greece	5.2
Spain	3.4
Total Developed countries	1395.7
Arab countries	
Saudi Arabia	612.4
United Arab Emirates	312.7
Kuwait	246
Bahrain	54.2
Qatar	42.2
Oman	11.3
Lebanon	10.3
Libya	3
Total Arab countries	1292.1

Source: Adapted by the author on Central Bank of Egypt, data available at: http://www.cbe.org.eg/Monthly Statistical Bulletin.htm, accessed 5 September 2008.

3.2 *Other indicators of marginalisation*

Apart from the economic indicators reported above, some softer economic indicators are used in the literature to identify the degree of integration of a country in the global economy.[16] The qualitative definition of globalisation adopted in this book starts from the assumption that the current phase of capitalist development is defined by some technological achievements that make it different from any other stages in the development of the world economy.[17] In particular, scholars refer to the telecommunication revolution and to the widespread use of Internet and digital resources that facilitate not only generic communication, but also learning and production processes.[18]

Hence, the analysis of indicators relating to the usage of telecommunications and internet or digital resources (so-called Information and Communication Technology, ICT indicators) can help in establishing whether or not a country is catching up with the globalisation process.[19] Reference is made below to some such indicators – for example, the number of computers, Internet access or mobile phone subscriptions per 100 people in Egypt. It is worth noting, however, that the author does not consider these indicators particularly revealing of the causes of marginalisation, as the reasons why a region or a country remains outside the globalisation process are very varied; the lack of recourse to modern technological means might not be the most important. Issues of political instability, lack of social capital or widespread corruption of the government, to mention just a few, may prevail. Additionally, symptoms of lack of integration via ICT indicators do not appear totally reliable. Indeed, if we look at indicators of access to technology for countries such as China, these are still very low, but this cannot and does not mean that the country is not being increasingly integrated in the global economy.

Given these considerations, Egypt is without doubt lagging behind in terms of access to the new technologies. For example, the number of mobile phone subscriptions per 100 persons in 2007 was only 39.8, compared to 83.51 in the USA (Figure 6.19).

Also, the number of Internet users was a mere 11.42 per 100 people, whereas in the USA this number was 71.94 (Figure 6.20). The use of broadband was almost non-existent in Egypt in 2007 (Figure 6.21).

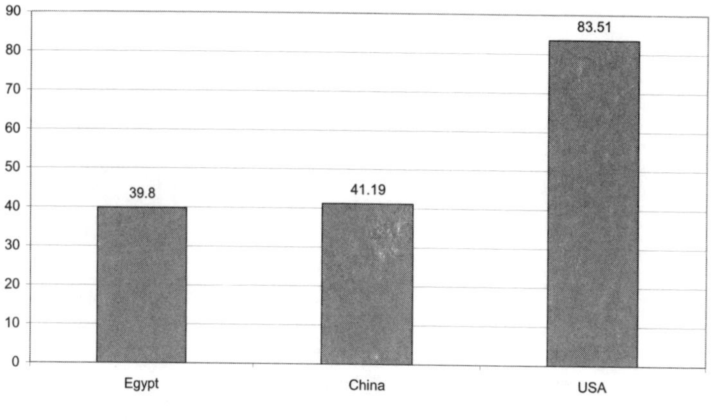

Figure 6.19 Egypt, China and the USA: Mobile phone subscribers per 100 inhabitants, 2007

Source: Adapted by the author on ITU data, available at: http://www.itu.int/net/home/index.aspx, accessed 5 September 2008.

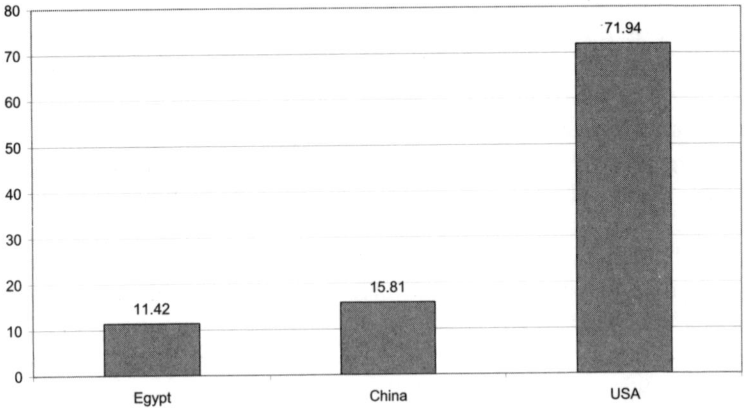

Figure 6.20 Egypt, China and the USA: Internet users per 100 inhabitants, 2007

Source: Adapted by the author on ITU data, available at: http://www.itu.int/net/home/index.aspx, accessed 5 September 2008.

The number of computers per 100 inhabitants is incredibly low – 4.19. However, this is also the case with China: 5.6 as compared to the USA's 79.89 (Figure 6.22).

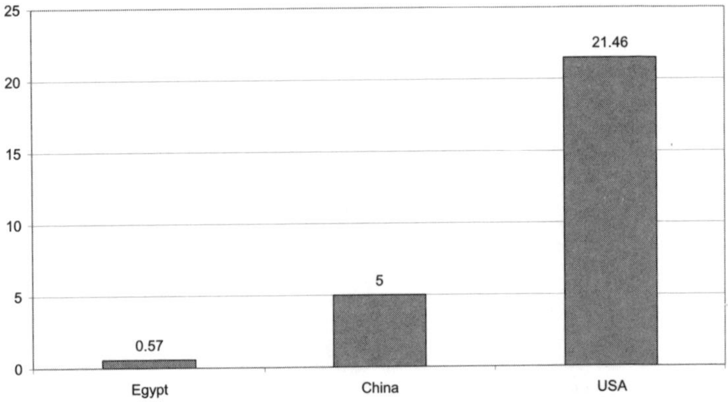

Figure 6.21 Egypt, China and the USA: Broadband Internet subscribers per 100 inhabitants, 2007

Source: Adapted by the author on ITU data, available at: http://www.itu.int/net/home/index.aspx, accessed 5 September 2008.

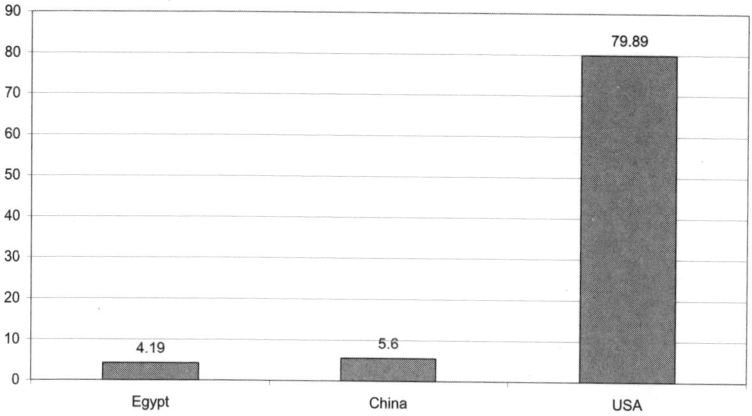

Figure 6.22 Egypt, China and the USA: Computers per 100 inhabitants, 2006
Source: Adapted by the author on ITU data, available at: http://www.itu.int/net/home/index.aspx, accessed 5 September 2008.

Finally, as might be expected, Egypt is basically not exporting high technology. Its share of high technology exports over total exports was 0.5 per cent in 2006, as compared to 30.1 per cent in the USA (Figure 6.23).

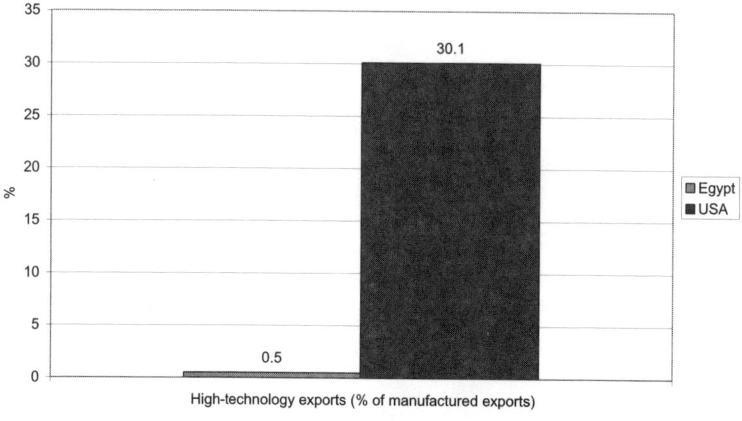

Figure 6.23 Egypt and the USA: High technology exports, 2006
Source: Adapted by the author on World Bank data, available at: http://go.worldbank.org/SI5SSGAVZ0, accessed 5 September 2008.

4 Conclusion

Rather than catching up with the process of globalisation, Egypt and the Middle East appear to be increasingly marginalised from the world economy. The MENA area is indeed the one area of the world, together with Sub-Saharan Africa, experiencing a decrease in its share of FDI stock in the last decades. Despite an aggressive policy of liberalisation and privatisation, which had begun in 1974 with the *infitah* of Sadat, Egypt has to date been unable to attract substantial FDI. Instead, both its share of FDI stock and its share of FDI inflows in the decade of the early 1990s/early 2000s have substantially decreased. Egypt is also very marginal in terms of mergers and acquisitions, and its trade openness has remained the same for the whole of the 1990s and is very low indeed.

This has occurred even though the country has undergone a substantial process of reorganisation and stabilisation of its economy under the supervision of the IMF and the World Bank, which has been successful to an extent in improving its macroeconomic performance. Nowadays, Egypt continues to rely heavily on remittances for the support of its economy; and these are increasingly coming from the most developed countries, first of all the USA, and less and less from its Arab neighbours.

But who are these Egyptian migrants? To this question we turn in the next chapter of this book.

Chapter 7

Who is the Egyptian migrant?

1 Introduction

The analysis so far has shown that, from a theoretical point of view, the following issues appear particularly relevant:

- the paradox of regionalisation within globalisation and its consequences in terms of increase of intraregional temporary migration;
- the paradox of marginalisation within globalisation and its consequences in terms of increase of permanent migration to the developed world;
- the paradox of 'Fortress Europe' and its consequences in terms of illegal migration.

These paradoxes impact on the decision of people to migrate, and on their modalities and motivations for migration. This makes it important to define the profile of migrants and their motivations for migration.

According to the theoretical paradigm adopted, the new global division of labour, which is a consequence of the restructuring induced by the globalisation process, increases the level of marginalisation of some countries, notably the MENA area and Sub-Saharan Africa. This results in an outflow of permanent labour migrants, both skilled and unskilled, to the developed world. So what should the characteristics of the Egyptian migrant be, to fit with the hypothesis that the last phase of migration from Egypt (namely, permanent migration to more developed countries, including the EU) is an example of globalisation-induced emigration?

In assessing the profile of the migrant, reference is made to the theory of migration as a social process.[1] Three constituent phases describe the model: (1) the homo economicus phase; (2) the goal reorientation phase; and (3) the community-formation phase. In the homo economicus phase, economically motivated migrants are thought to be mostly target-earners, persons with specific monetary goals. This helps to explain the frequent mismatch between migrants' skills and their job placements.[2] In the goal reorientation phase, families often form by adding female migrants from the sending countries to the originally male-dominated flow. Leisure time takes the place of multiple jobs, living conditions improve and require higher expenditures, and migrants enter the world of self-employment, initially only as a marginal activity, but later as their main occupation.[3] The last phase of the process is the formation of communities.

It is important to note that the process does not refer to a single migrant's experience, but to a group of migrants from a specific country and/or region. Also, the three phases in reality occur almost always contextually. However, there are some characteristics of each phase which prevail over the others according to which stage in the evolution of the migratory process the group analysed is experiencing. The transition from success to failure may occur after multiple migration episodes. Each is normally motivated by some monetary objectives, but overall they define the migrant's chances of social attachments in the receiving country, or his/her failure. The accumulation of many individuals' attempts to establish themselves in the host country results in the formation of networks between origin and destination communities.[4] These networks simultaneously:

- encourage continued migration if migrants are successful (according to this interpretation of communities, if failure to establish themselves in the host country prevails over successful stories, then the network does not form and the migratory process is definitively extinguished); and
- restrain return migration, because the formation of a social community results in the overcoming of purely monetary objectives and favours the stabilisation of migrants. A turning-point is usually represented by the birth of children who have a higher degree of attachment to the migrants' new country than to their original one.

For the purposes of this book, the model of migration as a social process assists in understanding the characteristics of Egyptian migrants. Through the definition of their profiles, the author can establish in which phase of the migratory process the Egyptian community in Europe is to be inserted. For the sake of completeness of the analysis, the chapter includes a comparison with migrants from another MENA country – Morocco. This is based on a questionnaire implemented by the author in Rabat.

Contemporary migration from Egypt is viewed almost unanimously as economically motivated.[5] Most research and opinion would place Egyptian migrants in the target earner category discussed in the exposition of the social process model.[6] Therefore, we should expect the Egyptian migrant to be typically male, unmarried, relatively young and with a very clear-cut preference for earning money, with no attention being paid either to the conditions of work or to the modalities of entry in the receiving country.

Given Egypt's history of non-emigration, the search for potential contextual factors to explain the change to an emigrant country is made relatively easy, as it may pragmatically be narrowed to a search for structural changes that occurred at about the same time. For the migration dynamics after the increase of oil prices, the hypothesis is made in this book that the reasons must be traced in the marginalisation of Egypt from the process of globalisation and the lack of integration of the MENA region. A similar hypothesis is made for Morocco, despite the fact that Moroccan migration is not as new as the Egyptian one. Therefore, in the profile of the Moroccan migrant, we would expect a higher rate of female migration, and a higher incidence of the aim of family reunification. A fundamental role should be played by the already-existing networks of family and friends in deciding to migrate. This, however, should exist alongside a still-important component of strongly economically motivated migration and acceptance of working conditions that can hardly be considered ideal.

To conclude, this chapter will investigate the micro-dimensions of Egyptian and Moroccan migration to the EU within the theoretical context so far defined. The main hypotheses are the following:

- migration from the MENA area to the EU is motivated primarily by economic considerations; political or religious issues do not play a major role in the decision to move;
- migration includes not only unskilled labour, but also skilled personnel (brain drain) fleeing the two sample countries as a consequence of their marginalisation;
- migrants from the MENA area are not 'documented' in all phases of their migration process;
- the same migrants do not have a job contract at the point of departure;
- familial or national networks play a major role in the choice of the destination country, especially if the migratory process has already passed the first phase of the model of migration as a social process;
- migrants are inserted in the labour structure of the receiving country in activities that do not necessarily correspond to their preferred sectors of employment;
- the existence of an underground economy positively influences the decision to move to a given country;
- migrants have some knowledge of the existence of an underground/ informal economy.

In turn, the difference between the Egyptian and the Moroccan case should mainly be represented by a higher percentage of female migration in the Moroccan case, and a lower share of migrants who are mainly economically motivated.

In the next section, we look at the case of Egypt.

2 The profile of the Egyptian migrant: The 'homo economicus'

As mentioned above, Piore[7] and Bohning[8] devised a model of migration as a social process to be applied to the case of permanent migrants from less developed countries to industrialised societies with the aim of finding out whether migration is still in its early phases or is more mature. A survey carried out by the author[9] shows that migration from Egypt to post-industrial European countries is still in the first phase of the migration process. From this point of view, we can say that it is a very new instance of migration. Egyptian migrants are predominantly concentrated in young age groups, with more males than females, and with a relatively high educational status, especially among those from an urban background.[10] This section, which emerged from the survey, sheds some light on the characteristics of Egyptian migrants in general.

In 1987, a survey by CAPMAS[11] indicated that Egyptian migrants were almost exclusively males (97.7 per cent of current migrants). The age group was, in 89.8 per cent of cases, between 20 and 44 years old. In 63.5 per cent of cases, emigrants were married. The results of the author's 2003 survey largely confirm the profile of the Egyptian migrant outlined above. The majority of prospective migrants interviewed in the Emigration section of the Egyptian Ministry of Manpower were, indeed, males (71.8 per cent), although the percentage of females (28.2) was far above the figures reported by CAPMAS in 1987 (2.4 per cent) – see Figure 7.1.

As in the official figures, the majority of migrants were young people between 20 and 50 years of age (86.4 per cent) – see Figure 7.2.

The figures relating to marital status coincide exactly with the official ones indicated by the Egyptian statistical office in 1987. Indeed, 63.1 per cent of Egyptian migrants interviewed were married (63.5 per cent in the CAPMAS data) – see Figure 7.3.

Moreover, the 2003 survey shows that 80.6 per cent of interviewed migrants possess some form of education, with 69.9 per cent of the sample having at least secondary education (see Figure 7.4). These figures are much higher than those reported by the official statistics, according to which only 41 per cent of migrants have education at the secondary level and above.

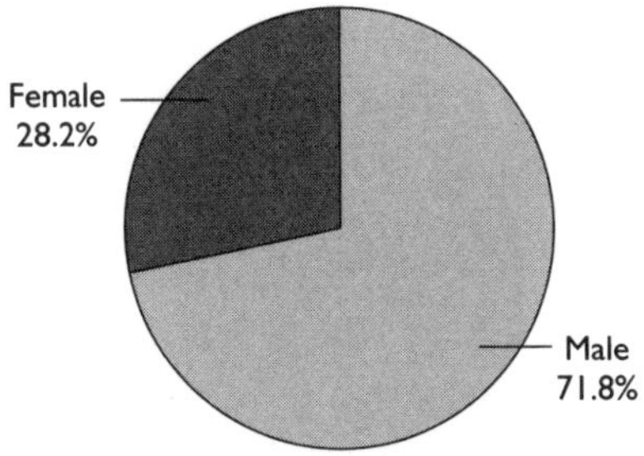

Figure 7.1 Gender division of Egyptian migrants

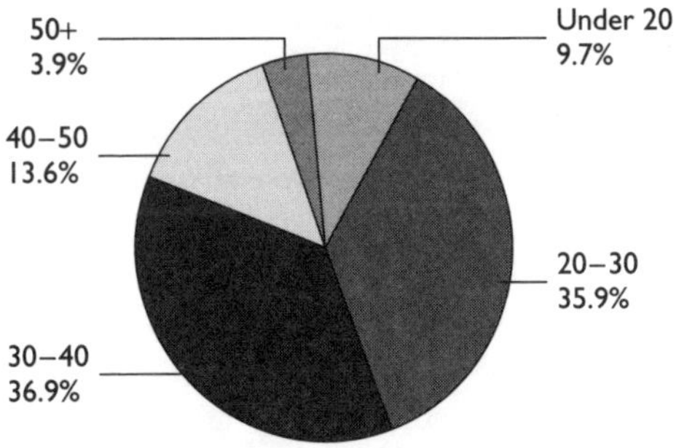

Figure 7.2 Age of potential Egyptian migrants

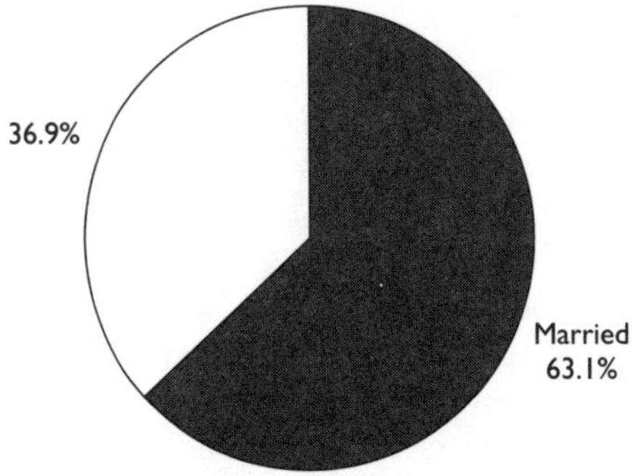

Figure 7.3 Marital status of Egyptian migrants

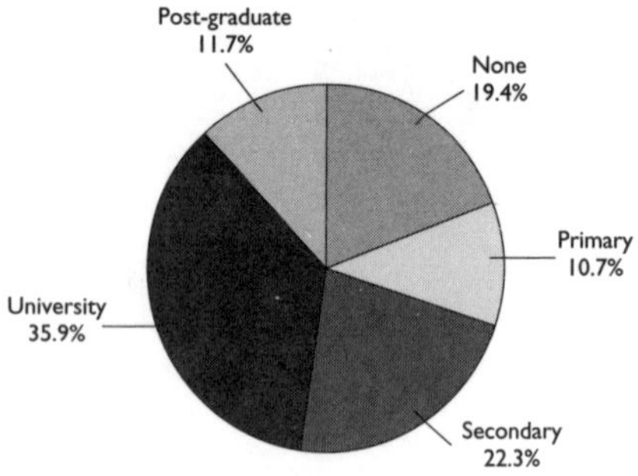

Figure 7.4 Level of education of Egyptian migrants

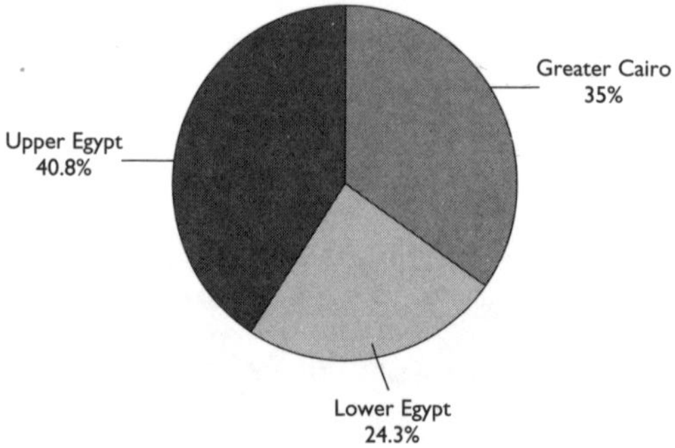

Figure 7.5 Birthplaces of Egyptian migrants

Finally, the sample includes potential migrants from all parts of Egypt, although the survey was conducted in Cairo. As reported in Figure 7.5 above, 35 per cent of the sample was born in greater Cairo, 40.8 per cent in Upper Egypt, and 24.2 per cent in Lower Egypt.

To conclude, with respect to the official sources on the profile of the average Egyptian migrant, the sample analysed by the survey over-represents both the female component and the level of education. Whether this result is related to an effective change in the migrant profile, to include more educated people and more women, is not possible to infer from such a limited number of questionnaires.

In relation to the motivations for migration at the point of departure, the results of the 2003 survey show that Egyptian migration is mainly based on economic grounds. When asked specifically about the motivations to migrate, the respondents to the questionnaire answered in 65 per cent of cases that their reasons were mainly economic (see Figure 7.6).

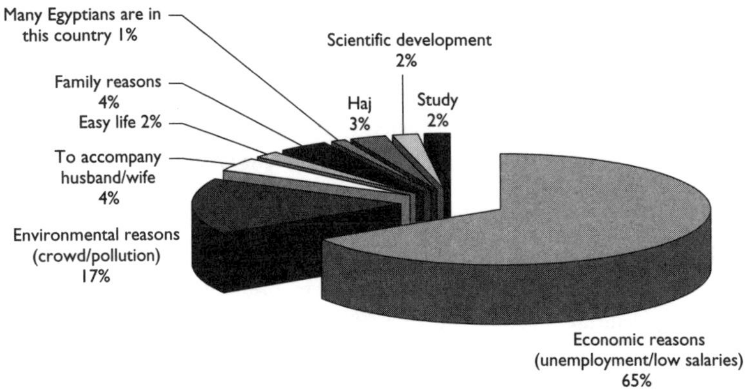

Figure 7.6 Egypt: Motivations to emigrate

Of course, a sizeable difference can be noted by disaggregating the data by gender. Indeed, economic motivations represent the main reason for male migration in 73 per cent of cases, while for female migration it was so in only 48 per cent of cases, whereas family unification represented the main motivation for female migration in 14 per cent of cases and 0 per cent of male cases.[12]

Further adding to the conclusion that the majority of potential migrants have an economic interest in moving abroad is the fact that, when asked about their expectations from migration, around 74 per cent of the sample answered that they would like to earn a good income, as opposed to increasing their expertise and skills (see Figure 7.7).

The main source of information about the potential destination country is represented by family and relatives abroad (68 per cent) – see Figure 7.8.

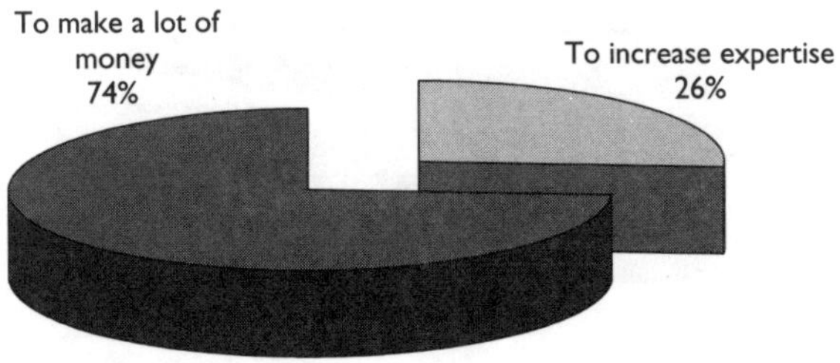

Figure 7.7 Expectations of experience of working abroad (multiple answers)

This substantiates the idea that community networks play a vital role in the choice of the destination country, as expected by the theory of migration as a social process.

In terms of the insertion into the labour market of the receiving countries, potential migrants expected to be working first and foremost in the services sector (56 per cent), with 40 per cent wanting to be involved in general services, 9 per cent in tourism and restaurants, and 7 per cent in home services. To this, we should add the people who wanted to work in banking (1 per cent), in government (1 per cent), and in education (5 per cent). Only 14 per cent were willing to work in industry, and even less (3 per cent) in agriculture – see Figure 7.9.

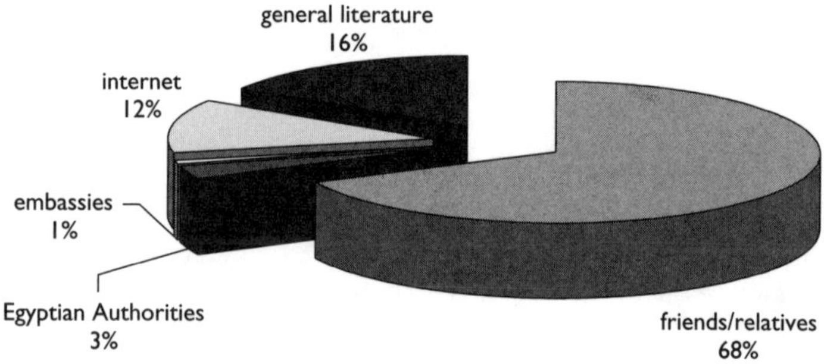

Figure 7.8 Egypt: Sources of information on preferred country of destination

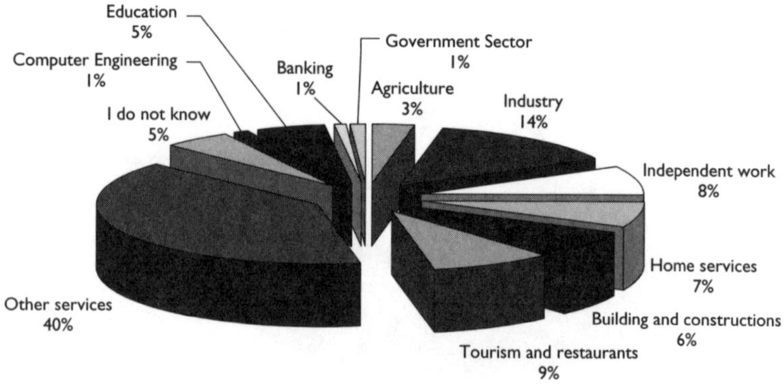

Figure 7.9 Egypt: Preferred sector in which to work abroad

Although there are no data available on the insertion of Egyptian migrants into the European labour markets, pointing to the necessity of more research in this field, a comparison may be made between their expectations and the reality of their integration in the labour markets of the Arab countries. The data collected by the Egyptian Ministry for Manpower and Emigration[13] show that, in 2002, 33.8 per cent of Egyptian migrants were working in industry, while according to our survey only 14.7 per cent were willing to be employed in the industrial sector. The agricultural sector was absorbing 8.6 per cent of the Egyptian migrant labour force, against 3 per cent of people expecting to do so; and finally, the services sector was employing only 12.7 per cent of those migrating to the Arab states, whereas more than 50 per cent would have liked to be integrated into the services sector. The existence of this incongruity between the expectations and the actual integration of migrants in the labour markets might point to the existence of a mismatch between the demand and supply of migrants' labour, and to a less-than-efficient utilisation of resources.[14]

As far as the legal/illegal dimension of migration is concerned, it seems important to note that, while 64 per cent of the overall sample claims that they chose a specific destination country for general job opportunities, only 12.6 per cent of Egyptian migrants have a specific job offer, let alone a contract (Table 7.1). Considering that in many EU member states having a job contract is a necessary precondition to being admitted legally into the hosting country, it might be possible to speculate on the lack of proper documents by Egyptian migrants.

It is true that, when asked about whether it was possible to enter a destination country without appropriate documents, 93.2 per cent of the respondents answered 'no', but obviously no different answer could have

Table 7.1 Egypt: Main reason for choice of destination country

	Frequency	*Percent*	*Valid Percent*	*Cumulative Percent*
Family ties	16	15.5	15.5	15.5
Language	1	1.0	1.0	16.5
A specific job offer	13	12.6	12.6	29.1
General job opportunities	66	64.1	64.1	93.2
Beauty of country	1	1.0	1.0	94.2
Company of husband/wife	1	1.0	1.0	95.1
Near to Egypt	1	1.0	1.0	96.1
Haj	2	1.9	1.9	98.1
Scientific Development	1	1.0	1.0	99.0
Study	1	1.0	1.0	100.0
TOTAL	103	100.0	100.0	

been expected; and, yet, almost 7 per cent of the respondents were not aware of the necessity of holding appropriate entry documents (see Figure 7.10).

A more in-depth survey of the characteristics of irregular migration from Egypt has been carried out by the Emigration sector of the Egyptian Ministry of Manpower and Emigration on the basis of a questionnaire devised in cooperation with the author. The study explains the reasons for irregular migration from eight Egyptian Governorates known to send irregular migrants mainly to Italy and France. One important objective of the survey was to gather information about the level of awareness of potential migrants about the smuggling of migrants and irregular migration from Egypt to the EU. The study interviewed only males between 18 and 40 years of age, as they represent the main population of Egyptian migrants, both legal and illegal. The total number of individuals interviewed was 1,552. Moreover, six focus group discussions were conducted to gather qualitative data.[15]

This more extensive survey confirms that the majority of migrants do not have a formal job offer before starting their migration process. Only 14.6 per cent of the respondents claimed to have some job offer; however, in the focus groups, this was revealed to be only a promise from relatives or friends to introduce the migrant into the European labour market.

Again, almost all migrants were aware of the necessity of proper documents to migrate to Europe (about 85 per cent of respondents), but an almost identical percentage of them (82) also knew that there are groups facilitating illegal migration. An even higher number of respondents mentioned that they had heard about deported migrants (94.7 per cent). Almost 75 per cent of the respondents were aware of the consequences of

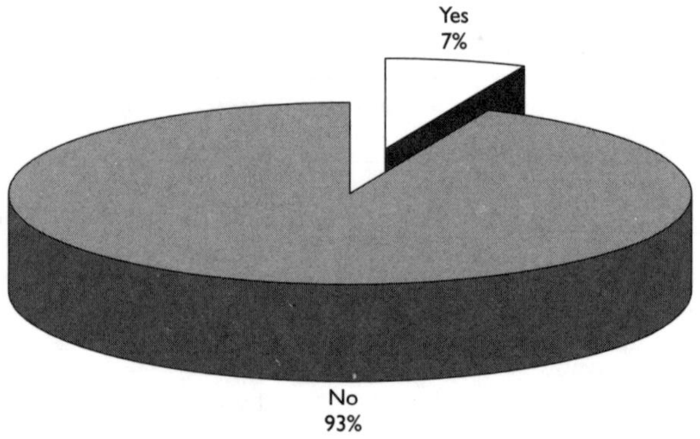

Figure 7.10 Egypt: Understanding of respondents as to whether one could go abroad without the required papers

illegal migration, but 78 per cent believed that legal migration to Europe was not easy, which could give hints on their availability to initiate their migration process in an irregular fashion.[16] To substantiate these suspicions, migrants who had already migrated to Europe were asked about the cost they paid to migration 'facilitators'. Of the respondents, 78.8 per cent admitted they paid money to migrate, and the average cost was 15,890LE (around £1,400). The focus groups' discussion with return migrants pointed to the existence of two main illegal routes to Europe.[17] The first is the route by desert and sea through Libya and Italy, and this costs around 15,000LE; the second is by plane with tourist visa, and this is more expensive – around 50,000LE. These amounts do not include any other services apart from those relating to facilitating entry into the countries of destination. Finally, only 6.9 per cent of respondents had a work contract before migration, and almost 40 per cent did not even try to obtain an official visa.[18]

The surveys and the analysis carried out for the case of Egypt make it possible to provide some preliminary answers to the set of hypotheses set out in the introduction of this chapter. In particular, it is possible to conclude that Egyptian migration to Europe is mainly motivated by economic considerations. Moreover, it concerns not only unskilled labour, but also skilled personnel (brain drain) fleeing the country as a consequence of its marginalisation. Concerning the legal/illegal dimensions of Egyptian migration, although it is impossible to find out how many migrants have proper documents in the different phases of the migration process, the surveys clearly show that only very few of those wishing to migrate to Europe have a job contract, which makes it very likely that they will become irregular migrants at a certain point after their entry into the receiving country. Familial and national networks play a major role in the choice of the country where to move. Finally, Egyptian migrants are inserted into the labour structure of the receiving country in activities that do not correspond to their preferred sectors of employment. No conclusions can be drawn about the insertion of Egyptian migrants into the underground economy from the data so far collected.[19]

Let us move now to the comparison with the profile of migrants from another MENA country – Morocco.

3 The profile of the Moroccan migrant: From the homo economicus to the community-formation phase

The data on the profile of the Moroccan migrant have been gathered through a field survey by the author, which took in March 2006 in Rabat.

The survey included 73 structured interviews of people willing to migrate, and the questionnaire was devised to be able to give some preliminary answers to the hypotheses detailed above. Given the limited sample of the survey, the author is aware that no final conclusions can be drawn. However, the survey might help in providing some insights to the issues posed by the theoretical analysis of this chapter. Of the 73 people interviewed, only one respondent had no intention to migrate to work abroad. We can therefore assume that the whole sample comprises potential migrants. Moreover, around one-third of the overall sample (31.5 per cent) had already been abroad to work.

As far as the main characteristics of the respondents are concerned, they were mainly males (75.3 per cent) aged between 18 and 44 years (35.6 per cent between 18 and 24; 35.6 per cent between 25 and 34; and 28.8 per cent between 35 and 44). Only a third of the sample was married, with very little difference in terms of gender (27.3 per cent males as opposed to 33.3 per cent females). As expected, the level of education is pretty high, with 20.5 per cent of the respondents having university education, and only 6.8 per cent of the sample being completely uneducated.[20]

The motivations for migration are overwhelmingly economic: 47.9 per cent of the sample refers to the lack of employment opportunities in Morocco, and 46.6 per cent to the fact that wages are lower than in Europe. For 58.9 per cent of the sample, the main reason to migrate to Europe is the difference in living standards, whereas 34.2 per cent of respondents want to help their families by migrating to Europe. Contrary to the Egyptian case, economic motivations are as important for women as they are for men – see Table 7.2.

Political motivations for migration are relevant only for men, but to a very limited extent: only 8.2 per cent of total answers. The motivation of family reunification is almost as important for Moroccan men as it is for Moroccan women. This confirms the hypothesis that many Moroccans,

Table 7.2 Motivations for migration: The case of Morocco (multiple answers)

	Male %	*Female %*	*Total %*
Lack of employment opportunities in Morocco	47.3	50	47.9
Lower wages in Morocco	50.9	33.3	46.6
Low standards of living	60	55.6	58.9
To escape family oppression	5.5	5.6	5.6
To help my family	41.8	11.1	34.2
Family reunification	20	33.3	23.3
To increase knowledge	20	5.6	16.4
To escape political problems	10.9	0	8.2
Other	0	11.7	2.9

both male and female, are in the second phase of the migratory process, according to Piore's classification, and are therefore forming families in the host country. Indeed, the main source of information on the country of destination for Moroccan migrants is represented by already-existing networks of nationals or, better, friends and family (87 per cent of the overall sample) – see Figure 7.11.[21]

Moreover, 81 per cent of respondents have family and/or friends working in Europe already (Figure 7.12); and in explaining why they want to migrate to Europe, 46.4 per cent of the sample answered that it was because they had family there, while 31.9 per cent explained that they had friends living in Europe (Figure 7.13).

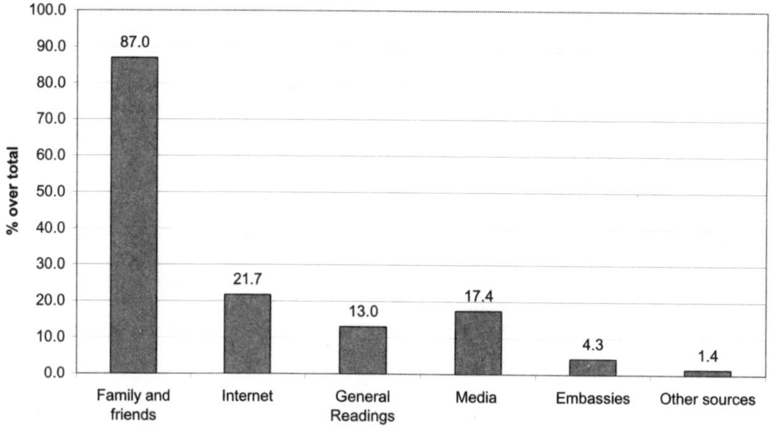

Figure 7.11 Morocco: Sources of information on the destination country (multiple answers)

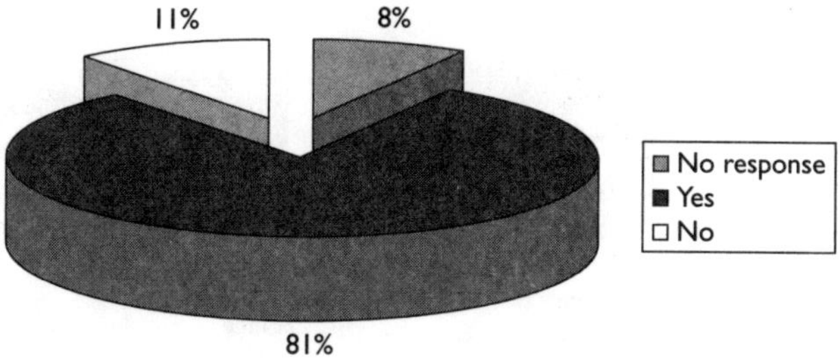

Figure 7.12 Morocco: Respondents with relatives or friends working in Europe

The three main countries of destination in Europe – France, Spain and Italy – are also the three countries where the majority of respondents claim they have families and friends (55.9 per cent).[22] Indeed, the survey confirms that the main countries of destination for Moroccans are France, Spain and Italy. The accumulated percentage of responses is such that around 65 per cent of those interviewed would like to go and work in one of these countries – see Figure 7.14.

The country perceived as the easiest to move to is Spain.[23] More interestingly, however, the perception of migrants about the permeability

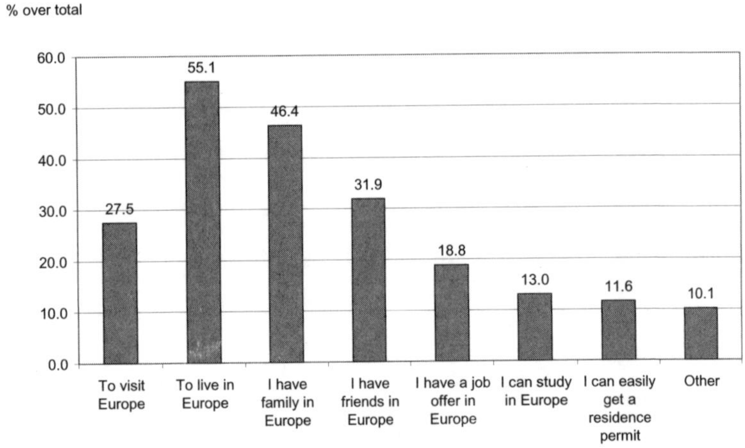

Figure 7.13 Morocco: Motivation in choosing destination country (multiple answers)

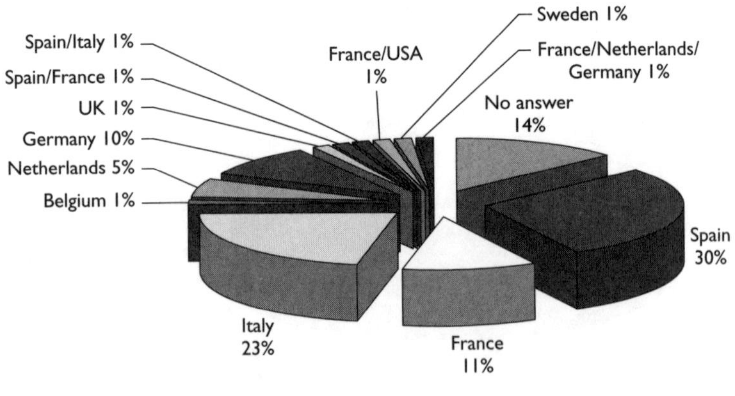

Figure 7.14 Moroccan migration: Preferred destination countries

of the Spanish borders refers not only to regular, but also undocumented entry. As detailed in Table 7.3, around 58 per cent of those interviewed thought that Spain was the easiest way into the EU both for legal and for illegal migration. This is a clear acknowledgement on the part of Moroccan migrants of the existence of the Spanish route for undocumented entry.

The issue of illegal migration has been approached in the questionnaire both directly and indirectly. The indirect way to obtain information on the legal or illegal status of migrants' entry and stay in an EU country is to ask whether they have a formal job contract. The reason why this is relevant in assessing the regularity of the migrants' status is because EU countries require a job contract to issue a working permit, which in turn is the necessary requirement to have a long-term visa and a residence permit.[24] As it is an indirect question, it is more likely that the respondents will give genuine answers; therefore, it is easier to assess the phenomenon of illegal entry and permanence. In the questionnaire, the issue has been raised on various occasions.

First, only 18.8 per cent of those interviewed answered that they wanted to migrate to Europe because they already had a job offer (Figure 7.13). Moreover, of those who had already proposed to migrate to Europe (49 people of 73), only 20.4 per cent had a formal job contract, while 40.8 per cent had a generic promise from a friend or member of the family that they would find a job for them in the receiving country (see Figure 7.15).

Finally, around 35 per cent of the sample had received other, unspecified proposals to enter Europe. Cross-checking with those who had already been in Europe, only 3 per cent had a job contract when they entered, and 42.5 per cent had entered the host country without a valid visa.[25]

Of course, when asked directly whether they would seek the help of an intermediary to cross the border, only 2 per cent answered yes. However, the amount of money they perceived as necessary to migrate is consistent

Table 7.3 Morocco: Opinions on the easiest country into which to migrate (in a regular or irregular way)

Countries of Destination	*% of Answers*
Spain	57.5
France	6.8
Italy	16.4
Spain/Italy	12.3
Spain/Belgium	1.4
France/Italy	1.4
Belgium/Holland	1.4
I do not know	1.4
Everywhere in Europe	1.4
Total	100

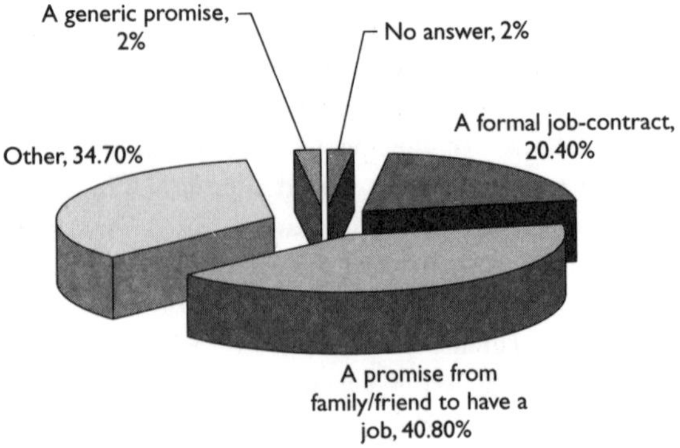

Figure 7.15 Moroccan migration: Type of emigration offer received

with the evidence that most Moroccan migrants do tend to access Europe through irregular means. Indeed, almost 80 per cent of respondents claimed that they would need between 15,000 and 200,000Dhr to migrate (which is between £1,000 and £12,000). Cross-checking with those in the sample who had already migrated to Europe, the survey confirms that an astonishing 73.4 per cent of respondents have paid more than 8,000Dhr (around £500) to migrate, with 56.7 per cent having paid more than 15,000Dhr (around £1,000) and 20 per cent more then 35,000Dhr (around £2,200).[26]

In terms of insertion into the labour market of the receiving countries, as hypothesised in the introduction of this chapter, only 21.2 per cent of those who had been employed in the receiving countries did obtain a job at their skill and educational level. The majority of migrants were occupied in the construction and agricultural sector (47 per cent) – see Figure 7.16.

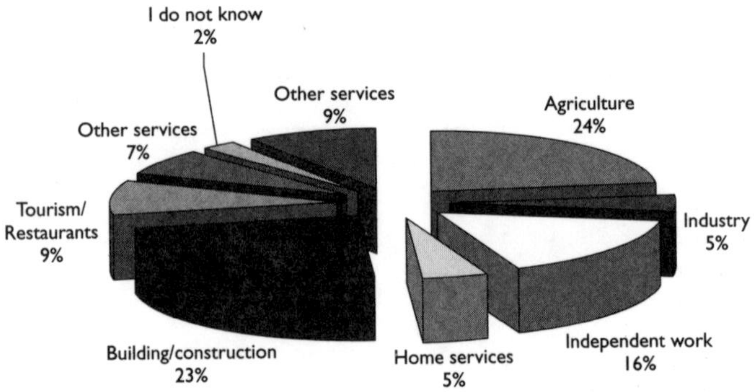

Figure 7.16 Moroccan migration: Occupation in destination country

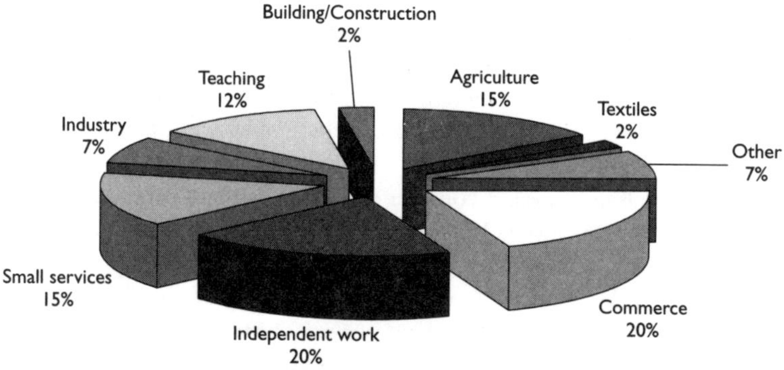

Figure 7.17 Moroccan migration: Occupation at the point of departure

However, if we look at the sectors in which the respondents were employed in their original country, only 2 per cent were occupied in building and construction, 15 per cent in agriculture, and the majority in commerce and services of various kinds (67 per cent) (see Figure 7.17).

To conclude, it is possible to claim that Moroccan migration is no doubt favoured by the existence of well-established communities of nationals in receiving countries. However, the characteristics of the 'homo economicus' phase of migration do not seem to have disappeared. Indeed, the majority of migrants are still young males who are motivated exclusively by economic considerations and are willing to initiate the migratory process through illegal means. The majority of Moroccan migrants interviewed were aware of the existence of illegal means of migration, and have internalised the possibility of migrating without the relevant documents. Finally, their insertion into the labour markets of the hosting countries does not seem to coincide with their capabilities and does not match the kinds of activities migrants were carrying out in their home country.

4 Conclusion

This chapter has stressed the importance of assessing the motivations for migration at the point of departure so as to be able to define the profile of the migrant and ascertain the relation between migration and globalisation.

According to the classification of Piore/Bohning, the newer the migratory process, the more the characteristics of the migrants should resemble those of the 'homo economicus'. Looking at the profile of the Egyptian migrant, it seems possible to claim that Egyptian migration is still prevalently in the first phase of the model of migration as a social process. Therefore, permanent Egyptian migration to Western developed countries is a new phenomenon. This is consistent with the idea that the most recent wave of emigration from Egypt is a consequence of the marginalisation of the country from the globalisation process, and is therefore a recent event.

In our analysis, we also consider the effect of globalisation on the entire MENA area, and its lack of regionalisation is used as a variable to explain the increase of mass migration from the whole region. The chapter therefore includes a comparison between the profile of the Egyptian and of the Moroccan migrant based on surveys carried out by the author. From this comparison, it emerges that there are some differences between Egyptian migration and Moroccan migration. The two countries seem to be at different stages in the evolution of their migratory dynamics. The characteristics of the Egyptian migrant are more similar to those described by Piore/Bohning as entailing the homo economicus phase. At this stage, emigrants are almost exclusively young men, motivated only by economic considerations and therefore more likely to engage with facilitators at home to initiate their migratory processes through illegal means. Moreover, they are more vulnerable to being lured into illicit or illegal economic networks.

Naturally, the presence of strong national communities in the receiving countries limits the extent to which migrants will find themselves striving alone against the risks of exploitation and marginalisation in Europe. These communities are clearly more developed in the case of Moroccan migration. Indeed, in the case of Morocco, the percentage of females and males migrating with the aim of family reunification is similar. This means that emigration from Morocco is already sufficiently well-established to have more migrants who have entered the second and the third phase of the migration process.

However, it seems that many of the elements of the homo economicus phase continue to prevail in the dynamics of Moroccan migration, which is still mainly represented by men who enter destination countries through illegal means. This entails some consequences for the receiving countries, as the involvement of migrants in organised crime networks, and the fact that they do not care too much about their living conditions in the receiving countries, does increase the likelihood that migrants will find themselves embedded in illicit or illegal economic activities. Moreover, they are more likely to be exploited by employers in destination countries, and certainly their expectations in terms of integration into the European labour markets are not met.

Despite the fact that the surveys show a high degree of awareness of the dynamics of irregular migration and of the costs involved, it seems to the author that more should be done to increase the information relating to the conditions of work and of life in destination countries for those who do not possess proper job contracts at the point of departure. The elaboration of information campaigns with regard to the risks connected to the smuggling of migrants and indentured migration might help to limit the risks for migrants. But what exactly are the risks for Muslim migrants in receiving countries? What are the dynamics of integration of emigrants from the MENA area in general and from Egypt in particular?

To this subject we turn in the next chapters of this book.

Chapter 8

What do Muslim migrants do in receiving countries?

1 Introduction

September 11 modified the perception and the reception of Muslim migrants in the Western world. One of the most controversial effects of September 11 on migration is the acceleration of the process of 'securitisation'. It is certainly difficult to deny that the terrorist threat from Muslim fundamentalism reshaped the EU attitude towards Muslim migration in a much more security-oriented fashion, and reinforced phenomena such as anti-Muslim behaviour (Islamophobia), social unrest in Muslim communities and right-wing extremism.[1]

However the challenges for Western industrialised countries, especially the EU, arising from the increase of Muslim migration predates the events of September 11. They range from the difficulty of integration in the labour markets of the receiving countries, to the exploitation by organised crime, and they include marginalisation from the social, political and cultural life of the host community, to straightforward hostility.

This chapter addresses some of the issues relating to the integration of the Muslim migrant in the labour markets of the destination country. It sketches the situation of the labour markets in receiving countries for Muslim workers in general and for Egyptian workers in particular. The chapter then tackles the question of the insertion of foreign-born workers in the underground economy. The aim is to verify to what extent the existence of a thriving underground economy, especially in southern European countries, may represent a strong pull factor, attracting especially undocumented migrants to the EU.

2 The integration of Muslim workers in the labour markets: General patterns in Europe

Data from the OECD help in the identification of general patterns of employment of Muslims in European labour markets, their level of employment and unemployment, and their conditions of work.[2] This represents the starting point for the assessment of the modalities of integration of European Muslim communities in the different European countries and the discussion, from an informed standpoint, of the phenomenon of Islamophobia in the next chapter.

On the basis of these data it is possible to reach the conclusion that all over Europe Muslim migrant communities suffer discrimination, unemployment, and marginalisation, for both genders.

Given the fact that data on the integration of the 'Muslims' as such in the European labour markets are not available, the way to identify their integration is to look at the patterns of integration of the different national or ethnic communities in the labour markets of the different receiving countries.

Starting from the study of the sectors in which foreign labour is mostly employed, the first instance of discrimination is represented by the fact that, according to OECD data, compared to the native-born, immigrants are overrepresented in the low-skilled jobs of the agricultural and industrial sectors.[3]

Table 8.1 shows the situation of European OECD countries, highlighting the differences between foreign-born and native workers in their patterns of employment in the different economic sectors. The table points at the existence of a clear gap between the percentages of foreign-born labour employed in the low-skilled sectors of agriculture and industry and the percentages of native-born labour working in the same sectors. The gap is particularly clear in the case of Greece, where 24.3 per cent more foreign men than natives work in the agricultural and industrial sectors, Luxembourg (+14.1 per cent), Italy (+10.7 per cent) and Spain (+4.5 per cent).

As far as foreign women are concerned, they tend to be overrepresented in the low-skilled personal and social services sectors, such as services for the elderly and for children, or services for restaurants and hotels. Although also native-born women are significantly involved in these activities, there still is a gap between the percentage of foreign-born women employed in these sectors and the percentage of native-born ones. This phenomenon is more pronounced in Southern European countries: Greece, where 16.3 per cent more foreign women are involved in the personal and social services sector, Portugal (+7.9 per cent), Italy (+7 per cent), and Spain (+3.3 per cent). (See Table 8.1.)

Table 8.1 Sectors of activity of the native-born and foreign-born by country of residence

	Country	*Sector*	*Native-born*		
			Men (%)	*Women (%)*	*Total (%)*
AUT	Austria	Agriculture and industry	40.9	19.6	31.4
		Producer services	11.7	13.0	12.3
		Distributive services	23.7	24.1	23.9
		Personal and social services	23.7	43.3	32.4
BEL	Belgium	Agriculture and industry	39.5	14.1	28.8
		Producer services	11.2	11.4	11.3
		Distributive services	23.4	20.4	22.1
		Personal and social services	25.9	54.1	37.7
CHE	Switzerland	Agriculture and industry	38.8	16.0	29.1
		Producer services	18.5	15.8	17.3
		Distributive services	22.8	25.3	23.9
		Personal and social services	20.0	42.9	29.8
CZE	Czech Republic	Agriculture and industry	55.3	32.6	45.1
		Producer services	6.9	9.4	8.0
		Distributive services	18.5	18.5	18.5
		Personal and social services	19.3	39.5	28.4
DNK	Denmark	Agriculture and industry	38.0	14.4	27.0
		Producer services	13.7	12.8	13.3
		Distributive services	25.3	17.2	21.5
		Personal and social services	23.0	55.5	38.2
ESP	Spain	Agriculture and industry	48.0	20.6	37.9
		Producer services	8.7	12.2	10.0
		Distributive services	22.4	23.3	22.7
		Personal and social services	21.0	43.9	29.5
FIN	Finland	Agriculture and industry	46.5	17.5	32.4
		Producer services	12.7	13.6	13.2
		Distributive services	22.5	16.8	19.7
		Personal and social services	18.3	52.1	34.7
FRA	France	Agriculture and industry	38.6	15.9	28.3
		Producer services	3.5	5.0	4.2
		Distributive services	32.5	26.6	29.8
		Personal and social services	25.4	52.4	37.7
GBR	United Kingdom	Agriculture and industry	36.6	11.7	25.2
		Producer services	16.9	17.1	17.0
		Distributive services	25.1	22.1	23.7
		Personal and social services	21.4	49.1	34.1
GRC	Greece	Agriculture and industry	41.0	28.5	36.4
		Producer services	7.7	12.0	9.3
		Distributive services	25.6	20.2	23.6
		Personal and social services	25.7	39.3	30.7
HUN	Hungary	Agriculture and industry	47.8	27.5	38.5
		Producer services	9.2	9.7	9.4
		Distributive services	22.9	20.6	21.9
		Personal and social services	20.1	42.2	30.2

and gender (Percentage of the employed population aged 15 and above)

Foreign-born			*Total*			*Difference foreigners minus natives*		
Men (%)	*Women (%)*	*Total (%)*	*Men (%)*	*Women (%)*	*Total (%)*	*Men*	*Women*	*Total*
43.3	19.3	32.9	41.3	19.5	31.6	2.4	–0.3	1.5
11.9	16.4	13.8	11.7	13.5	12.5	0.2	3.4	1.5
22.5	19.9	21.4	23.5	23.6	23.5	–1.1	–4.2	–2.5
22.3	44.4	31.9	23.5	43.4	32.4	–1.4	1.1	–0.6
39.3	10.9	28.7	39.5	13.9	28.8	–0.2	–3.3	–0.1
12.0	15.0	13.1	11.3	11.7	11.5	0.7	3.6	1.8
22.3	19.2	21.2	23.3	20.3	22.0	–1.1	–1.2	–1.0
26.4	55.0	37.0	25.9	54.2	37.7	0.6	0.9	–0.7
43.3	19.0	33.0	39.9	16.7	30.0	4.6	3.0	3.9
15.1	15.2	15.1	17.7	15.6	16.8	–3.3	–0.6	–2.2
19.4	19.9	19.6	21.9	24.0	22.8	–3.4	–5.5	–4.3
22.1	46.0	32.3	20.5	43.7	30.4	2.1	3.1	2.5
50.8	35.8	44.2	55.1	32.7	45.0	–4.5	3.2	–0.8
7.4	7.8	7.6	6.9	9.3	8.0	0.5	–1.5	–0.4
22.1	19.1	20.8	18.7	18.5	18.6	3.5	0.6	2.2
19.7	37.3	27.4	19.3	39.5	28.3	0.5	–2.2	–0.9
29.3	15.3	22.9	37.5	14.5	26.7	–8.7	0.8	–4.0
16.2	19.2	17.6	13.9	13.2	13.6	2.5	6.3	4.2
25.2	16.1	21.1	25.3	17.2	21.5	–0.1	–1.1	–0.4
29.2	49.4	38.4	23.4	55.2	38.2	6.2	–6.1	0.2
52.5	15.5	37.6	48.3	20.2	37.8	4.5	–5.1	–0.2
7.3	10.6	8.6	8.6	12.1	9.9	–1.4	–1.6	–1.4
18.5	16.8	17.8	22.1	22.8	22.4	–3.8	–6.6	–4.9
21.7	57.2	35.9	21.0	44.9	29.9	0.7	13.3	6.5
34.6	17.5	27.3	46.2	17.5	32.3	–11.9	0.0	–5.1
17.4	16.0	16.8	12.8	13.7	13.2	4.7	2.4	3.7
19.5	19.5	19.5	22.4	16.8	19.7	–3.0	2.7	–0.2
28.4	47.0	36.3	18.5	52.0	34.7	10.1	–5.1	1.6
38.6	13.4	28.3	38.6	15.7	28.3	0.0	–2.6	0.0
3.3	5.8	4.3	3.5	5.1	4.2	–0.3	0.8	0.1
32.8	27.3	30.5	32.5	26.7	29.9	0.3	0.6	0.7
25.3	53.5	36.9	25.4	52.5	37.6	–0.1	1.1	–0.8
22.4	10.1	16.7	35.3	11.6	24.4	–14.2	–1.7	–8.4
21.6	20.1	20.9	17.3	17.4	17.4	4.7	2.9	3.9
25.0	18.8	22.2	25.0	21.8	23.6	–0.1	–3.2	–1.5
31.1	51.0	40.2	22.3	49.2	34.7	9.6	1.9	6.1
65.3	21.5	49.7	44.4	27.6	38.2	24.3	–7.1	13.3
4.0	9.8	6.1	7.2	11.7	8.9	–3.7	–2.2	–3.2
16.7	13.1	15.4	24.4	19.2	22.5	–8.9	–7.0	–8.2
14.0	55.6	28.8	24.1	41.4	30.5	–11.7	16.3	–1.9
40.4	25.0	33.3	47.6	27.4	38.4	–7.4	–2.4	–5.2
10.5	10.2	10.3	9.3	9.7	9.5	1.2	0.5	0.9
25.9	22.9	24.5	23.0	20.7	21.9	3.0	2.3	2.7
23.3	41.9	31.8	20.2	42.2	30.2	3.2	–0.4	1.6

Table 8.1 Sectors of activity of the native-born and foreign-born by country of residence

	Country	Sector	Native-born Men (%)	Native-born Women (%)	Native-born Total (%)
IRL	Ireland	Agriculture and industry	47.2	14.9	33.8
		Producer services	11.9	16.5	13.8
		Distributive services	21.6	20.0	21.0
		Personal and social services	19.3	48.6	31.4
ITA	Italy	Agriculture and industry	46.6	26.1	38.6
		Producer services	9.3	11.0	10.0
		Distributive services	20.3	17.8	19.4
		Personal and social services	23.7	45.1	32.0
LUX	Luxembourg	Agriculture and industry	25.4	15.6	21.3
		Producer services	15.3	17.6	16.3
		Distributive services	24.2	19.2	22.1
		Personal and social services	35.2	47.6	40.3
NLD	Netherlands	Agriculture and industry	35.6	12.0	25.9
		Producer services	15.5	14.6	15.1
		Distributive services	23.7	21.3	22.7
		Personal and social services	25.3	52.1	36.3
NOR	Norway	Agriculture and industry	38.5	10.2	25.3
		Producer services	13.2	10.4	11.9
		Distributive services	25.3	19.5	22.6
		Personal and social services	23.0	59.9	40.3
POL	Poland	Agriculture and industry	55.9	33.7	45.7
		Producer services	6.7	8.7	7.6
		Distributive services	21.2	20.5	20.9
		Personal and social services	16.1	37.2	25.8
PRT	Portugal	Agriculture and industry	50.1	28.8	40.7
		Producer services	6.9	8.4	7.5
		Distributive services	23.3	18.5	21.1
		Personal and social services	19.8	44.3	30.6
SVK	Slovak Republic	Agriculture and industry	51.7	29.2	41.2
		Producer services	7.5	7.9	7.7
		Distributive services	20.1	19.3	19.8
		Personal and social services	20.7	43.5	31.4
SWE	Sweden	Agriculture and industry	40.7	11.6	26.8
		Producer services	15.6	12.3	14.0
		Distributive services	22.5	15.4	19.1
		Personal and social services	21.1	60.8	40.1

Source: Database on Immigrants in OECD Countries (DIOC)

Notes: The last three columns refer respectively to the difference between foreigners and natives: men, women and total.
Among the employed men aged 15 or above born and living in Australia, 35.9% work in the agriculture and industry sector, 14% in the producer services sector, 28.2% in the distributive services sector and 21.9% in the personal and social services sector.

and gender (Percentage of the employed population aged 15 and above) (*Continued*)

Foreign-born			*Total*			*Difference foreigners minus natives*		
Men (%)	*Women (%)*	*Total (%)*	*Men (%)*	*Women (%)*	*Total (%)*	*Men*	*Women*	*Total*
37.9	14.6	28.0	46.1	14.9	33.1	−9.3	−0.4	−5.9
17.9	18.3	18.1	12.6	16.7	14.3	6.0	1.8	4.3
18.3	17.4	17.9	21.3	19.7	20.6	−3.3	−2.6	−3.0
25.8	49.8	36.0	20.1	48.7	32.0	6.5	1.2	4.6
57.3	26.2	45.2	47.2	26.1	39.0	10.7	0.2	6.5
5.1	7.7	6.1	9.1	10.8	9.8	−4.2	−3.3	−3.9
16.4	14.0	15.5	20.1	17.6	19.2	−3.9	−3.8	−3.9
21.1	52.1	33.3	23.6	45.5	32.1	−2.6	7.0	1.2
39.5	8.0	26.5	31.3	12.5	23.5	14.1	−7.6	5.2
21.2	26.6	23.4	17.7	21.4	19.2	5.9	9.0	7.2
17.2	15.7	16.6	21.3	17.8	19.8	−6.9	−3.5	−5.5
22.1	49.7	33.5	29.7	48.4	37.5	−13.1	2.1	−6.9
35.6	13.2	26.2	35.6	12.1	25.9	0.1	1.2	0.4
16.4	21.3	18.5	15.5	15.2	15.4	1.0	6.7	3.4
20.7	18.3	19.7	23.4	21.0	22.4	−3.0	−2.9	−3.0
27.2	47.1	35.6	25.4	51.7	36.3	1.9	−4.9	−0.7
27.7	8.7	18.8	37.7	10.1	24.8	−10.9	−1.5	−6.5
15.8	12.3	14.2	13.4	10.5	12.0	2.6	1.9	2.3
22.2	15.8	19.2	25.0	19.3	22.3	−3.1	−3.8	−3.4
34.3	63.2	47.8	23.8	60.1	40.8	11.3	3.3	7.6
44.7	31.9	39.4	55.8	33.7	45.6	−11.2	−1.8	−6.3
11.1	9.4	10.4	6.8	8.7	7.7	4.4	0.7	2.8
19.6	17.7	18.8	21.2	20.4	20.9	−1.7	−2.8	−2.1
24.6	41.1	31.4	16.2	37.2	25.8	8.5	3.9	5.6
46.6	16.8	33.1	49.8	27.8	40.1	−3.5	−12.1	−7.7
9.8	13.0	11.3	7.1	8.8	7.9	3.0	4.7	3.8
20.3	17.9	19.2	23.0	18.4	21.0	−2.9	−0.5	−1.9
23.3	52.3	36.4	20.1	45.0	31.1	3.5	7.9	5.9
45.3	29.1	37.4	51.6	29.2	41.1	−6.5	−0.1	−3.8
8.6	7.8	8.2	7.5	7.9	7.7	1.1	−0.1	0.5
20.7	18.5	19.6	20.1	19.3	19.7	0.6	−0.8	−0.1
25.4	44.5	34.8	20.8	43.5	31.5	4.8	1.0	3.4
35.2	14.4	25.0	40.2	11.9	26.6	−5.5	2.8	−1.8
14.7	13.9	14.3	15.5	12.4	14.0	−1.0	1.6	0.3
22.3	12.6	17.5	22.5	15.1	18.9	−0.3	−2.8	−1.6
27.9	59.1	43.2	21.8	60.6	40.4	6.7	−1.6	3.1

Table 8.2 Sectors of activity of the foreign-born population from the five main countries of origin (Percentage of the employed population aged 15 and above)

	Country	*Country of birth*	*% (x thousand of total pop.*	*Agriculture and industry (%)*	*Producer services (%)*	*Distributive services (%)*	*Personal and social services (%)*
AUT	Austria	Former Yugoslavia	53.8	39.5	13.4	20.5	26.6
		Turkey	18.6	45.9	12.2	20.7	21.1
		Germany	17.0	24.1	15.7	22.3	37.9
		Poland	6.5	30.7	14.2	21.8	33.2
		Romania	4.9	38.8	12.1	22.6	26.5
BEL	Belgium	France	12.6	23.2	11.9	22.6	42.3
		Italy	11.5	44.7	8.3	18.6	28.5
		Morocco	9.1	36.1	16.6	19.5	27.8
		Netherlands	8.6	32.0	16.2	23.8	28.1
		Germany	8.0	23.9	15.9	21.1	39.1
CHE	Switzerland	Former Yugoslavia	43.0	46.5	9.2	18.4	25.8
		Italy	36.2	42.6	13.2	22.0	22.3
		Germany	26.8	23.8	20.4	17.9	37.9
		Portugal	20.5	41.1	9.6	17.8	31.5
		France	14.7	20.7	18.5	20.5	40.4
CZE	Czech Republic	Slovak Republic	24.7	46.4	7.6	15.5	30.5
		Former USSR	4.9	52.3	8.4	15.7	23.5
		Vietnam	2.5	3.5	1.4	92.4	2.7
		Poland	2.2	62.3	3.9	12.1	21.7
		Former Yugoslavia	0.8	32.8	9.5	32.7	24.9
DNK	Denmark	Turkey	5.4	21.9	19.5	21.8	36.8
		Germany	4.7	26.0	14.5	19.1	40.4
		Former Yugoslavia	4.7	34.9	18.4	21.0	25.7
		Sweden	4.0	19.2	16.7	20.2	44.0

		Norway	2.9	17.7	16.2	18.4	47.7
ESP	Spain	Morocco	10.1	55.5	5.2	15.9	23.4
		Ecuador	8.7	42.8	5.3	12.8	39.1
		Colombia	5.3	31.3	8.6	14.2	45.9
		France	5.2	34.1	10.8	23.6	31.5
		Germany	3.6	29.5	12.6	25.3	32.5
FIN	Finland	Sweden	6.2	32.8	13.0	22.0	32.2
		Former USSR	6.0	27.1	16.2	24.8	31.9
		Germany	0.7	25.5	20.5	16.7	37.3
		United Kingdom	0.7	20.7	20.3	11.0	47.9
		Vietnam	0.5	52.6	6.5	13.8	27.1
FRA	France	Algeria	21.6	22.2	4.4	30.7	42.6
		Portugal	13.7	44.4	5.9	23.9	25.9
		Morocco	9.4	29.5	3.6	31.8	35.2
		Tunisia	5.0	24.7	4.8	33.4	37.1
		Spain	4.2	34.1	5.4	26.0	34.4
GBR	United Kingdom	India	8.6	24.2	16.9	28.8	30.1
		Ireland	8.6	23.9	17.7	17.8	40.6
		Germany	5.1	18.6	20.4	21.8	39.1
		Pakistan	4.3	22.6	12.8	38.7	25.9
		Kenya	3.2	17.4	22.4	31.8	28.4
GRC	Greece	Albania	54.1	67.6	3.2	9.1	20.0
		Former USSR	22.3	44.6	5.9	14.7	34.7
		Germany	12.9	25.0	10.3	27.0	37.8
		Bulgaria	5.9	52.0	3.6	6.4	38.0
		Romania	4.1	62.4	4.0	8.8	24.7
HUN	Hungary	Romania	16.1	38.4	9.6	20.9	31.1
		Former USSR	3.4	25.6	10.8	25.5	38.0
		Former Yugoslavia	2.6	33.7	10.5	28.5	27.3

Table 8.2 Sectors of activity of the foreign-born population from the five main countries of origin (Percentage of the employed population aged 15 and above) (*continued*)

	Country	*Country of birth*	*‰ of total pop.*	*Agriculture and industry (%)*	*Producer services (%)*	*Distributive services (%)*	*Personal and social services (%)*
		Slovak Republic	1.9	34.4	10.9	16.1	38.7
		Germany	1.2	34.1	13.5	22.2	30.2
IRL	Ireland	United Kingdom	76.8	30.2	16.6	19.3	33.8
		United States	4.8	23.5	21.3	13.6	41.6
		Former USSR	3.9	47.6	10.7	17.2	24.4
		France	2.8	22.4	26.9	15.8	35.0
		Germany	2.8	28.4	24.5	17.7	29.3
ITA	Italy	Switzerland	5.0	42.1	8.4	18.6	30.9
		Morocco	3.9	65.3	2.1	17.4	15.1
		Albania	3.6	70.5	2.1	9.5	18.0
		Germany	3.4	41.0	7.6	18.4	33.0
		Former Yugoslavia	3.3	54.6	4.7	16.2	24.5
LUX	Luxembourg	Portugal	150.3	44.7	12.0	17.0	26.4
		France	57.6	14.1	31.3	17.9	36.6
		Belgium	45.2	13.9	39.1	17.7	29.9
		Italy	30.4	25.4	19.6	17.1	37.3
		Germany	29.6	14.8	30.3	17.2	37.7
NLD	Netherlands	Turkey	10.2	44.6	13.7	18.5	23.2
		Indonesia	9.8	22.3	18.3	14.2	45.2
		Morocco	8.2	34.3	15.4	21.4	28.9
		Germany	7.2	22.2	14.0	27.9	35.9
		United Kingdom	3.8	23.2	28.4	20.4	28.0
NOR	Norway	Sweden	7.3	18.8	14.5	21.5	45.2

		Denmark	5.0	23.5	12.3	19.0	45.3
		Former Yugoslavia	3.3	24.8	13.6	20.0	41.5
		United Kingdom	3.3	24.5	19.7	16.1	39.7
		Germany	2.4	20.0	12.8	15.3	52.0
POL	Poland	Former USSR	5.9	40.0	10.3	17.5	32.2
		Germany	1.2	44.5	10.3	18.8	26.5
		France	0.3	45.6	11.5	17.4	25.5
		Czech Republic	0.1	37.2	10.0	19.1	33.7
		Former Yugoslavia	0.1	51.7	7.1	23.5	17.7
PRT	Portugal	Angola	25.9	26.2	12.5	19.8	41.4
		Mozambique	12.0	19.7	15.4	23.1	41.7
		France	11.4	38.2	8.3	23.3	30.2
		Brazil	6.5	35.2	9.5	18.2	37.1
		Cape Verde	6.1	47.6	11.9	9.4	31.1
SVK	Slovak Republic	Czech Republic	17.9	36.8	8.6	19.4	35.3
		Former USSR	2.0	37.6	7.0	18.7	36.7
		Hungary	1.1	44.4	5.7	17.1	32.8
		Poland	0.6	44.0	6.2	17.0	32.9
		Romania	0.5	61.4	4.2	14.9	19.6
SWE	Sweden	Finland	23.1	31.6	12.8	14.7	41.0
		Former Yugoslavia	14.4	38.4	12.2	17.6	31.8
		Iran	5.7	15.7	11.5	23.4	49.4
		Poland	4.9	21.5	15.2	16.4	46.9
		Norway	4.1	23.5	14.3	19.4	42.8

Source: Database on Immigrants in OECD Countries (DIOC).

Note: Among the employed men aged 15 and above born in the United Kingdom and living in Australia, 24.8% work in the agriculture and industry sector, 17.9% in the producer services sector, 22.6% in the distributive services sector and 34.7% in the personal and social services sector.

Analysing the integration in European labour markets of Muslim workers from the MENA area by country, it emerges that the majority are indeed employed in the agricultural and industrial sectors. The OECD European countries with the highest numbers of Muslim workers are France, Belgium, Italy, Spain, Greece, the Netherlands, the UK, and Sweden (data on Germany are not available) (Table 8.2).

In France there is the highest number of foreign workers from the MENA area: 21.6 per thousand of the total population are from Algeria, 9.4 per thousand are from Morocco, and 5 per thousand are from Tunisia. They are mostly involved in the personal and social services, in the distributive services and in agriculture and industry. In Belgium, Moroccans (9.1 per thousand of working population) are mainly involved in agriculture and industry (36.1 per cent of the Moroccan employed population). In Spain 55.5 per cent of Moroccans are working in agriculture and industry. A similar situation for Muslim workers is to be found in Greece where Albanians are overwhelmingly in agriculture and industry (67.6 per cent); and in Italy where 65.3 per cent of Moroccans and 70.5 per cent of Albanians work in these sectors. In the UK, on the contrary, Pakistanis are mainly involved in distributive services. (See Table 8.2.)

Apart from the discrepancies between native and foreign-born workers in terms of sectoral employment, there is the problem of high unemployment amongst Muslims. Not all OECD countries present a similar situation in terms of labour market outcomes for migrants. In general, however, the level of employment is lower for foreign-born than for native-born residents (Table 8.3). In some cases this difference is extremely relevant, notably in northern European countries where it is 25.2 per cent in Denmark, 21.2 per cent in Sweden, 18.9 per cent in Finland and 16.7 per cent in Norway (Table 8.3). This is reflected in the difference in the unemployment rates (Table 8.4). In Belgium and Finland, the level of employment for the foreign-born is below 50 per cent while it is above 65 per cent in Canada, Switzerland, Luxembourg and Portugal.

Moreover, migrant workers are overrepresented among the unemployed in all OECD countries except the Slovak Republic, Mexico, Poland, Hungary, and Greece. In the Nordic countries, and in Switzerland and Belgium, the unemployment rate of the foreign-born is more than twice that of the native-born. In France it is 7.6 per cent higher and in Germany 9.4 per cent.[4]

Looking at the employment rate of Muslim migrants in European OECD countries, Table 8.5 shows how low this is. Moroccans present a level of employment of below 50 per cent in Belgium, France, and the Netherlands. By the same token, the unemployment rate of Moroccans is extremely high in Belgium (34.2 per cent), France (25.3 per cent), Spain

Table 8.3 Employment rate by country of residence, place of birth and gender (Percentage of the 15–64 population)

		Native-born			*Foreign-born*			*Total*			*Difference between foreigners and natives*		
	Country	*Men* (%)	*Women* (%)	*Total* (%)	*Men* (%)	*Women* (%)	*Total* (%)	*Men* (%)	*Women* (%)	*Total* (%)	*Men*	*Women*	*Total*
AUS	Australia	76.6	64.0	70.3	72.5	54.8	63.6	75.5	61.6	68.5	–4.1	–9.2	–6.6
AUT	Austria	76.5	61.7	69.1	75.0	56.8	65.9	76.3	61.0	68.6	–1.4	–4.9	–3.2
BEL	Belgium	67.8	52.9	60.4	54.9	34.5	44.6	66.2	50.6	58.4	–12.9	–18.4	–15.8
CAN	Canada	77.8	68.5	73.1	78.1	62.5	70.1	77.8	67.2	72.5	0.4	–6.0	–3.0
CHE	Switzerland	87.6	69.5	78.6	83.3	62.7	72.8	86.5	67.6	77.1	–4.3	–6.8	–5.8
CZE	Czech Republic	74.1	60.9	67.5	68.3	52.2	60.1	73.8	60.5	67.1	–5.8	–8.7	–7.4
DEU	Germany	74.2	60.4	67.3	68.8	52.0	60.5	73.4	59.3	66.4	–5.4	–8.5	–6.9
DNK	Denmark	83.7	75.5	79.7	59.8	49.2	54.4	81.7	73.3	77.6	–23.9	–26.4	–25.2
ESP	Spain	67.2	39.7	53.5	68.1	47.0	57.7	67.2	40.1	53.7	1.0	7.3	4.3
FIN	Finland	66.1	63.5	64.8	52.1	39.7	46.0	65.7	62.8	64.3	–14.1	–23.8	–18.9
FRA	France	67.2	54.8	61.0	65.2	46.4	56.0	66.9	53.9	60.4	–2.0	-8.4	–5.0
GBR	United Kingdom	76.3	64.2	70.2	69.9	53.4	61.2	75.7	63.1	69.3	–6.3	–10.8	–9.0
GRC	Greece	68.2	39.9	54.1	78.5	45.6	62.5	69.5	40.6	55.1	10.3	5.6	8.4
HUN	Hungary	58.6	47.6	53.0	63.3	46.9	54.6	58.8	47.5	53.0	4.7	-0.6	1.6
IRL	Ireland	72.2	51.1	61.7	72.7	53.3	63.0	72.3	51.3	61.8	0.6	2.2	1.3
ITA	Italy	67.1	42.4	54.7	75.4	42.6	58.0	67.4	42.4	54.9	8.3	0.2	3.2
JPN	Japan	86.2	60.0	73.2	78.6	50.9	63.9	86.1	59.9	73.1	–7.5	–9.1	–9.2
LUX	Luxembourg	70.7	49.0	60.0	78.2	56.5	67.5	73.7	52.0	62.9	7.5	7.5	7.5
MEX	Mexico	81.7	34.7	57.2	78.6	36.1	57.7	81.6	34.7	57.2	–3.1	1.4	0.5
NLD	Netherlands	84.2	65.0	74.7	69.4	50.5	59.9	82.4	63.2	73.0	–14.8	–14.4	–14.8
NOR	Norway	75.4	68.9	72.2	59.6	51.6	55.6	73.9	67.2	70.6	–15.8	–17.3	–16.7
NZL	New Zealand	82.1	68.9	75.3	73.3	58.6	65.7	80.2	66.6	73.2	–8.7	–10.3	–9.6
POL	Poland	55.5	46.6	51.0	45.5	27.5	35.8	55.4	46.3	50.8	–10.1	–19.1	–15.3
PRT	Portugal	75.1	56.9	65.9	79.1	65.6	72.4	75.5	57.6	66.4	4.0	8.6	6.5

Table 8.3 Employment rate by country of residence, place of birth and gender (*ccnt.*):

		Native-born			*Foreign-born*			*Total*			*Difference between foreigners and natives*		
	Country	*Men* (%)	*Women* (%)	*Total* (%)	*Men* (%)	*Women* (%)	*Total* (%)	*Men* (%)	*Women* (%)	*Total* (%)	*Men*	*Women*	*Total*
SVK	Slovak Republic	59.7	48.4	54.0	61.5	46.0	53.1	59.7	48.3	54.0	1.9	–2.4	–0.9
SWE	Sweden	75.2	72.0	73.6	54.4	50.5	52.4	72.2	68.7	70.5	–20.8	–21.4	–21.2
TUR	Turkey	74.1	42.7	58.6	62.8	37.4	49.7	73.9	42.6	58.4	–11.3	–5.3	–8.9
USA	United States	78.1	68.4	73.2	73.3	54.6	64.1	77.4	66.4	71.8	–4.8	–13.8	–9.1
OECD	(weighted)	75.7	56.3	66.0	71.7	52.9	62.3	75.3	56.0	65.6	–4.1	–3.4	–3.7
OECD	(unweighted)	73.5	57.1	65.3	68.6	49.5	58.9	73.1	56.3	64.7	–4.9	–7.6	–6.4

Source: Database on Immigrants in OECD Countries (DIOC).

Notes: The three last columns refer respectively to the difference between foreigners and natives: men, women and total.
This data excludes people with unknown gender or place of birth.

Table 8.4 Unemployment rate by country of residence, place of birth and gender (percentage of the employed population aged 15 and above)

		Native-born			*Foreign-born*			*Total*			*Difference between foreigners and natives*		
		Men	*Women*	*Total*	*Men*	*Women*	*Total*	*Men*	*Women*	*Total*			
	Country	(%)	(%)	(%)	(%)	(%)	(%)	(%)	(%)	(%)	*Men*	*Women*	*Total*
AUS	Australia	7.7	6.1	7.0	8.5	8.0	8.3	7.9	6.6	7.3	0.8	1.9	1.3
AUT	Austria	5.4	5.8	5.6	11.1	11.3	11.2	6.3	6.6	6.4	5.6	5.5	5.6
BEL	Belgium	7.1	12.4	9.5	16.4	26.4	20.6	8.2	13.8	10.7	9.3	14.0	11.1
CAN	Canada	7.8	7.0	7.4	6.9	8.2	7.5	7.6	7.2	7.4	–0.9	1.2	0.1
CHE	Switzerland	2.2	3.1	2.6	5.5	10.2	7.6	3.0	5.0	3.9	3.2	7.2	5.0
CZE	Czech Republic	8.6	9.5	9.0	13.2	14.6	13.9	8.8	9.8	9.2	4.7	5.1	4.9
DEU	Germany	7.4	8.0	7.7	17.7	16.2	17.1	8.9	9.0	9.0	10.2	8.2	9.4
DNK	Denmark	3.2	3.9	3.5	8.2	8.3	8.2	3.5	4.2	3.8	5.0	4.4	4.7
ESP	Spain	10.7	18.9	13.9	15.2	18.9	16.7	11.0	18.9	14.1	4.4	0.0	2.8
FIN	Finland	12.0	12.2	12.1	23.3	30.6	26.6	12.3	12.7	12.5	11.3	18.4	14.5
FRA	France	10.0	14.1	11.9	17.7	22.0	19.5	11.0	15.0	12.8	7.7	7.9	7.6
GBR	United Kingdom	6.3	4.5	5.5	8.9	7.5	8.3	6.5	4.7	5.7	2.6	3.0	2.8
GRC	Greece	9.7	13.3	11.1	9.3	13.3	10.7	9.6	13.3	11.0	–0.5	0.0	–0.3
HUN	Hungary	11.5	8.7	10.2	6.4	7.5	6.9	11.3	8.7	10.1	–5.1	–1.3	–3.3
IRL	Ireland	9.2	7.6	8.5	11.8	10.7	11.3	9.5	8.0	8.9	2.6	3.1	2.8
ITA	Italy	9.4	14.6	11.5	9.3	18.4	13.1	9.4	14.8	11.6	–0.2	3.8	1.6
JPN	Japan	5.1	4.1	4.7	5.7	5.8	5.7	5.1	4.2	4.7	0.6	1.6	1.0
LUX	Luxembourg	2.3	2.6	2.4	3.3	4.7	3.9	2.7	3.5	3.0	0.9	2.1	1.4
MEX	Mexico	1.4	0.9	1.2	1.0	1.0	1.0	1.4	0.9	1.2	–0.4	0.1	–0.2
NLD	Netherlands	2.0	3.5	2.6	6.6	6.9	6.7	2.5	3.9	3.1	4.6	3.4	4.1
NOR	Norway	3.5	2.7	3.1	9.6	7.6	8.7	4.0	3.1	3.6	6.1	4.9	5.5

Table 8.4 Unemployment rate by country of residence, place of birth and gender (*cont.*):

		Native-born			*Foreign-born*			*Total*			*Difference between foreigners and natives*		
		Men	*Women*	*Total*	*Men*	*Women*	*Total*	*Men*	*Women*	*Total*			
	Country	(%)	(%)	(%)	(%)	(%)	(%)	(%)	(%)	(%)	*Men*	*Women*	*Total*
NZL	New Zealand	6.6	7.6	7.1	8.6	9.5	9.0	7.0	8.0	7.4	2.1	1.8	2.0
POL	Poland	20.6	22.0	21.3	13.8	14.3	14.0	20.6	22.0	21.2	–6.8	–7.7	–7.3
PRT	Portugal	5.2	8.6	6.7	5.7	9.8	7.6	5.2	8.7	6.8	0.6	1.1	0.9
SVK	Slovak Republic	22.0	21.3	21.7	19.1	21.0	20.0	21.9	21.3	21.6	–2.9	–0.3	–1.7
SWE	Sweden	3.1	2.7	2.9	8.6	6.9	7.8	3.7	3.1	3.5	5.5	4.3	4.9
TUR	Turkey	9.8	7.1	8.9	13.6	14.4	13.9	9.9	7.3	9.0	3.8	7.2	5.0
USA	United States	5.6	5.5	5.6	6.0	7.9	6.8	5.6	5.8	5.7	0.4	2.4	1.3
OECD	(weighted)	6.9	7.6	7.2	9.3	10.8	10.0	7.2	7.9	7.5	2.4	3.2	2.7
OECD	(unweighted)	7.7	8.5	8.0	10.4	12.2	11.2	8.0	8.9	8.4	2.7	3.7	3.1

Source: Database on Immigrants in OECD Countries (DIOC).

Notes: The three last columns refer respectively to the difference between foreigners and natives: men, women and total.
This data excludes people with unknown gender or place of birth.

Table 8.5 Employment rate by country of residence, main country of origin and gender (percentage of the population aged 15–64)

	Country	*Country of origin*	*‰ of total pop*	*Men (%)*	*Women (%)*	*Total (%)*
BEL	Belgium	France	16.7	57.5	40.1	48.2
		Italy	15.3	52.3	28.2	41.3
		Morocco	13.4	47.4	18.5	34.4
		Netherlands	10.5	69.8	46.4	58.1
		Germany	8.6	64.6	45.4	54.3
DEU	Germany	Former USSR	20.2	68.9	57.2	62.9
		Turkey	17.3	64.7	35.0	50.3
		Poland	15.1	72.5	61.2	66.5
		Former Yugoslavia	9.4	65.3	49.8	57.8
		Romania	5.7	81.1	66.4	73.3
DNK	Denmark	Turkey	6.7	63.2	41.1	52.8
		Former Yugoslavia	6.2	58.5	44.0	51.4
		Germany	5.7	71.5	60.7	66.4
		Sweden	4.0	74.6	71.4	72.8
		Norway	3.4	67.2	64.2	65.4
ESP	Spain	Morocco	8.0	71.3	35.3	58.0
		Ecuador	5.5	75.8	63.5	69.5
		France	4.3	73.6	48.8	60.5
		Colombia	4.1	63.8	51.2	56.3
		Germany	3.6	58.9	39.5	48.7
FRA	France	Algeria	25.2	61.5	43.7	52.9
		Morocco	14.3	60.8	37.2	49.7
		Portugal	11.8	79.1	65.3	72.4
		Italy	8.4	65.2	47.2	56.8
		Spain	7.0	69.1	53.2	60.6
GBR	United Kingdom	Ireland	11.0	70.9	60.9	65.5
		India	9.5	76.7	50.7	63.2
		Pakistan	6.3	64.5	18.2	41.6
		Germany	4.9	76.2	64.9	69.8
		Bangladesh	3.0	58.7	16.2	37.4
GRC	Greece	Albania	36.4	85.1	41.6	67.9
		Former USSR	19.9	69.7	46.4	56.2
		Germany	9.8	70.3	49.5	59.0
		Turkey	8.2	79.5	34.3	56.5
		Bulgaria	3.9	84.4	65.7	72.8
ITA	Italy	Switzerland	3.7	75.8	48.7	61.4
		Former Yugoslavia	3.6	72.3	35.6	54.0
		Germany	3.4	58.9	35.3	45.6
		Morocco	2.8	80.1	26.8	60.4
		Albania	2.8	79.9	30.2	58.7
NLD	Netherlands	Indonesia	14.4	72.5	55.2	64.1
		Turkey	12.6	64.6	36.7	51.3
		Morocco	10.8	61.3	31.5	47.7
		Germany	8.5	77.4	55.8	64.9
		Belgium	3.7	83.4	64.6	72.7

Table 8.5 Employment rate by country of residence, main country of origin and gender (*cont.*):

	Country	*Country of origin*	*‰ of total pop*	*Men (%)*	*Women (%)*	*Total (%)*
NOR	Norway	Sweden	8.5	74.0	70.6	72.3
		Former Yugoslavia	6.8	58.1	50.9	54.7
		Denmark	6.2	76.9	73.5	75.2
		Pakistan	4.3	59.0	26.2	43.4
		United Kingdom	3.8	71.3	61.0	67.2
SWE	Sweden	Finland	25.4	65.1	66.9	66.1
		Former Yogoslavia	17.3	56.3	47.6	52.0
		Iraq	7.5	34.9	21.8	29.2
		Iran	7.0	51.8	44.1	48.3
		Norway	5.7	57.3	60.4	59.0

Source: Database on Immigrants in OECD Countries (DIOC)
Note: This data excludes people with unknown gender or place of birth.

(17.6 per cent), the UK (12.8 per cent) and Italy (12.1 per cent), although other African Muslim workers are in an even worse situation. Somalis, for example, suffer an unemployment rate of 58.4 per cent in Belgium, 52.3 per cent in the UK, 46 per cent in France, 35.3 per cent in Switzerland, 31 per cent in Norway, and 28.6 per cent in Spain. (See Table 8.6.)

Pakistanis in the UK have an employment level of only 41.6 per cent, and Bangladeshis of 37.4 per cent. Pakistanis also experience a low level of employment in Norway (43.3 per cent), and Iraqis in Sweden have an employment rate of only 29.2 per cent while Iranians are at 48.3 per cent.[5]

As could be expected, the level of employment and unemployment of Muslim workers is affected by their level of education. OECD data (Table 8.7) confirm that the unemployment rate drops as the level of education rises. However, this difference becomes relevant only for tertiary education, whereas the difference between the employment status of Muslim migrants with primary and secondary education is minimal, and there is even an increase in the unemployment level of migrants with secondary education. (See Tables 8.7 and 8.8.)

Workers coming from North Africa, who are, in almost all cases, Muslims, consistently present the highest rate of unemployment, whatever the level of education. This phenomenon could easily conceal some form of discrimination against Muslims. Indeed, from Table 8.8 we can see that workers of North African origins have a total rate of unemployment of 11.2 per cent, higher even than the level of unemployment of workers from Sub-Saharan Africa (8.8 per cent). This is the case for each level of education.

Table 8.6 Unemployment of migrants from eight African countries in the main receiving countries (percentage of the population aged 15 and over)

	Belgium	*France*	*Norway*	*Spain*	*Switzerland*	*Sweden*	*Italy*	*Canada*	*United Kingdom*	*Portugal*	*Australia*	*United States*
Somalia	58.4%	46.0%	31.2%	28.6%	35.3%	24.8%	14.4%	26.9%	52.3%		46.2%	13.8%
Morocco	34.2%	25.3%	12.4%	17.6%	14.9%	12.3%	13.1%	15.6%	12.8%	6.9%	14.6%	5.1%
Senegal	35.6%	23.9%		16.7%	16.9%	12.1%	10.2%	12.6%	17.2%	8.4%	13.1%	10.5%
Nigeria	33.2%	27.6%	14.4%	16.5%	14.3%	13.2%	16.6%	14.8%	13.0%	5.6%	9.4%	6.1%
Ghana	37.6%	26.6%	9.9%	16.7%	11.2%	9.2%	8.0%	11.0%	10.6%	11.1%	8.1%	6.5%
Ethiopia	28.0%	26.7%	10.5%	25.0%	19.7%	9.9%	10.0%	11.6%	23.3%		19.1%	6.2%
Kenya	23.5%	18.6%	9.1%	12.5%	15.7%	9.2%	11.2%	6.5%	5.8%	6.0%	8.4%	5.2%
South Africa	12.5%	14.5%	7.5%	19.4%	6.4%	6.0%	10.2%	5.1%	5.3%	7.9%	5.8%	3.1%

Source: Database on Immigrants in OECD Countries (DIOC).

Table 8.7 Labour force status of the foreign-born population of the main Muslim origin countries in the OECD area, by education level (percentage of the employed population aged 15 and above)

Country of birth	*Primary* Employed (%)	Unemployed (%)	Inactive (%)	Total (000)	*Secondary* Employed (%)	Unemployed (%)	Inactive (%)	Total (000)	*Tertiary* Employed (%)	Unemployed (%)	Inactive (%)	Total (000)	*Total* Employed (%)	Unemployed (%)	Inactive (%)	Total (000)
Turkey	40.0	12.0	48.0	1,438	61.0	11.9	27.1	452	74.5	4.4	21.1	132	46.9	11.5	41.6	2,022
Morocco	41.7	12.3	46.1	918	57.0	13.6	29.5	340	68.0	9.7	22.3	210	49.0	12.2	38.8	1,467
Algeria	28.1	11.5	60.5	729	53.3	13.6	33.1	366	66.5	8.8	24.7	216	41.4	11.6	47.0	1,311
Pakistan	35.3	6.3	58.4	292	54.1	6.3	39.5	145	66.1	5.2	28.7	204	49.3	6.0	44.7	641
Iran	24.8	6.0	69.3	97	55.4	5.8	38.8	206	71.9	4.8	23.4	272	58.0	5.3	36.6	574
Albania	58.9	6.8	34.3	283	66.5	6.9	26.6	182	64.0	7.8	28.2	46	62.1	6.9	31.0	511
Tunisia	35.0	12.7	52.4	239	53.8	12.4	33.8	120	66.1	7.6	26.3	69	45.3	11.8	43.0	427

Source: Database on Immigrants in OECD Countries (DIOC)

Notes: This data excludes people with unknown education level or place of birth.

Table 8.8 Labour force status of the foreign-born population in the OECD area, by region of origin and education level (percentage of the employed population aged 15 and above)

Region of birth	*Primary* Employed (%)	Unemployed (%)	Inactive (%)	Total (000)	*Secondary* Employed (%)	Unemployed (%)	Inactive (%)	Total (000)	*Tertiary* Employed (%)	Unemployed (%)	Inactive (%)	Total (000)	*Total* Employed (%)	Unemployed (%)	Inactive (%)	Total (000)
North Africa	35.5	11.7	52.8	1,974	54.4	12.4	33.3	943	66.8	7.9	25.3	656	46.2	11.2	42.6	3,573
Sub-Saharan Africa	50.2	10.8	38.9	954	62.2	9.1	28.7	928	75.8	6.4	17.8	952	62.7	8.8	28.5	2,834
Asia	40.6	5.5	53.9	4,582	57.9	5.1	37.0	4,978	69.8	3.7	26.5	5,932	57.3	4.7	38.0	15,492
Latin America	48.3	6.2	45.5	10,192	62.1	5.5	32.5	6,083	70.8	4.2	25.0	2,637	55.9	5.7	38.4	18,912
Oceania	52.2	6.8	41.0	296	67.4	5.7	26.9	429	80.1	3.5	16.4	304	66.8	5.4	27.8	1,028
North America	31.2	2.9	65.9	363	52.6	3.4	43.9	673	71.5	2.4	26.1	811	56.7	2.9	40.4	1,846
Europe EU 15	38.5	4.4	57.0	5,829	57.5	4.0	38.5	5,132	71.8	3.0	25.3	3,654	53.5	3.9	42.6	14,615
Europe EU A10	28.3	5.8	65.9	1,183	55.6	6.5	38.0	1,640	66.9	3.9	29.2	782	49.1	5.7	45.2	3,605
Other Europe	39.0	8.2	52.8	4,671	58.0	7.7	34.3	3,310	64.3	6.1	29.6	1,622	49.8	7.7	42.5	9,603
OECD	42.7	5.9	51.4	14,967	58.2	4.9	36.9	10,860	70.5	3.1	26.4	6,822	53.7	5.0	41.4	32,649

Source: Database on Immigrants in OECD Countries (DIOC)
Note: This data excludes people with unknown education level or place of birth.

Workers with only a primary level of education from North Africa present a rate of unemployment of 11.7 per cent, as opposed to 10.8 per cent of workers of sub-Saharan Africa; those with secondary level of education are unemployed in 12.4 per cent of cases (Sub-Saharan workers in 9.1 per cent of cases); while those possessing tertiary education have a rate of unemployment of 7.9 per cent (whereas workers from Sub-Saharan countries with tertiary education have an unemployment rate of only 6.4 per cent).

Another more general example of discrimination in the integration of foreign-born workers in Western labour markets is shown by the fact that the majority of foreign-born workers are employed in jobs below their qualifications; or, in other words, they are overqualified for their job placements. This applies also in the case of Muslim migrants.

Taking the distribution of native-born employment by main occupation categories in OECD countries, operators and labourers normally represent 40 to 60 per cent of total jobs, and technicians are around 30 per cent.[6] The situation is very different as far as foreign-born employees are concerned. The OECD distinguishes three categories of receiving countries in relation to the distribution of their migrant workers' communities among the different occupation categories. The first group of host countries, including Germany, Austria and most southern European countries, presents a much higher percentage of jobs as operators and labourers for immigrant employees (almost 70 per cent) than for natives.

In the second group are countries with selective migration policies or dynamic highly-skilled labour markets such as Australia, the United Kingdom, Ireland, and New Zealand. Here more than 30 per cent of immigrant employment consists of professional jobs. In the third group, including France and most Nordic countries, there is a comparable share of foreign-born employment in professional and technician occupations, around 20 to 25 per cent.[7]

Although the phenomenon of over-qualification is characteristic of much of the working situation of foreign-born employees, especially from less developed countries, this becomes even more relevant for migrants coming from Muslim countries, especially from MENA countries.

Indeed, the majority of migrants from North Africa are employed as operators (57.9 per cent) in receiving OECD countries (Table 8.9). This is a very high percentage (amongst the highest in the world) and conceals instances of over-qualification and, therefore, discrimination against Muslim workers. Analysing the data relating to countries of origin one by one, the picture does not change.

Moroccan workers are overwhelmingly operators (67.1 per cent) as are Albanians (with a staggering 90.5 per cent), Pakistanis (60.7 per cent), and Tunisians (59.1 per cent). (See Table 8.10).

Table 8.9 Occupations of the foreign-born population in the OECD area (excluding Japan, Turkey and the United States), by region of origin (Percentage of the employed population aged 15 and above)

Region of birth	*Professionals* (%)	*Technicians* (%)	*Operators* (%)	*Total* (000)
North Africa	21.0	21.2	57.8	1,456
Sub-Saharan Africa	27.0	26.9	46.1	1,295
Asia	26.9	22.4	50.7	3,426
Latin America	19.5	23.8	56.7	1,480
Oceania	30.1	26.8	43.1	542
North America	45.5	26.6	27.9	507
Europe EU 15	28.5	24.1	47.4	5,077
Europe EU A10	17.7	24.5	57.8	1,238
Other Europe	11.4	14.6	73.9	3,395
OECD	26.1	23.3	50.6	8,266

Source: Database on Immigrants in OECD Countries (DIOC).

Notes: Among the employed people born in North Africa and living abroad in the OECD area, 21 per cent are professionals, 21.2 per cent are technicians and 57.8 per cent are operators. This data excludes people with unknown occupation or place of birth.

There is indeed plenty of evidence of the over-qualification of foreign-born employees. Data show that in some countries the percentage of foreign-born workers holding a job for which they are overqualified is very high: 32.4 per cent in Greece, 24.5 per cent in the Slovak Republic, 21.6 per cent in Finland and so on (Figure 8.1).

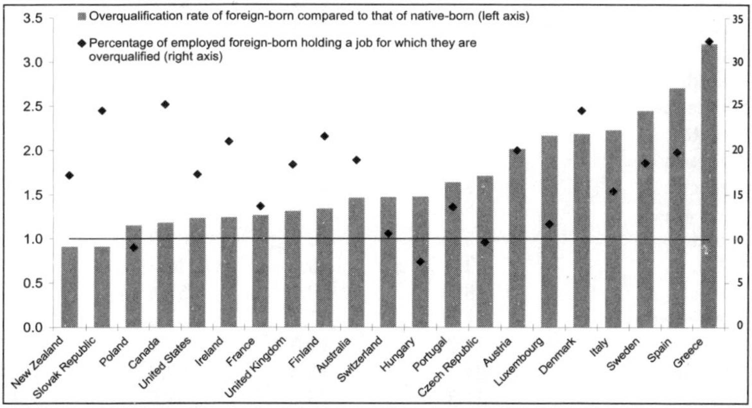

Figure 8.1 Overqualification of foreign and native-born immigrants in OECD countries, circa 2000
Source: OECD 2008.

Table 8.10 Occupations of the foreign-born population from the 50 main origin countries in the OECD area (excluding Japan, Turkey and the United States) (Percentage of the employed population aged 15 and above)

Country of birth	*Professionals* (%)	*Technicians* (%)	*Operators* (%)	*Total* (000)
United Kingdom	36.9	27.4	35.8	1,277
Germany	31.0	29.3	39.7	852
Turkey	6.3	10.4	83.3	808
Poland	13.1	24.7	62.2	748
Italy	18.2	17.2	64.5	690
Morocco	16.2	16.7	67.1	668
India	29.8	21.2	49.0	556
Algeria	22.6	27.7	49.8	531
Russia	11.6	18.6	69.8	518
Portugal	8.0	11.0	81.1	467
France	33.1	26.1	40.8	446
Romania	18.2	22.4	59.5	406
United States	46.9	25.4	27.7	396
Philippines	14.5	26.6	58.9	332
China	30.7	17.8	51.6	326
Albania	4.5	5.0	90.5	299
Ireland	30.6	26.5	42.9	287
New Zealand	30.4	26.1	43.5	269
Vietnam	21.1	18.5	60.4	243
Serbia and Montenegro	10.1	10.9	79.0	239
Bosnia-Herzegovina	5.2	10.0	84.8	234
Hong Kong, China	37.1	30.0	33.0	219
Pakistan	23.4	16.0	60.7	200
South Africa	42.2	31.2	26.7	197
Netherlands	35.5	26.3	38.2	195
Spain	24.7	20.7	54.6	191
Kazakhstan	10.0	25.4	64.5	189
Switzerland	22.7	26.6	50.7	181
Croatia	10.8	15.0	74.2	177
Sri Lanka	23.2	23.1	53.7	157
Greece	22.4	14.9	62.7	152
Australia	37.8	31.0	31.1	151
Ecuador	5.3	8.9	85.8	150
Belgium	33.2	30.0	36.7	148
Jamaica	18.7	28.9	52.4	145
Slovak Republic	18.4	23.8	57.8	143
Tunisia	24.8	16.0	59.1	136
Ukraine	21.7	15.6	62.7	135
Angola	21.3	28.8	49.8	130
Former Yugoslavia	11.1	16.5	72.4	123
Iran	40.5	22.0	37.5	122
Finland	22.7	27.5	49.8	119

Colombia	13.3	14.9	71.8	113
Canada	40.6	30.7	28.7	111
Kenya	37.2	30.6	32.2	108
Indonesia	31.3	32.1	36.6	106
Argentina	30.8	23.1	46.1	105
Lebanon	32.5	22.7	44.7	103
Brazil	25.0	23.1	51.8	100
Austria	36.5	27.7	35.8	96
Average	23.9	22.0	54.1	

Source: Database on Immigrants in OECD Countries (DIOC).

Notes: Among the employed people born in the United Kingdom and living abroad in the OECD area, 36.9 per cent are professionals, 27.4 per cent are technicians and 35.8 per cent are operators. 'Professionals' refers to ISCO major groups 1 and 2, 'technicians' refers to ISCO major groups 3 and 4, and 'operators' refers to ISCO major groups 5, 6, 7, 8, and 9. Armed forces (ISCO group 0) are excluded. For more details on definitions, please refer to the annex.

This data excludes people with unknown occupation or place of birth.

The data above clearly demonstrate that foreign-born populations in general, and people of Muslim religion in particular, live with labour market conditions that conceal instances of discrimination. They have a higher rate of unemployment than the native-born population for each level of education, and the most overrepresented in terms of unemployment rate are migrants of North African origins. Moreover foreign-born labourers are more likely than locally born workers to be employed in the low skilled agricultural and industrial sectors, and they are also overqualified for their job placements.

Before addressing whether these examples of discrimination in the labour markets are reflected in an overall hostile attitude of the local population vis-à-vis the immigrant communities, especially Muslim ones, it is worth focusing a bit more on the situation of Egyptian migrants.

3 Egyptians abroad: Brain drain or mass migration?

As seen in Chapter 7, no specific data are available about the integration of Egyptian migrants in the different European labour markets. There are however some data relating in general to the occupation of Egyptians in receiving countries and, more specifically, about their employment in other Arab countries. These data allow the identification of general trends in the patterns of integration of Egyptian workers abroad and to draw conclusions about the dynamics of their migratory experiences as far as labour opportunities are concerned.

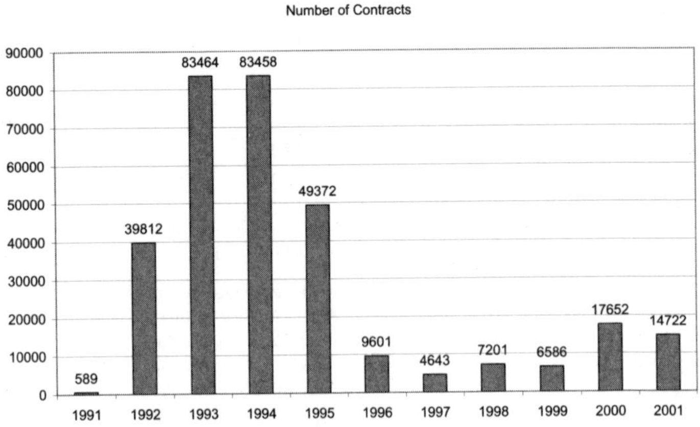

Figure 8.2 Work permits granted to Egyptians in Arab countries, by year (1991–2001)
Source: General Directorate for External Employment, Ministry of Manpower and Emigration, as reported by CARIM 2008.

To start with the number of job contracts granted to Egyptian citizens in Arab countries, their dynamics in the period between 1991 and 2001 closely followed the dynamics of political events in the region.

Figure 8.2 shows how the number of contracts was very low during the war in Iraq in 1991; it then increased in the course of the first half of the 1990s, to decrease again at the end of the 1990s. These figures refer to the contracts registered with the General Directorate for External employment of the Egyptian Ministry of Manpower and Emigration and are by no means an exhaustive record of all the contracts granted to Egyptians in Arab countries.

More recent figures by CAPMAS for 2005 give an idea of the official numbers of contracts granted all over the world to Egyptians (Table 8.11). However the figures relating to the EU and other developed Western countries obviously do not include migrants who have jobs in the informal economy and those who are undocumented workers. They are therefore much lower than the numbers for Arab countries, although, as detailed in a previous chapter, Egyptian permanent migration to Western industrialised countries has increased substantially in recent years.

Looking at the characteristics of Egyptian workers abroad, they are on average more educated than the non-migrant population. From Table 8.12 we learn that the total of Egyptian migrants who did not receive any formal education is more than 20 per cent less than in the non-migrant population.

Table 8.11 Work Permits granted to nationals abroad by country of residence in 2005

Country	*First Time*	*Renewal*	*Total*
Albania	21	21	42
Greece	1,704	3,272	4,976
Turkey	10	16	26
Cyprus	703	503	1,206
Russia	21	8	29
Spain	64	122	186
Portugal	13	48	61
Austria	58	111	169
U.K.	68	115	183
Ireland	29	134	163
Italy	5,994	16,007	22,001
Belgium	19	13	32
Germany	26	40	66
Switzerland	10	20	30
France	114	178	292
Malta	18	38	56
Netherlands	59	15	74
Others	37	46	83
Total European Countries	**8,968**	**20,707**	**29,675**
Syria	122	170	292
Jordan	73,717	47,311	121,028
Algeria	148	82	230
Iraq	32	9	41
Saudi Arabia	141,945	215,051	356,996
Yemen	269	622	891
Lebanon	1,633	4,183	5,816
Kuwait	66,621	84,454	151,075
Bahrain	918	1,479	2,397
U.A.E.	34,993	42,610	77,603
Qatar	12,288	12,152	24,440
Oman	3,306	4,541	7,847
Djibouti	33	59	92
Others	50	51	101
Total Arab Countries	**336,075**	**412,774**	**748,849**

Source: Central Agency for Public Mobilization and Statistics, as reported in CARIM 2008.

On the other hand, the total of migrants that received secondary education exceeds by more than 20 per cent the number of non-migrants who received it. Also the percentage of migrants with a university degree or a higher level of education is more than the percentage of non-migrants who possess university or higher education. This is already an indication of

Table 8.12 Educational level of migrants and non-migrants at last emigration (migrants) or five years previously (non-migrants)

Educational Level	*Migrants*	*Non-Migrants*
Non-Formal Education	15.4	37.7
Incomplete Primary	18.7	18.5
Primary	7.8	8.8
Preparatory	4.2	4.9
Secondary	32.7	15.7
University or Higher	21.2	14.5
Total (%)	100	100
Number	1.121	3.672

Source: Ministry of Manpower and Emigration as reported by CARIM 2008; updated 7 February 2005.

brain drain. This trend is indeed confirmed if we look at the dynamics of the occupations of Egyptian migrants abroad.

Analysing the data relating to the occupation categories of Egyptian workers in Arab countries from 1985 to 2002, the tendency towards an increase in the numbers of highly qualified migrants is clear. Indeed, the percentage of work permits granted to scientists and technicians was 20.4 per cent in 1985. In 2002 it had doubled (41 per cent) (Table 8.13). The number of managers has also increased, whereas production workers were reduced by 10 per cent and clerical workers went from 8.8 per cent to 1.5 per cent (Table 8.13).

Egyptian brain drain is mainly directed towards Saudi Arabia, Libya, Kuwait, UAE, Qatar, Oman and Yemen. In these countries the percentage of work permits granted to technicians and scientists over total work permits ranges from 69.1 in Yemen to 40.5 in Saudi Arabia. Unskilled labour, on the other hand, is mainly going to Lebanon, where it comprises about 75 per

Table 8.13 Work permits granted to Egyptians in Arab countries, by occupation and year (%) (1985–1990–2002)

Occupation	*1985*	*1990*	*2002*
Scientists and technicians	20.4	40.2	41.0
Managers	0.3	0.3	2.4
Clerical workers	8.8	8.0	1.5
Sales and services	18.5	17.3	12.7
Agriculture, animal husbandry and fishing	8.9	5.3	8.6
Production workers	43.0	28.9	33.8
Total	100	100	100

Source: Ministry of Manpower and Emigration as reported by CARIM 2008; updated 7 February 2005.

Table 8.14 Work Permits granted to Egyptians in some Arab countries by occupation (1985–2002) (%)*

Countries/ Occupations	*Scientists and technicians*	*Managers*	*Clerical Workers*	*Sales and Services*	*Agriculture, animal husbandry and fishing*	*Production workers*
Bahrain	27.2	5.5	24.3	24.3	0.0	33.7
Iraq	2.6	0	1.5	1.5	33.0	62.9
Jordan	1.4	0.0	1.7	1.7	31.9	62.9
Kuwait	53.5	1.1	21.5	21.5	0.2	14.1
Lebanon	0.0	0.0	2.3	2.3	21.1	76.6
Libya	57.0	9.0	0.0	0.0	0.0	34.0
Oman	52.9	8.1	4.1	4.1	1.4	31.5
Qatar	51.5	1.9	6.1	6.1	1.0	37.4
Saudi Arabia	40.5	0.4	0.3	20.6	7.1	31.1
United Arab Emirates	41.1	4.0	2.9	2.9	0.9	50.1
Yemen	69.1	18.1	1.1	1.1	0.0	7.7

Source: Ministry of Manpower and Emigration, as reported by CARIM 2008; updated 7 February 2005

* The data has been reported as provided by the official sources although they do not look convincing to the author

cent of the total number of work permits granted to Egyptian migrants; Iraq and Jordan rank second with 62.9 per cent; in the UAE the total is 50 per cent, and in other Arab countries it ranges from 37.4 per cent in Qatar to 7.7 per cent in Yemen. Overall, the GCC plus Libya absorb most of the skilled Egyptian workers while Iraq, Jordan and Lebanon are the preferred destination countries for Egyptian unskilled labour (Table 8.14).

As far as permanent migration to more developed countries is concerned, this has always mainly interested more educated workers. More than 77 per cent of Egyptians heading to OECD countries or to the USA have tertiary education, around 19 per cent have secondary education, and only 4 per cent have primary education alone.[8] Moreover, this trend has increased in the last years, leading to a higher rate of brain drain.[9] Nassar reports that 18.3 per cent of highly skilled migrants were in the medical sciences, 32.2 per cent were engineers, 36.5 per cent were in social sciences, 8 per cent in basic sciences, and 5 per cent in agriculture.[10] These conclusions on the dynamics of highly skilled permanent migrants leaving Egypt and heading to more developed OECD countries confirm the hypotheses made in the theoretical section of this book. Indeed, the lack of integration of Egypt and the MENA region in the global economy reduces the possibilities of employing highly skilled personnel in the country, thus further adding to its marginalisation. It is a vicious circle which is becoming more and more difficult to break.

The analysis above only tackles the issue of the insertion in the labour markets of legal or 'documented' migrants. In the previous sections of this book, however, we have stressed that the majority of Egyptian and Muslim migrants to EU countries are likely to be 'undocumented' at a certain point in their migratory processes. Moreover, insertion in the local communities is likely to be hindered by the fact that as 'illegal' migrants they are very likely to be employed in the 'underground', or even in the 'illegal' economy of the receiving countries. This is especially true as far as migration to Southern European countries is concerned. Below we report the findings of a research project financed by the EU which addresses precisely the question of the insertion of migrants in the informal/illicit/illegal economy of receiving countries and what impact this has on receiving societies.

4 The insertion of migrants in the 'informal economy' and its consequences for receiving societies

The results of the project *Migrants' Insertion in the Informal Economy: Deviant Behaviour and the Impact on Receiving Societies* reported below represent an extremely valuable source to assess the consequences for receiving societies of the integration of migrants in general, and Muslim migrants in particular in the informal or illegal economies of host countries.[11]

The aims of the project under analysis were of both a theoretical and a more empirical nature.[12] At the theoretical level, the authors tried to overcome the usual division among the different scientific approaches to immigration reported in Chapter 1 of this book by adopting an interdisciplinary analytical perspective whose results must be read within an interdisciplinary context.

Going to the specifics of the theoretical debate, the study criticised the common opinion that neglects the important 'mirror effect' of immigration, that is, it highlights the inner problems of the receiving societies. The study clarified the following notions:

- migrants' projects: reasons behind the migrants' decisions to leave their countries of origins and migrate to southern Europe;
- underground/informal economy: sector of the national economy offering irregular job opportunities to both nationals and particularly non-nationals;
- receiving countries: destination countries for the migratory flows;
- irregular jobs: jobs available to both nationals and non-nationals outside the definition of the legal economic activities;
- pull factor: existing realities within the receiving countries representing an element of attraction for both legal and illegal migrants;
- unauthorised migrants: migrants entering the receiving countries without the required documentations or staying on once the permit for entry has expired;
- competitive threat: fear by nationals of the existence of a competition with migrants for the same jobs;
- ethnification of illegal activities: tendency towards a disproportionate representation of migrants in the criminal records of receiving countries;
- deviant behaviour: tendency of migrants to take part in or be involved in illegal activities.[13]

The theoretical approach used by the researchers discarded a merely rationalist and economic approach. The decision to emigrate is not explained as a rational comparison between the costs and benefits – albeit, admittedly, not necessarily only economic ones – of the migratory process, as the economists would approach it. The decision to emigrate is analysed from a holistic perspective because it is a 'crucial' (non-reversible) event.

It therefore involves the whole of the personality and identity of the migrant, as well as the whole system of people and values in which this personality and identity was formed. However the authors also refuse to adopt a relativistic approach, within which the definition of the aims of the emigration process is confused and mutable and it is therefore impossible to identify the motivations and the reasons why the decision is taken. If it is true that emigration is often the answer to a moment of temporary crisis (the death of a relative, scholastic failure, loss of a job, economic or political misfortune of a friend, etc.), it is equally true that the motivations to migrate are rationalised by the migrant only after the migratory process has taken place. They are therefore very likely to be crucially influenced, at least when made explicit by the migrants, by the conditions in which they find themselves in host societies, from their chances of staying to the possibilities of earning. This is where the question becomes important as to whether the host society and economy is facilitating the integration of migrants or is making their experience painful and negative. Indeed, the authors stress how the ways that migrants 'relive' their decision to emigrate and experience their stay in receiving countries, as well as their expectations for the future, deeply condition their behaviour, both in the labour market and in society at large. In short, migrants who are not welcome in receiving societies, who find themselves marginalised and involved in illicit if not illegal activities to survive or to pay the debts incurred in the course of their migratory processes, are more likely to adopt deviant behaviour or to become straightforward criminals. Their behaviour is deeply embedded in the conditions and opportunities they find in receiving societies, which makes the latter co-responsible of the migrants' reactions.[14]

This approach informs the field studies and the interviews and surveys contained in the project. Here the migrants are asked to describe their motivations for migration, their 'projects' in general terms, clarifying why they left their country of origin and how they are experiencing their stay in the receiving country. All the surveys involve people who have been living in the host country for a more or less long time, which mean that their motivations for migration, their projects, are always reconstructed after the fact, and are re-elaborated through the lenses of their experiences so far in the receiving societies. This is exactly what the authors consider of assistance in grasping immigrants' orientations to action, and better understanding their behaviour, expectations, and inclinations. This methodological introduction is necessary because by adopting a similar approach the study is able to overcome the traditional distinctions between temporary emigration and definitive settling down, short or long distance, economic or extra-economic motivations. The emigrants' orientations to action depend crucially on the way in which they re-live and re-elaborate their experience which, in turn, is a consequence of the way in which the host country has treated them from the moment they entered. This means that it is not possible to exclude the possibility that more than one 'life project', more than a single set of 'intentions' could co-exist in the same person, thus exerting a contradictory influence on his/her behaviour.[15]

From an empirical point of view, the research focuses on the comparative analysis of integration of immigrants in the economic and social structures of Southern European countries, namely Italy, Spain, Greece, and Portugal, with particular attention to their inclusion in underground or informal economic networks and the impact of these on receiving countries.

The choice of Mediterranean countries is justified by various considerations. First of all, southern European countries present the most developed 'informal' economic sectors, which in some cases, like the case of southern Italy, are straightforwardly illegal.[16] Second, in all these countries immigration is a relatively new phenomenon. Indeed, they have historically been sending countries and did not experience migratory inflows in the 1960s and 1970s like traditional European receiving countries, mainly Germany and France.[17] This makes it more interesting to study the reaction of these hosting societies, as they are not used to being receiving societies and represent a sort of 'pure' case study. Finally, southern European countries present a very typical form of welfare state, what has been termed the 'Mediterranean' model.[18] This is often characterised as familial, i.e. one based on the assumption that the family male is the only breadwinner. This would explain why exceedingly high levels of female and youth unemployment are not inconsistent with a high level of labour protection and a low level of social protection. The family is the locus of social protection, and wife and children remain dependent on the income of the father up to a very advanced age. The protection of the job of the latter thus becomes of fundamental importance for the entire society. However, as labour protection becomes more and more complicated in the era of globalisation, a rigid labour market structure in reality favours the development of the informal economy. This model differs substantially from the liberal model prevailing in Anglo-Saxon countries, where in the trade-off between flexibility and exclusion there is a tendency towards the former with all that it implies in terms of decrease in equality.[19] From the methodological point of view, the project also relies on a qualitative analysis of already existing bibliographical or statistical sources.

The analysis draws on data gathered by EUROSTAT or national statistical offices sources, or on a wealth of secondary sources quoted by the authors in the final report. In relation to specific issues, field studies were carried out within the context of the project. These used mainly a qualitative methodology and were conducted throughout interviews with migrants or other relevant people.

The field research work concerned mainly three areas. The first is the integration of migrants in the informal labour market with the aim of verifying whether it is possible to identify any competitive threats for domestic workers. The second objective is the assessment of deviant behaviour among migrants, from micro-criminality to the illegal economy. Finally, the field research focused on identification of the social attitudes towards migrants in receiving countries with particular attention to the issues of segregation and the rise of urban movements to defend the security of local communities from micro-criminality.

The micro-data gathered through this field-work are then related to more general issues represented by: the resurgence of the informal economy in Mediterranean countries; the role of migrant workers in the informal economy; the question of whether the informal economy constitutes a powerful pull factor in attracting immigrant workers, especially unauthorised ones; the relation between the insertion of mainly unauthorised migrants in the underground economy and both their deviant behaviour and their social exclusion; and, finally, the reaction of the receiving society.

The project's deliverables consisted of a series of in-depth reports, which are of interest to both policy makers and scholars. The main result was the final report, which included a set of comparative reports on specific issues by different members of the research group. The reports and the data produced provided a wealth of material, which is very useful for further analysis.

The first report was on *New Migrants in South European Countries and Their Insertion in the Underground Economy*, by Emilio Reyneri and Maria Baganha. The report contained an analysis of the typology of migration in the four countries considered, their status at entry, the modalities of their insertion in the labour market, their activities at destination, the issues of competition with the local working force and the role of the underground economy as a pull factor for documented and mainly undocumented migration.[20]

The second report, by Salvatore Palidda, Maria Frangoulis and Antonios Papantoniou, was *Les Conduits Deviantes et la Criminalisation des Immigrés* [*Deviant Behaviour and the Criminalisation of Immigrants*]. This report contained an analytical account of the results of immigration in terms of criminalisation of migration with special attention to the Italian and Greek cases.[21] It was mainly concerned with theoretical issues and, therefore, not particularly suitable for the general public, nor had it a specific and concrete outlook which could appeal to practitioners. However it addressed and analysed legal problems whose relevance at the political level should not be underestimated.

The Impact of Immigration on South European New Receiving Societies, by Carlota Solé, compared society's reactions to immigration in Spain, Greece, Italy and Portugal, in order to discover which factors determine the impact of immigration in Southern European countries. This was done by analysing the impact of immigration from the standpoint of the material factors and conditions (position in the occupational structure, immigration legislation in the receiving country) encountered by the immigrant population.[22]

Finally, the report on *New Forms of Immigration and the Informal Labour Market in Old Receiving Countries: France and Germany*, by Czarina Wilpert and Smain Laacher, deals with the new forms of migration in two traditional migration countries: Germany and France. At the outset, it provided for a thorough historical account of migratory phenomena in the two countries. Then the authors moved on to compare their responses to new migrations. The three basic lines of comparison were: the relation between migratory inflows, types of migration and official policies; the formal and informal labour market and the connection between the migratory inflows and the presence of new migrants in the informal market.[23]

Overall, the results of the study showed that the underground economy represents a major factor in defining the dynamics of migratory flows to Southern European countries.[24] The underground economy employed an overwhelming majority of the migrants included in the study at some stage in their migratory processes. However, the migrants did not create the informal economy, which is an endogenous phenomenon pre-existing migratory flows.[25] On the contrary, the study demonstrates that it is exactly the existence of opportunities of work within the underground economy which constitutes a strong incentive for migrants to enter southern European countries, even if they do not have the possibility of entering legally or of legalising their status once they are in.[26] Indeed, the majority of immigrants are undocumented and they remain so throughout most of their time in the hosting country. On the basis of the number of unauthorised migrants entering regularisation schemes (Table 8.15), the authors of the project estimated how many migrants lived in each of these receiving countries without any documents for a specific period of time: three out of four migrants in Italy, more than half in Spain, more than a quarter in Portugal, and one out of ten migrants in Greece.[27]

The authors demonstrate that in all the countries of Southern Europe, there is a vicious circle of unauthorised residence and irregular work.[28] This is due to the fact that citizens of a non-EU country are forbidden to

Table 8.15 Unauthorised immigrants filing for regularisation schemes (thousands)

Italy population	*57,000*	*Spain population*	*39,000*	*Portugal population*	*9,000*	*Greece population*	*10,000*	*France population*	*58,000*
1986–87	118.7	1985–86	43.8	1992–93	39.2	1998–99	373.0	1981–82	121.1
1990	217.7	1991	108.3	1996	21.8			1998–99	80.6
1995–96	238.2	1996	21.3	2001	147.5				
1998–99	193.2	2000	200.0						
2002	695.0								

Source: Reyneri 2003.

work regularly without a residence permit for work reasons and in turn, to obtain such a permit is not easy for migrants (Chapter 3). In many EU countries, for example, a work permit may be restricted in terms of jobs allowed, or its time duration, or its geographical validity. Moreover, the work permit is normally not renewed automatically, but requires a long wait for the documentation to be approved by the related authorities. Sometimes, the work permit is renewed when it is too late and the migrant is already 'undocumented' again. On other occasions, the migrant undergoes the whole regularisation process and when the work-permit is obtained he/she has already lost the job for which the work permit was obtained. The duration of the work permit is in general limited to only one or two years and that makes it unlikely that migrants can hold a work permit for their entire period of residence in the hosting country – and having the work permit is necessary to stay legally in a country. In short, it is very likely for immigrants who entered the country without a residence permit for work reasons, or who lost their permit in the course of their stay in the receiving country, to seek for alternative working opportunities in the irregular economy.[29] Indeed, a migrant can also enter a country legally with a tourist or a student visa. However these visas have a very limited duration and do not entitle the holder to work in the destination country. They are in fact often used to aid the migrant to enter the country and look for a job, but obviously the status of the worker is then not a regular one. Finally, there are the residence permits issued for family re-unification purposes but in this case the members of the migrants' family are also allowed to work only under certain conditions. Moreover they are not issued on an automatic basis but require the migrant to show that he/she is able to support and maintain the members of his/her family. Also, the definition of family varies according to the different countries but it never includes the extended family.[30]

To sum up, there are many occasions for the migrant to enter or remain illegally in a receiving country. In general terms it is possible to categorise the entry or exit of a migrant as follows:

- legal–legal: The migrant applies for immigrant status, gains legal entry and remains in the country as a legal migrant;
- illegal–legal: This includes those migrants who enter a country illegally, using false documents or evading immigration restrictions, and who seek to change their status after arrival;
- legal–illegal: This group is considered the one including the largest percentage of the 'illegal' migrant population; they enter the country legally, but remain illegally after they were supposed to return home;

- illegal–illegal (independent): This group enters the country illegally and remains illegal but without the assistance of organised criminal groups;
- illegal–illegal (indentured): This is the most vulnerable category. They are undocumented migrants at the mercy of the criminals who procured their passage and employment. They have incurred large debts for their passage which require long periods of time to re-pay;
- legal–legal (indentured): These are those migrants who paid criminal organisations to gain legal access to and a legal stay in the host country. Legal status may improve job prospects, however the amount of money owed still means that crime is a necessary or attractive option.[31]

The phenomenon of illegal migration is particularly worrying in the relations between Europe and its Mediterranean counterparts. Smuggling illegal immigrants into Europe has become a profitable business. It is estimated that illegal immigration into Europe from the south and east raised sharply in the last years. Some 500,000 illegal migrants are believed to have arrived in 2000, up from 40,000 in 1993.[32] As we saw in Chapter 4, there are several favourite routes in: via boat from Albania, Tunisia or Morocco into southern Europe; via Libya through the desert route from sub-Saharan Africa; from Sarajevo airport via Croatia and Slovenia into Italy and Austria; or overland starting from Istanbul and often ending up in Germany.[33]

What is most important to stress is that unauthorised residence and irregular work very often go together.[34] On the basis of the interviews conducted within the context of the project, for example, in the case of Italy, only a few migrants interviewed knew the difference between 'regular' and 'irregular' jobs before migrating. This however did not stop them from entering the country without a residence permit, as the prevailing view was that work was easy to find in Italy. Actually some migrants were motivated to enter Italy instead of, for example, Greece, as they knew that the amount of money to be earned in the Italian underground economy was higher and it was easier to become involved. The opportunity for irregular jobs was cited as a reason for coming to Italy by many Moroccans, who normally enter Europe through Spain and who often leave that country heading to Italy to find jobs in its thriving underground/illegal sector.[35]

Entering a country and being employed easily in its informal economy, as in the case of Italy, does not mean that the expectations of the migrant are met in terms of living standards and conditions. However this never stops a migrant from deciding to migrate. Among the migrants interviewed within the context of the project and finding themselves in a difficult situation in the hosting country, not even one hinted at the possibility of returning to their own country, and they all said that their negative opinion would never stop their friends and relatives from undergoing their own migratory process.[36] This is consistent with the hypotheses made in Chapter 7 relating to migration as a social process. Particularly at the beginning of their migratory experience, migrants do not care about their conditions of life in the receiving country, as their motivations are mainly economic, in the sense that they would like to make a lot of money. That was the case for both the Egyptian and Moroccan migrants studied above. Moreover, they are very unlikely to go back home without money, and show that their migration experience was a failure. This makes it even more likely that they will become involved in the non-legal economy of the hosting country and that they will prolong their stay even if their life is difficult and unlikely to become more comfortable.

They will always depict their life in the host country as much better than it is, thus inducing their friends and relatives to follow their path. However, even if they did tell the truth about their life abroad, according from what emerged from the interviews conducted in the project, this would not serve as a deterrent at all.[37] Indeed, quite apart from the fact that messages coming from a returning migrant can be pretty contradictory, their negative experience would be discarded as irrelevant by the local population willing to flee the country. Migration is a self-fulfilling process. Migration leads to further migration, regardless of the information it transmits or its success or failure for the migrant.

Indeed, from the evidence it emerges that the recent immigration in Italy is seldom a success story. However this does not stop other illegal migrants from entering the country and going down the same road of becoming implicated in the informal, or illegal economy, being criminalised and being further incentivised to misbehave.

All this supports the hypothesis that the existence of the underground economy is a strong 'pull' factor of migration to the EU. This is particularly true in the context of 'Fortress Europe' (Chapter 3), where borders are firmly closed. Those who are unable to obtain a work permit to enter legally and work legally in an EU country are obviously cut off from the regular labour market, but, thanks to the existence of the irregular economy, they do not need to go back to their home country. Thus, the research concluded, the ready availability of employment in the underground economy, where no documents are required, promotes undocumented immigration.[38] There is a feedback process between undocumented migration and work opportunities in the underground economy which can hardly be underestimated. It is actually the engine allowing for the entry of illegal migrants to continue unhindered.

Far from being an effect of illegal immigration, the submerged economy would appear to be one of its causes. In a nutshell, if the underground economy did not offer the possibility of employment to undocumented migrants, according to the study in question, many of them would not enter Southern European countries in the first place.

This outcome is further strengthened by the evidence that the majority of the migrants do not come from the poorest countries, but from those with an intermediate level of development and who have therefore enough information and resources to go looking for a better life abroad.[39] Thus, more than the necessity of survival, these migrants are attracted by the possibility of improving their standard of living and getting closer to the idea of the West proposed by the media. Whether this happens or not, as we have already elaborated, is not actually the point. The point is that they think it can happen.

The issue of whether immigrants represent a competitive threat for domestic workers should be addressed in the context of the labour structure of the receiving countries. Southern European countries are certainly characterised by high levels of unemployment. However such unemployment concerns mainly educated young people living with their families, who can afford to wait for the right job proposal. They are therefore unlikely to compete with migrant workers for low-skilled jobs.[40] This brings the authors of the research to conclude that a demand for migrant workers does exist in Southern European countries, although the overall employment rate is high. Indeed, as underlined at the beginning of this chapter, nearly all migrants are employed in low-level jobs, often below their qualifications and educational level. They are employed in personal and social services and in the industrial and agricultural sectors (see above). In all southern European countries migrants hold a wide range of jobs in the least skilled services, while the proportion of self-employed migrants is negligible (see above). In conclusion, there is little if any competition because both in the formal and even more in the underground economy, most activities carried out by migrants are below the level accepted by local workers.

Finally, the insertion of the vast majority of immigrants in the underground economy is one of the main reasons why Southern European countries have so quickly adopted a very negative attitude towards the new phenomenon of immigration. Working in an underground economy, as well as living without documents, contributes hugely both to the marginalisation of migrants and in provoking negative attitudes in migrants towards local people.

The reasons why these happen are reported to be the following. First, working in the underground economy makes the migrants look like criminals and does not allow the general local public to recognise the migrants' contribution to the overall economy and well-being. This is even more true because as unregistered workers they do not pay income tax and social contributions, whereas they are entitled to use some public services and goods (like schools, hospitals, or even water and streets). Moreover, although in South European countries local people working in an underground economy are legitimised by social consensus, migrants are highly stigmatised if they do. This happens because on the one hand, in-group free-riders are more tolerated than out-group free-riders. On the other hand, migrants are supposed to be more likely to cross the line between irregular work and illegal activities.[41] This leads directly to the analysis of the issues relating to the myth and reality of migrants' 'deviant behaviour'.

A careful analysis both of the social construction of criminal statistics, and of the proceedings of police activities and penal trials, allowed the authors of the project to depict to what extent immigrants are discriminated against.[42] Especially in Italy and more recently in Greece, a 'short circuit of securisation'[43] made it more likely that the authorities would adopt policies of repression than policies of support towards migrants.[44] Although the number of people in prison has increased in general, in all southern European countries, this increase is especially marked for foreigners, producing a phenomenon of ethnification of the jailed population and an allegedly related process of ethnification of illegal activities.[45] Amongst the many reasons that contribute to this, the authors stress that an underground economy willing to accept migrants may contribute to increase their deviant behaviour, although in an indirect way.

In general, the fact that migrants can easily find work in the underground economy, as is the case in Italy and in the other Mediterranean countries, can have contradictory effects on the migrants' tendency to adopt deviant behaviours. From one point of view, the migrants might not want to risk being caught by the authorities and therefore might reduce their level of engagement in deviant behaviour. On the other hand, however, the fact that when they lose an irregular job, migrants are not eligible for any public support might convince them to look for survival at any cost, therefore engaging in criminal activities more easily. It is estimated in the project that generally the second effect prevails.[46]

The connection between deviant behaviour and working in the underground economy is also the consequence of a self-selection process. Indeed, people who are willing to enter a country illegally, even risking their lives to do so, are also more likely to undertake more risky but more lucrative activities, even if they entail engaging with criminal organisations or becoming criminals themselves. Indeed, 'making money', for migrants in the first phase of their migratory process, is an overwhelming priority and the less they have to lose in the receiving countries, which is the less they are integrated in hosting societies, the more they might be willing to enter criminal activities to achieve their aims. Finally, the fact that the receiving country offers easy unauthorised entry and easy illegal work, may give migrants the impression that, in the receiving society, rules are not to be respected.[47]

In conclusion, the most important findings of the project are the following:

1. The new immigrants are mostly unauthorised, but have different personal characteristics and migratory projects;
2. There is more replacement and complementarity than competition, in the receiving labour markets, except for the self-employment field;
3. Migrants are inserted in well-rooted and flourishing underground economies;
4. The domestic underground economy promotes unauthorised immigration;
5. The underground economy prevents immigrants from settling in a steady way;
6. The underground economy makes migrants' marginalisation easier;
7. The underground economy may contribute in increasing migrants' deviant behaviour;
8. *Medice cura te ipsum*: Southern European countries should realize that only by curbing the size and relevance of the underground economy for the domestic labour market will it be possible to tackle the problems of unauthorised immigration.[48]

What kind of policy implications does this analysis suggest? The project under analysis could provide suggestions on a number of areas of intervention in relation to the issues of migration to southern European countries. In particular, it would be important to stress the extent to which undocumented migrants are creating wealth in their hosting countries, providing services and performing jobs that the labour force would not supply otherwise. Awareness of the relevance of the migrant communities for the local economy could help in their integration in the local civil societies, creating the necessary level of integration between the migrants' and the local social capital to avoid violent outbursts of discontent (Chapter 9).

In practical terms, the project suggests intervention in the following areas of governance:

- to inform migrants about their rights to work, live and reside in the receiving countries as well as to provide them with basic legal and training support;
- to inform local population about the extent to which migrant communities contribute to the overall economy and welfare, to stress the lack of competition in the labour markets and provide vital information about migrants' cultural and religious backgrounds to avoid clashes and misunderstandings.[49]

In more general terms, it would be advisable to adopt governance measures at the EU level aimed at the progressive eradication of the phenomenon of illegal migration. That could be obtained by, on the one hand, reversing the tendency towards the creation of Fortress Europe, and on the other, by adopting migratory policies more realistic in terms of acceptance of migratory flows not only as an inevitable event, but also as a positive development for receiving countries.[50] Moreover, the research findings actually identify a powerful pull factor for migration in the existing thriving informal sectors of Southern European countries, especially Italy. This plays a very crucial part in understanding what is happening to the relationship between migrants and hosting societies. The level of hostility can only be worsened by the factors facilitating the introduction of unauthorised migrants in the informal/illegal economies of receiving countries, and these factors are all reinforced by official migratory policies denying the right to entry on the basis of the existence of high unemployment level in receiving countries. Moreover, this activates a vicious cycle between illegal entry, insertion into the informal/illegal sector, stigmatisation and an increased likelihood to adopt a deviant behaviour. The interruption of such a cycle is not an easy task, but the research shows that tightening border controls is not going to be a solution.[51]

Indeed, the project suggests that a complex and difficult strategy at both the national and the regional level should be implemented, if EU institutions and Southern European countries want to solve the problems of unauthorised immigration.

First, EU countries, and especially southern European ones, should come to terms with the fact that they have become countries of immigration. This means also recognising the existence of segmented labour markets in which there coexists a high level of unemployment as regards the local educated youth, and also a demand for less skilled jobs which should be filled by foreign labourers.

Second, the policy of Fortress Europe does not lead anywhere close to the solution of the problems of migration. EU institutions should devise a common migratory policy under the new immigration regime introduced after the entry into force of the Amsterdam Treaty, which allows the entry of those labour migrants necessary to cover the needs of the EU labour markets.

Finally, the third and most important step of this complex strategy must be a set of policies aiming at reducing domestic underground economy. Indeed, evidence shows that an underground economy is not the heritage of past backwardness, but, on the contrary, is an emerging phenomenon even in some of the wealthiest regions of the EU, for example in Northeast Italy.[52]

Overall, it seems necessary to allow for a gradual opening of EU borders to immigrant workers although with effective control of their insertion in the labour market of the receiving countries. Indeed, from the analysis of the labour markets of EU countries there does not seem to be competition between the domestic labour force and the immigrant workers, despite the high level of unemployment recorded in some EU member states. To this we should add considerations about the difficulty of sustaining the welfare states of EU countries in the context of an ageing population which makes even more evident the need to integrate immigrant workers in the social and political life of receiving countries.

Finally, the legalisation of migration and the extension of social and political rights to foreign workers would contribute to the elimination of any instance of social prejudice against the local labour force, ensuing from the wage depression effect that the use of unauthorised migrant workers in the illegal or even legal economy necessarily has. It would also contribute to the eradication of the underground economy, since migrant workers with a legal status are undoubtedly more likely to denounce situations of exploitation and illegality than unauthorised migrants might be.[53]

What remains to be seen at this point is how receiving societies have reacted to the increase of migrants, mostly undocumented ones, from less developed countries, especially Muslim ones. In the next chapter we will elaborate on some examples of 'Islamophobia' pre-dating the terrorist attacks of 2001, with the aim of showing how much of the hostility towards Muslim migrants is not related to recent terrorist threats but is rooted in the cultural, social, political and religious clashes engendered by the increase of mass migration and brain drain from Muslim countries as a consequence of globalisation. This is in line with the theoretical considerations made in Chapter 2 of this book.

5 Conclusion

The analysis so far demonstrates that foreign-born populations in general, and people of Muslim religion in particular, live in labour market conditions that conceal instances of discrimination. They have on average a higher rate of unemployment than the native-born populations at each level of education. The most overrepresented in terms of the unemployment rate are migrants of Northern African origins. Moreover foreign-born labourers are more likely to be employed in the low-skilled agricultural and industrial sectors than locally born workers, and they are also generally overqualified for their job placements.

As regards the situation of Egyptian migrants, the dynamics of highly skilled permanent migrants leaving Egypt and heading to more developed OECD countries confirm the hypotheses made in the theoretical section of this book. Brain-drain seems to be an unstoppable phenomenon and this further hinders the chances of the country overcoming its difficulties in joining the globalisation process. Indeed, the lack of integration of Egypt and the MENA region in the global economy reduces the possibilities of employing highly skilled personnel in the country, thus further adding to its marginalisation. It is a vicious circle which is becoming more and more difficult to break.

The considerations above only refer to the case of the insertion in the labour markets of legal or 'documented' migrants. In the previous sections of this book, however, we have discovered that the majority of Egyptian and Muslim migrants to EU countries are likely to be 'undocumented' at a certain point in their migratory processes. Moreover, insertion in the local communities is likely to be hindered by the fact that as 'illegal' migrants they are very likely to be employed in the 'underground', or even in the 'illegal' economy of the receiving countries. This is especially true as far as migration to Southern European countries is concerned.

The findings of a research project financed by the EU support the hypothesis that the existence of the underground economy is a strong 'pull' factor of migration to the EU. This is particularly true in the context of Fortress Europe, where borders are strictly closed. Those who are unable to obtain a work permit to enter and work legally in an EU country are obviously cut off from the regular labour market, but, thanks to the existence of the irregular economy they do not need to go back to their home country. Thus, the research concludes, the ready availability of employment in the underground economy, where no documents are required, promotes undocumented immigration. There is a feedback process between undocumented migration and work opportunities in the underground economy which can hardly be underestimated. It is actually the engine allowing for the entry of illegal migrants to continue unhindered. Far from being an effect of illegal immigration, the submerged economy would appear to be one of its causes. In a nutshell, if the underground economy did not offer the possibility of employment to undocumented migrants, many of them would not enter Southern European countries in the first place.

The issue of whether immigrants represent a competitive threat for domestic workers should be addressed in the context of the labour structure of the receiving countries. Southern European countries are certainly characterised by high levels of unemployment; however, such unemployment mainly involves educated young people, living with their families, who can afford to wait for the right job proposal. They are therefore unlikely to compete with migrant workers for low-skilled jobs. Overall, there is little if any competition because both in formal and even more in the underground economy, most activities carried out by migrants are below the level accepted by local workers.

Finally, the insertion of the vast majority of immigrants in the underground economy is one of the main reasons why Southern European countries have so quickly adopted a very negative attitude towards the phenomenon of immigration. Working in an underground economy, as well as living without documents, contributes hugely both to the marginalisation of migrants and in provoking migrants' negative attitudes towards local people. This leads directly to the analysis of the issues relating to the myth and reality of migrants' 'deviant behaviour'.

In general, the fact that migrants can easily find work in the underground economy, as is the case in Italy and in the other Mediterranean countries, is considered an incentive to 'misbehave'. In turn, however, the reaction of receiving societies is often a hostile one, to the extent that, as we will find out in the next chapter, scholars have started talking about 'Islamophobia'.

Chapter 9

Islamophobia and social capital

1 Introduction

This chapter touches upon the complex issue of the integration of Muslim migrants' communities in the civil society of European hosting countries without any ambition to be exhaustive, or even to highlight the main terms of the question. By making reference to original research on the subject, it stresses how co-habitation between Muslims and national communities was already problematic before the occurrences of September 11, to the extent that it was possible to talk about straightforward hostility against Muslims, or Islamophobia. This produced in response the widespread establishment of Muslim social, political and religious organisations all over Europe and the related debate of whether they constitute genuine social capital. After defining social capital and analysing the issue of how to measure it, the chapter finds that the emergence of 'Muslim voices', instead of increasing the level of trust between Muslim communities and the local civil society, may have indeed reduced it. This, in turn, enhances difference, and multiplies the occasions of confrontation between original communities and communities of migrants. In a few words, it reduces social capital and facilitates Islamophobia and social unrest. The solution, as some authors point out, is an increase of social capital measured in terms of trust and respect for civic norms. This is a result which might also be obtained by introducing adequate urban policies.

2 'Muslim voices': The enemy within

The outcome of a project financed by the European Union[1] which took place between February 1997 and April 1999 provides the evidence we need to assess the degree of hostility towards Muslim migrant communities before September 11. The aim is to show that, although the new emergency following the terrorist threat exacerbated the problems of Muslims in developed Western countries, these predated the terrorist attacks and are related to the cultural, social, political, and religious clashes resulting from the increase of migration from Muslim countries as a consequence of globalisation.

The primary concern and focus of this project was the production of an analytical, descriptive and comparative account of the different forms and processes by which European Muslims (and the religious affiliation is assumed as the main determinant of their identity) have been socially excluded and marginalised in eight European countries: Belgium, France, Germany, Greece, Italy, Switzerland, the Netherlands and the UK.

The project relies mainly on qualitative research commissioned by the co-ordinating partners in the UK, namely the Centre for the Study of Globalisation, Euro-Centrism and Marginality (CGEM) and the Cathie Marsh Centre for Census and Survey Research (CCSR) at the University of Manchester, with their partners in the eight member states included in the study. The partners in the member states were: Facultes Universitaires Saint Louis, Bruxelles (Belgium); Institut Europeen de Sciences Humains (France); Zentrum for Turkeistudien, Essen (Germany); University of the Aegean (Greece); Il Poliedro, Milano (Italy); University of Geneva (Switzerland); and EGA/University of Amsterdam (the Netherlands). Each partner in the member states produced a report on the issues relevant to the project, to which we will make reference later on. The project ran for three years, from 1997 until 1999. At the empirical level the research aimed at:

1 obtaining evidence on the different national forms and processes by which European Muslims have been socially excluded in each of the eight countries;
2 mapping the mechanisms generating socio-economic and cultural conditions within which European Muslims have experienced a progressive process of marginalisation and how this has led to economic deprivation and various forms of social and cultural disadvantage;
3 verifying whether these forms of social exclusion have been favoured by transnational European 'path-ways';
4 identifying national and European public policies aimed at contrasting social exclusion amongst migrant communities especially those from Muslim countries.[2]

To achieve these aims, the project was divided into two phases. Phase one focused on the identification of the general characteristics of the European Muslim populations. Phase two addressed the problems and the forms of discrimination related to the employment of Muslims in the national labour structures with particular reference to gender issues.

From the theoretical point of view the project addressed two debates in the social and political sciences: the sociology of employment and work, and the politics of identity. In particular, the study argues that the analysis of European Muslims, and the way in which they express their socio-political and cultural identities, should be located in an analytical framework where they are agents of their own history. Thus, in the first instance, the project highlights the economic, social, and political structures within which European Muslims have organised politically as a means of expressing their identities and bringing attention to their demands. Finally, the project focused on the political organisations of Muslim communities within the European Union, the so-called 'Muslim voices', and the articulation of their political demands at both the national and European level.[3]

According to the authors of the project, a number of 'Muslim voices' emerged across Europe as a consequence of the discrimination against Muslim communities in member countries (so-called Islamophobia). These 'Muslim voices' started making demands for equal access to social, economic and cultural resources, thus articulating the need for the recognition of a 'Political Islam' not only at the national but also at the level of European Institutions.[4] The project not only took on the descriptive task of confronting the different European member states' experiences in terms of the political organisation of exclusively Muslim communities but also fulfilled the normative task of accounting for their requests in all policy realms, from education to political representation.

The scientific findings have been subdivided by the authors of the project into two main categories:

1 trans-national characteristics;
2 particular specificities identified in some of the countries under investigation.

The transnational findings were summarised under four major headings and represented the basis for the articulation of Muslim communities' political demands to European institutions.[5] The first heading was demographics, or the quantification of Muslims in Europe. Here the primary problem was the identification of the Muslim population in many of the countries which do not have the category of 'religion' in their census statistics. Indeed the project's theoretical premise that religious affiliation prevails over any other component of identity, from ethnicity to citizenship, is debatable and it has been criticised by scholars such as Fred Halliday[6] who argued that it is more constructive and accurate to talk about national identities and ethnicity than it is to talk about Islamophobia or anti-Muslimism'. Since, however, the real aim of the authors of the project was normative and is related to the articulation of the demands of 'Political Islam' and to their proposition at the level of European institutions, the identification, also in numerical terms, of the European Muslim community becomes an evident necessity.

The second findings referred to the identification of patterns and forms of social exclusion at a national, transnational and European level. The authors claim that in all eight countries the research has highlighted the existence of forms of discrimination targeting Muslim communities as such, and not as immigrants, foreigners, women or other discriminated groups.[7] The ensemble of these discriminatory practices, ranging from education to political representation and from general legislation to gender, is called by the authors 'Islamophobia'. This is what we will make reference to in the rest of the chapter. In this context, the report made a policy recommendation for the establishment of a Directorate for European Muslim Affairs as part of a broader Commission for the Future of Multi-Ethnic Europe.[8]

The research then identified the network of social organisations that represent Muslims in each country, and their political leaders. The research shows that these organisations have complex structures and it is difficult to differentiate between social, cultural, religious, and political groups. This is a very important finding which is however easily explained by the comprehensive nature of Islam, in which religious, political, legal and social issues are all regulated by the Islamic Law (*Sharia*) based on the Quran and its interpretations (*Fiqh*).

Finally, the research allowed for the production of case studies and ethnographies.

On the basis of these findings, the authors made some policy recommendations. At the national level they proposed:

1 the organisation of publicly funded training courses, conferences and meetings on Islamic culture and religion for all those who have a direct or indirect relationship with Muslims in the work-place (for example, teachers, etc.);
2 the establishment of a national commission to carry out the revision of school textbooks in order to eliminate the stereotyped use of words and images referring to Muslims and Islam;
3 the revision of curricula in schools which exclude or denigrate the histories, religion and cultures of Muslim people;
4 the encouragement of fairer representation in state organisation (for example the judicial system, policing, etc.);

5 the establishment of a national commission in each EU country, to monitor the media in order to eliminate the stereotyped use of words and images referring to Muslims and Islam;
6 to facilitate access to national and local broadcast media by Muslim organisations;
7 the recognition and inclusion of Islamic religious observance in all areas of public life (the workplace, education, etc);
8 the development of socio-economic ties between Muslim communities and the varying national authorities to create better links with those communities' countries of origin;
9 the promotion of financial support for Muslim socio-cultural and religious associations (for example mosques);
10 the recognition of religious discrimination as an integral factor in the application of equal opportunities legislation;
11 the development of awareness within state-funded organisations of the specific needs and requirements of Muslim communities.[9]

At the European level, they proposed:

1 the establishment of a commission for religions in order to undertake cultural and information campaigns on religious matters in Europe;
2 the consultation of Islamic socio-cultural organisations by the EU representatives in order to create increased awareness of their concerns.[10]

Apart from these proposals, the report also included policy measures that the EU should adopt to ensure that EU member states are not Islamophobic.[11] The report even proposed to base national family law on *sharia*:

> the recognition of Islamic family law (*shar'ia*) would also constitute a constructive step towards allowing Muslims to participate fully within the host communities and ensuring the respect for civil rights. Islamic legal requirements for marriage, divorce and inheritance at present are secondary to those prescribed by the state, and ceremonies have to be conducted according to state laws before they are officially recognised. According Islamic laws the same status as national laws, that is, once a marriage ceremony has been conducted according to Islamic law (*nikaah*) it is recognised as a legal contract and does not have to be confirmed at a Registry Office, will endorse equity for Muslim citizens. Indeed this should be extended to *all* marriage ceremonies in all religions.[12]

In the light of these policy proposals, the final report of the project, as well as a good part of the research itself, could appear instrumental to the aim to propose to the relevant EU authorities the demands of Muslim political/religious organisations spread across the EU. Similar demands do not only take the form of anti-discriminatory measures, but of the proposition of more straightforward Islamic practices whose legitimacy within the secularised Western democratic political systems is at least controversial.

Whereas some proposals could be inserted within the broader context of a universal recognition of the political and civil rights of ethnic minorities, other propositions might seem to infringe on the political and civil rights of other minority groups as well as appear inconsistent with the secularised legal, political and value systems of EU member states. This is clearly the case as regards the subordination of EU member states' civil law, particularly in relation to marriage, divorce and inheritance, to Islamic Law (*Sharia*). This might not only clash with the distinction between state and religion and the privatisation of religion typical of secular States, but also directly harm the principle of gender equality given the nature of *Sharia*'s provisions in civil matters where women are often attributed less rights than men. The same applies to the prohibition on girls taking part in certain activities, like swimming, for reasons of decency. This is clearly not the place to address similar matters which require a much more sophisticated analysis than the author can provide and have engendered the most heated debates and controversies not only in the academic context but also in the social and political one.

However, the outcomes of the project are extremely relevant for the issue of integration of Muslim communities, in that they point out and document the existence of a very lively political debate within the European Muslim communities on their rights and prerogatives in the EU hosting countries.

This political debate is indeed accompanied by a very high level of political awareness, testified to also by the wide spread of Muslim social/religious and political organisations throughout the EU. Indeed, the widespread presence of Muslim organisations in the EU configures the definition of a distinct Muslim civil society in Europe which by itself modifies the terms of the governance in the EU. However, is this high level of political organisation enough to configure the establishment of a critical amount of 'social capital' not only within the Muslim communities but also between them and the hosting societies?

In practical terms, it would be advisable to start the dialogue between national and particularly local institutions with the 'Muslim Voices' in order not only to identify their needs, but also to increase the knowledge of the phenomenon on the side of local authorities and facilitate the identification of solutions to eventual cultural or religious clashes. Indeed, cultural and religious clashes related to the presence of very self-conscious Muslim minorities in the EU member states have already taken place[13] and are very likely to happen again.

In terms of counter-proposals, it might be useful to think about awareness campaigns targeting the Muslim communities, informing them accurately on the cultural, social, political and civil values prevailing in their hosting countries, in order to facilitate their assimilation within the local hosting communities.

One of the most salient insights of the project is that this politicisation of Islam, referred to as the phenomenon of 'Political Islam', takes place regardless of Muslims' countries of origins or of residence within the EU. This proves the existence of a distinct 'Muslim question' and, therefore, makes it imperative for EU institutions to treat Muslim issues as distinct from the issues relating to migration, social exclusion, race, gender and so on. Needless to say, this has become even more imperative after the events of September 11.

Though the proposal devised by the authors of the project to establish a distinct EU Institution dealing with Muslim Affairs, the so-called Directorate for European Muslim Affairs, might not be feasible, it might however be advisable to increase the level of knowledge of the phenomenon of 'Political Islam' and maybe to identify, within EU institutions, appropriate counterparts to the 'Muslim Voices' to increase the level of dialogue and communication with the aim of avoiding instances of violence and clashes such as happened in France.

Therefore, as suggested in the final report of the project,[14] action could be taken in the following realms of EU governance:

1 knowledge-increasing activities, for example, devising a distinct section within the EU research programmes dealing specifically with Muslim communities in the EU and related cultural/religious/social issues;
2 communication-increasing activities aimed at establishing and keeping open the dialogue with the political/religious organisations of European Muslims spread over the EU;
3 awareness-increasing activities on both sides, i.e. activities aimed not only at increasing the awareness of EU citizens and institutions about the existence and characteristics of Muslim communities but also, and this is extremely important, at increasing the awareness within Muslim groups of the values and characteristics of their hosting societies.

All these measures were and are still necessary to overcome instances of 'Islamophobia', which, as clarified below, predates September 11 and are therefore embedded in the social and cultural humus of receiving societies. At the more structural level, however, the increase of integrated social capital between Muslim and local communities seems to be the only possible way ahead.

3 Instances of Islamophobia before September 11

The research points at the existence of very different Muslim communities in the European countries studied, although they all share the Islamic religion. Coming from different regions of the world, they present very heterogeneous characteristics even as regards their relation with Islam.

It seems however possible to claim that the different forms of discrimination against these migrant communities identified by the researchers are a consequence of the fact that they are 'Muslims'. As we have seen above, Muslim migrants in EU as well as other OECD countries tend to be overqualified for their job placement and inserted in low-skill sectors of the economy like manufacturing, agriculture and personal and social services (Chapter 8). However the forms of discrimination that they experience exceed, according to this analysis, the general kind of discrimination faced by foreign-born labourers in hosting labour markets. It is a more pervasive form of discrimination directed at their distinct religious faith and it is highly politicised in the international arena.[15] As we have already seen, it is called 'Islamophobia'.

Islamophobia is present in different ways and in various contexts. The term is used by the authors to define 'a fear or hatred of Muslim peoples and Islam which manifests itself in various forms of discrimination'.[16] This definition is taken from the one provided by an organisation in the United Kingdom called the Runnymede Trust.[17] The research established that the instances of Islamophobia cover a wide number of issues and areas.

The main manifestations of this phenomenon are represented by: the perception of Islam as a threat both in the domestic and in the international arena; religious hatred adding to xenophobia and racism; the identification of Muslims as 'the others'; and a lack of consideration of the Muslim viewpoint in the general debate.[18]

Indeed the researchers were able to find out that, even before September 11, in political debates (especially international ones), the so-called 'Islamic threat' had replaced the threat of communism for Western societies. Islam was perceived 'to be the "enemy" both without and within'.[19] Muslim communities were found to be completely different from other migrants' communities and thus represented 'the other'. Another instance of Islamophobia was given by the frequent dismissal of Muslims' contribution to general social, political or cultural debates, which resulted in the marginalisation of the Muslim perspective in scholarly debates. Moreover, anti-Muslim behaviours seemed so embedded in the discourse of the countries analysed as to appear perfectly normal and acceptable.

The areas in which discrimination was particularly evident in the different countries studied are many. They range from legislation, to education, from political exclusion to employment and media. The absence of specific legislation against religious discrimination was perceived as a form of legislative discrimination in itself. There was indeed a strong conviction on the side of both Muslim and non-Muslim organisations that legislation against religious discrimination and hatred should be implemented.[20] The debate rotated around the possibility of distinguishing between anti-religious behaviour and racism or anti-immigrant sentiments. Researchers found that in countries like France, Italy and Switzerland, anti-immigrant feelings were more evident than anti-Muslim ones. It must be noted, however, that the majority of the immigrants in these countries are also Muslims, especially from the MENA area, and therefore the two discriminatory attitudes are confused and a lot of the anti-migrant sentiments are expressed as 'Islamophobic' ones and vice versa. The case of France analysed below in this chapter is indicative.

Of the eight EU Member States involved in the 'Muslim Voices' project, some had, at the time of the study, legislation banning religious discrimination, and some had not. Table 9.1 gives an overview of the situation.

Table 9.1 Legislation against religious discrimination in project countries

Country	*Law against Religious Discrimination*	*Law against Incitement to Religious Hatred*
Belgium	—	—
Britain	—	—
France	Yes	Yes
Germany	Yes	—
Greece	—	—
Italy	Yes	Yes
Netherlands	Yes	Yes
Switzerland	Yes	Yes

Source: Glavanis 1999: 76.

The evidence collected shows that, although legislation exists in some countries, it is rarely appropriately applied. Moreover, discrimination on religious grounds relating to access to housing, education and public services, continues unhindered as these issues do not receive any legal attention.

Apart from the lack of legislation directly addressing religious hatred, political exclusion is also cited as a clear form of discrimination. In countries, like Germany and Switzerland, where Muslims and other 'foreigners' were not allowed to vote, the consequences were significant. Turkish families living in Germany for generations were still not granted citizenship rights. However, even when citizenship is not denied, Muslims are marginalised and sidelined.

The typical example is that of French Muslims, especially young people living in the suburbs of large cities. The report claims that second- and third-generation immigrants, mainly from North African countries (e.g. Algeria, Morocco, Tunisia), were experiencing increasing levels of discrimination which had intensified following the state's crackdown on political Islamic activity. France also prohibited political parties, groups or activities based on religious beliefs.[21]

Political representation for Muslims varied in the different countries analysed. In Britain and Italy, for example, Muslims were establishing themselves in local politics, but they had still not acquired political rights at the national level. However the lack of a generalised recognition of political rights across the spectrum was considered an instance of Islamophobia.

The report also pointed at the existence of clear discriminatory behaviours in the educational systems of the countries analysed. Curricula were found to be discriminatory, the intolerance for the way Muslim women dress (headscarves and trousers for girls) was considered unacceptable, and the lack of attention to the dietary requirements in school meals as well the lack of facilities for prayers were considered serious problems. Other instances of Islamophobia were given by the fact that Islamic festivals were not always observed, nor did Islam receive state funding to establish Islamic schools as did other religions.[22] Combating Islamophobia in the schools was considered extremely important to benefit not only Muslim children, but also children of other faiths and ethnic communities. The curricula in most schools were found to be grounded in a very Eurocentric or 'Western' perspective, excluding more marginal cultures and non-Western, non-Christian, non-secular faiths.[23] A deeper understanding of these cultures as well as a more objective study of Islam would create a terrain more conducive to interreligious dialogue. Switzerland and Italy in particular were far from having achieved a significant level of respect of Islam in their educational systems, and cases of confrontation between schools and parents were still frequent.[24]

The area of employment was also one in which it was possible to identify many examples of discrimination against Muslims. In the previous chapter, we explored the questions relating to unemployment of Muslims, especially from the MENA. The research pointed also at the existence of discriminatory practices as far as pay was concerned. Immigrants, especially of Muslim origins, were often receiving lower incomes than local-born workers. Moreover, the Equal Opportunities Centre in Belgium reported that 7.5 per cent of the complaints they received about work and employment was represented by racist attitudes of employers during the hiring process (especially towards women with headscarves), in promotions and transfers, and discrimination about time off for Muslim festivities.[25]

One issue which was highlighted was discrimination against women wearing the *hijab* or veil, and which was not limited to employment. In the absence of specific legislation protecting women from similar discriminatory practices, employers were taken to court on grounds of racial or sexual discrimination. However such an issue needed addressing in more institutional terms.[26]

The media were another target of the research. They were considered to be the source of much of the hostility towards Muslims, and were denounced for stigmatising Muslims as a problem, generalising from particular incidents, for using irresponsibly charged and negative terms in their discourse over Islam, and for depersonalising the Muslims. In general, they were accused of perpetuating the negative images of Islam and Muslims. This was especially true for the national media, and only a little less so for local media.[27]

In terms of specific countries, in Belgium the presence of Muslim groups continued to spark controversy. These groups were discriminated against with respect to many aspects of social life, amongst which the freedom of worship was most prominent. Islam became visible in the country with the development of Muslim immigrant neighbourhoods. However, at the same time as Muslims acquired more visibility, in the period between 1975 and 1984, the economy was in recession. Therefore their employment status was never ideal and by the late 1970s they were already subject to a certain amount of hostility from 'native' Belgian public opinion. From the mid-1980s onwards delinquency, recurrent 'riots' in Brussels's blue-collar neighbourhoods and the rise of Islamic discourse and practices were stigmatised in the media as typical Islamic phenomena. In terms of organisation, Belgium's Muslim communities were starting to organise into networks. Some form of Muslim social capital was being built, but the integration with the local communities was still embryonic. Only recently had an ideologically pluralistic elite stratum of people from different Muslim communities started participating in public affairs, Belgian political parties, and/or associations and trade unions. There was a huge diversity of Muslim communities in Belgium, composed mainly of the Turks and the Moroccans. The Turkish community was reported to be cohesive and active. There was a high level of social capital in as much as the community's rules were traditionally respected and there was a lot of internal social control. The Turks were also more religious than the Moroccans who seemed to have started secularising. However Turks were less skilled in the local languages and Moroccans outperformed them at school. Moreover Moroccans were more likely to marry Belgians. Therefore they are theoretically more integrated than the Turks. Yet they were the object of more stigmatisation than the Turks, possibly because there are more of them.[28]

In the case of France, in the last decades there has been an evolution in the immigration model of the Muslim community. Before, Muslims were mainly temporary labourers, now they are a population settling down into the French society. The consequences of this process are enormous and some of them are addressed further on in this chapter. In terms of social capital, French Muslims started associative activities with trade unionism defending the Muslim workers' rights in factories. From the middle of the 1970s, young Muslims from North Africa started creating musical, theatrical and sporting associations. Only in the 1980s were cultural and religious Muslim associations established, although nowadays there are many thousands of them.[29] However there is not a high level of cohesiveness among them as they all compete to win recognition in terms of the representation of the Muslim community. Moreover they are scarcely integrated with non-Muslim associations and within the French civil society.

As far as Islamophobic attitudes are concerned, in the employment domain, many activities were forbidden for foreigners. As a consequence the grey economy throve and this put foreigners in an extremely weak position (see Chapter 8). Foreign citizens did not enjoy rights relating to all sections of the social security. Moreover, Islam was, even before September 11, within the competence of the Home Office, and the police had already been given a number of powers to control Muslim activities.

Finally, as we have seen, the secular nature of the State did not allow girls to wear the veil in schools and religious parties could not be established. Discrimination was evident also in the treatment of the jailed population. At the time of the research, the period of detention pending trial stands at 63.9 per cent for foreigners in comparison to 40.1 per cent for French citizens for the same offence. Moreover, the likelihood of being freed earlier for the same offence was higher for French citizens.[30]

In the educational sphere, the difficulties faced by immigrant children, even French nationals, were significant. Indeed, the percentage of those of Maghrebian origin without diplomas was 68 per cent, and 72.2 per cent for the Turks, while this figure was only 27.4 per cent for those who are French by birth and aged over 15.[31]

The high number of Muslims in Germany is the consequence of a huge immigration from Muslim countries, especially Turkey. Turks are by far the biggest Muslim group, which is why in Germany Islam is often considered a 'Turkish' phenomenon, both in its outward appearance and in the way it is perceived in the host society. However, there are also large numbers of Bosnian, Iranian, Maghreb and Afghan Muslims as well as Muslims of German origin.

The political organisation of German Muslims dates back to the 1970s, when the first communities of migrants started moving beyond the 'homo economicus' phase and settling in Germany. However the report stressed that the majority of the Muslims living in Germany had not yet acquired German citizenship, and instead of improving, their legal situation was becoming more and more insecure. Restricted measures were introduced with the reform of the Aliens Law in 1991, which was mainly aimed at making family reunification more difficult. Visas could be obtained only after proving sufficient income, housing accommodation and residential status. In 1997 visas also became compulsory for children under the age of 16. In 1993 the law on political asylum was changed in a more restrictive way.

Germany legally guarantees religious freedom in principle. However the report pointed at the existence of social mechanisms that often prevent the religious life of Muslims from being freely expressed. For example, the construction of mosques was often strongly objected to by local populations. This problem was exacerbated if the mosques wished to utter the prayer call (*Ezan*) in public. Other forms of discrimination were found in the fact that Islamic associations were not attributed corporate rights, and in the ban on slaughter according to religious rites.

Regarding employment, the report noted the existence of two forms of discriminatory practices in Germany. The first set was typical of Germany and of a more technical nature. This related to the fact that many Muslim immigrants had arrived in the Federal Republic in the framework of recruitment contracts. As those were only addressed to non-EU citizens, the migrants were automatically given second-class treatment. The second set of discriminatory practices was similar to other OECD countries. The immigrant population presented higher unemployment rates than the locally born working population (for example in 1996, Turkish immigrants had an unemployment level of 22.5 per cent, double that among Germans). This phenomenon was particularly serious for Muslim youths. The usual discriminatory practices against Muslim women wearing *hijab* were reported as well as evidence of discrimination against Muslim youths looking for work despite their qualifications and skills being at the same level as local workers.

In terms of education, Muslim immigrants of the second generation had to struggle with the problem of insufficient school and vocational qualifications which also limited their access to the labour market.[32]

In the case of Greece, Muslim communities are not only those living in the metropolitan area of Athens, Salonica, Patras and Heraklion in Crete, but also ethnic minorities in Thrace, Northern Greece (there are 100–120,000 people of Turkish origin, Pomaki and Gypsies living mainly in Rodopi and Xanthi), and in the Dodecanese Islands. There are also secondary migratory streams to rural areas but they are less significant. Integration of Muslim migrants in Greece, as in other Mediterranean countries, is not easy. This is due to the fact that Greece is a new immigration country and does not find it easy to put in place appropriate institutional arrangements, especially as the majority of migrants are undocumented. There is some legislation in place to protect religious minorities against racial and religious discrimination, namely law 927/1979. However, in 1991 Greece was condemned by the European Court of Human Rights, Amnesty International and the US Human Rights Report due to the enforcement of article 19 of the Greek Nationality Law withdrawing Greek nationality from those of non-Greek origin leaving Greece with the intention of not returning. In terms of the Muslim culture, Greece did not allow self-administration of the religious organisation of the community, as, for example, it does not allow the free election of the Mufti or the free establishment of Mosques without the consent of the local Church.

The report noted also that for historical reasons the level of discrimination against Muslims, especially those of Turkish origin, was especially evident and ranged from limited recognition of the studies of members of the minority who hold Turkish university degrees; to non-recognition of societies and organisations that represent the Turkish minority. In general, the researchers quoted evidence that most state services, from the police and job centres to local social services, approach Muslims with mistrust. As far as employment issues are concerned, Muslim men in rural areas often make up the numbers of seasonal workers who come to the Metropolitan Area of Athens for short-term employment. The majority of documented as well as undocumented workers in Athens are employed in construction (Polish, Albanian and mainly Turkish migrants), tourism (Albanian, Polish and Thai female workers), heavy industry (Egyptians, Pakistanis), domestic labour (Albanian, Polish, Bulgarian, Filipino women) and the leisure industry (Albanian, Thai, and African female workers).[33] Gypsies, on the other hand, are either blacksmiths, who tend to be more permanently established and identify more with the Turkish ethnic group, or vendors moving around the country. A third group of Gypsies consists mainly of unskilled, unstable workers living in the periphery of their own camps. They are employed in transport as assistants; they also work as cleaners, etc. As in other countries, undocumented migrants tend to be exploited, receive lower wages, work longer hours and suffer worse conditions of work.

In the realm of education the researchers report a widespread practice of institutionalised discrimination. Some examples refer to the withholding of permission to teach at community schools from qualified teachers from Turkish educational backgrounds. Measures against illiteracy were applied arbitrarily for Muslims. In Thrace, there were official provisions to create educational structures for the children of minorities. However, Muslim children in other areas were not given any special treatment and were not taught in their mother tongue.

Social capital among Muslims was mainly represented by minority and immigrant organisations of a cultural and educational nature and with solidarity purposes. Only rarely did they have an officially religious purpose.

In Italy discrimination against Muslims was very widespread especially in the form of 'cultural racialism'. This referred to the fact that religious difference based on everyone's own belief was not recognised and respected by non-Muslims but considered as based on cultural differences only.[34]

There was also a lot of criminalisation of Muslim communities which hindered the development of Muslim political organisations. Indeed the study points at a conflation between 'Political Islam' and 'religious–cultural Islam' which was the fault of the media discourse on Muslims in Italy. The analysis then also highlighted that the issue of education was a main concern, together with that of mosques, for Muslim communities in Italy. There were attempts to open private Muslim schools in Italy, outside the national educational system, where Koran studies could be available as the national provisions would not cater for religious needs.[35]

As far as employment was concerned, as noted above, in the case of Italy there did not seem to be a particularly discriminatory attitude against Muslims as such, but against migrants in general. However, the fact that the majority of immigrants are indeed Muslims makes it difficult to distinguish what kind of discrimination is in place.[36]

The report on the Netherlands mainly focused on the Turks and/or

Moroccans, as they are the largest Muslim populations in that country. A number of the Surinamese and Indonesians, and most of the Pakistani, Egyptians, Tunisians and other migrant groups living in Holland are Muslim but their number is more limited.[37]

Legislation on minorities dated back to 1983 with the Policy Document on Minorities. With the formalisation of minorities policy and the constant separation of church and state, the discussions about the relationship between Islam and state changed. Muslim organisations were increasingly recognised as actors who could play a role in the integration of Muslims in Dutch society and started receiving financial assistance provided that their objectives were 'non-religious' and their activities contributed to the integration of Muslims in Dutch society. In turn, integration and participation in society and people's willingness to integrate and participate are the principal preconditions of citizenship in the Netherlands. More complicated was the issue of the financing of mosques, given the fact that their main activities are clearly of a religious nature. However, mosques are dealt with by local authorities and not by national ones. In the Dutch legal system racism and xenophobia are outlawed, and the principle of non-discrimination is sanctioned in the Constitution and in many articles of the criminal code. Anti-discrimination legislation in Holland in general is very sophisticated although combating discrimination is not always easy. The Dutch legal system recognises some Islamic practices, like ritual slaughter and disposal of the dead, which are not allowed in other countries. However, some other Islamic institutions, like the headscarves, the call for prayer, Muslim dietary prescriptions or the recognition of Muslim feasts, were still under discussion.

Within the labour market, migrants, and Muslim ones in particular, were reported to suffer various forms of discriminations: they were overqualified for their job placements, especially Turks and Moroccans, and their employment was less stable than that of locally born workers. In 1995, unemployment among the four main groups of ethnic minorities was three times that of the indigenous population; moreover, long-term unemployment mainly affected the young ethnic population, not the indigenous one.[38]

In terms of education, Holland allowed the opening of Muslim schools, although the issue was still controversial. The first Muslim primary schools were opened in 1988, however the total number of Muslim children going to Muslim school was negligible (4 per cent in 1993).[39]

There were Muslim media like the NMO (Nederlandse Moslim Omroep), a broadcasting organisation run by Muslims and directed exclusively at Muslims. Other national and local broadcasting organisations transmitted radio programmes for migrants in their own language, but did not transmit programmes exclusively for Muslims. Studies conducted in the mid-1990s concluded that the representation of Muslims by the Dutch media was mostly negative. Nevertheless, the Dutch Association of Journalists was committed to promote the integration of minority journalists in the media and to stimulate a critical discussion of the media coverage of minorities through a 'Migrants and Media' working group initiated in 1984.[40]

Switzerland has always been a welcoming country for refugees and asylum seekers. Muslims have been present since the nineteenth century although Islam remained alien to Switzerland until the late 1960s. There is no official provision for Islam in Swiss law and Islam is not recognised as an official religion in Switzerland. Moreover, some forms of discrimination against Muslims resulted directly from the so-called 'three circles policy' in force since 1991, according to which foreigners of non-European ideology (third circle of foreigners), originally from distant countries like all Muslims, were attributed less rights. Moreover, foreign residents in Switzerland could not participate in political life. The report noted how violence against Turkish, Bosnian and Albanian refugees or asylum seekers in German-speaking cantons was very common. It also pointed out that, according to the study, discrimination against Muslims, in the juridical, political and social spheres, had increased. In the social sphere the state prohibited foreigners from performing certain jobs, like teaching in state schools. In the labour markets, the policy of the 'three circles' increased the level of unemployment amongst Muslims and stimulated other forms of discrimination. Also the two-tiered Swiss system of tax collection was fairly discriminatory in that foreigners had to pay as they earn, while Swiss citizens and permanent residents did not. Finally the housing policy of the Swiss government was considered discriminatory for foreigners who could not benefit from low or moderate rents. Moreover, Swiss law prevented non-residents from buying land or buildings. Overall, foreigners of the third circle suffered employment discrimination, higher unemployment rates, and lower wages, and were employed only in the low-skilled sectors. However the report could not directly relate these forms of discrimination to Islamophobia.[41] In the education sphere, no Muslim schools had yet been built, which meant that Muslim children attended state schools. However, if parents had no legal status in the country children had no right to enter any school, which was considered an infringement of the International Convention on the Rights of the Child. Finally Islamophobia was not so obvious in Swiss media apart from right wing and some local media.

Political Islam in Switzerland was not very well established, as national authorities did not formally recognise Muslim organisations as representative of Muslims. There were however around 140, amongst which the most important are:

- Vereinigung der Islamischen Organisationen in Zuerich (VIOZ) (Union of Islamic Organisations in Zurich) founded in 1994;
- La Fondation Culturelle Islamique de Genève (Islamic Cultural Foundation in Geneva) founded in 1978 by the Rabita and financed by Saudi Arabia;
- Le Centre Islamique de Genève (the Islamic Centre of Geneva) which is the oldest Islamic centre and was founded in 1961.[42]

Muslim communities in Switzerland were particularly worried by issues relating to teaching Islamic values, establishing mosques, ensuring an Islamic education for their children, guaranteeing their Islamic identity, and establishing Islamic cemeteries. The Swiss authorities reacted to these requests by allowing freedom of expression in the local media and freedom to celebrate religious rituals in public on special occasions.[43]

On the other hand, politicised 'Muslim voices' were a very relevant phenomenon in the UK and that was a direct consequence of the discrimination suffered by Muslims in that country. The biggest Muslim communities there are Pakistanis and Indians and more recently Bangladeshis. Small settlements of Arabs, Egyptians, Iraqis, Moroccans, Palestinians and Yemenis can be found in service industries in and around London. As a consequence of the marginalisation felt by Muslim migrant settlements, a distinct Muslim identity as opposed to the British one developed and found a way to articulate a 'Muslim voice'. Thus, Muslim voices were perceived by locally born populations as a threat to their identity, even before September 11 and were therefore treated as 'the enemy within'. The researchers found evidence of this phenomenon at all levels, from the international to the national and local level. Muslims felt discriminated against at the state level because of the lack of explicit legislation protecting them as a religious group. Discrimination was also to be found in employment, education and the media. Unemployment was high and was one of the major causes of social exclusion as it led to low income, low standards of living, poor health and poor housing. As analysed above, Muslims in Britain are likely to be marginalised in the labour markets, to be discriminated against and to obtain job placements below their qualifications and skills (see Chapter 8).

The question of education was also a very pressing one. Muslims complained about national curricula and their Eurocentric view of religious education, sexual education, the study of arts and music. Another source of acrimonious relations between Muslim organisations and the British state was the issue of state-funded Muslim schools, strongly demanded by Muslims.[44]

As far as the British media were concerned, Muslims' worries focused on the way in which Islam and Muslims were portrayed. Negative images of Muslims were common, while in the international context it was highlighted how the Western capitalist democracy was the only viable ideology and how there was no room for any other contender, especially not Islam. However, the spread of Muslim media in Britain provided a valid alternative to mainstream British sources. The level of Muslim associationism in Britain was already very high. Social, cultural, religious and political Muslim organisations were widespread although it was not easy to distinguish between their nature and scope. It was estimated that in 1986 therewere already more than 4,000 of these organisations, dealing mainly with issues of solidarity and welfare. This plethora was considered the source of much of the visibility of Muslim communities in the UK.[45] But is this enough to provide for the integration of Muslims in host societies? More generally, what is required to facilitate integration? How is social capital related to the integration of migrants? What kind of social capital is required for this? What is social capital? These issues are the focus of the next section of this chapter.

4 What is social capital?

Social capital as a notion was developed nearly a century ago, in 1916, with the work of L. Judson Hanifan.[46] In the tradition of Bourdieu, social capital is defined as resources embedded in social networks and accessed and used by actors for action.[47] On the other hand, the broadly used conception of social capital as defined by Coleman emphasizes its impact at the level of community.[48] This conception has acquired a substantial heuristic value thanks to the contribution of Robert Putnam.[49] The core idea of social capital is that the person's social assets, family, friends, associates, are not irrelevant in that person's life. On the contrary it is crucial to solve situations of crisis or to obtain economic or other advantages. This is not only true for individuals but for communities too, to the extent that the density of social capital in a given community can bring about material advantages and avoids or limits the impact of crises. In a few words social capital matters, or, in Putnam's words: 'civil society affects the health of our democracies, our communities and ourselves'.[50]

The link between social policy and social capital lies in the amount and quality of mutual welfare delivered informally by friends, mutual support groups and community (neighbourhood or identity-based) associations, which adds to and re-enforces the social service nets provided by law. Social capital represents communal assets produced and reproduced by interpersonal relations based on trust and reciprocity and sustained by solidarity norms and values, as well as (in some contexts such as family and friendship networks) by emotional investment. Social capital relations are by their nature inclusive rather than exclusive.

Three interrelated and cumulative dimensions of social capital are important. These are: bonding social capital (relationships at the basic level of the family, built on identity and sense of belonging); bridging social capital (relationships that tie together different families and neighbourhoods into a larger civic community able to pursue common goods and outcomes); and linking social capital (relationships that connect the civic community and political/policy making institutions). In our conception, it is the bridging social capital that can connect migrant communities to the broader civic community. Moreover, it is the linking social capital that brings together, in a synergic and sustainable relationship, the informal welfare and the formal (institutional) welfare arenas.

Besides, the amount of social capital in a community is not given; it varies across time and space, which makes it imperative to study this notion in different societies and different historical periods.

How do social networks and relations matter? They matter first of all for the people who belong to them, providing for psychological and social comfort, but also for plain economic returns. This is what the economists would call 'the internal value' of social capital and it defines social capital as a private good. One classical example is the case of employment opportunities created by the intervention of friends or relatives or, more generally, 'social connections'.

However there is also an external value of social capital, as its existence also provides benefits for those who do not belong to the social networks in question. In the economists' jargon, there are some positive externalities from social capital. For example a neighbourhood watch against crime also produces a safer environment for those who do not take part in it. From this point of view, social capital also represents a public good. Even more important, it helps to solve problems through collective action as it produces trustworthy relations. In other words, the existence of a social interaction based on trust can help people to act for the collective good without coercion or immediate reciprocity.

In operative terms, scholars distinguish between a narrow and a wider definition of social capital.[51] In a narrow sense, social capital refers only to the networks and groups joined voluntarily by individuals and involving regular face-to-face meetings. These could be cultural associations, or sport clubs. In a broader sense, individuals can also belong to social groups by chance, or birth, or constraint, as in the case of a family or a social class or a neighbourhood. Finally, in the widest meaning, social capital refers to situations where meetings are irregular and casual, like groups of commuters, or participants in a public demonstration.

Moreover, the social cohesion of a society can be measured at various levels:

- within each group and community;
- between different groups and communities.

This distinction, as well as the distinction between the narrow and the wider definition of social capital, is especially relevant when dealing with multicultural and multi-ethnic environments. Indeed, whereas voluntary associations and grassroots social groups can acquire a multicultural dimension more quickly, wider forms of social capital, like neighbourhoods, do require more time and more structural intervention to become multicultural. Also, a high level of social capital *within* different ethnic communities does not mean that there is a high density of social capital *between* them.

Finally what is most relevant is whether social capital is created through public intervention or it is a completely private venture. Indeed the relations between state and society are very complex ones. The state is shaped by society but society is also shaped by the state and its political institutions and legislation.

Can the lack of social capital between and within different ethnic communities be used as an explanatory variable to understand instances of hostility against Muslim communities or Islamophobia? Can diversity and lack of integration of migrant communities lead to the phenomena of social unrest and violence? To answer these questions it is important to understand how to measure social capital. There is indeed an ongoing debate in the social sciences about whether the level of participation in voluntary associations and, in a related way, the density of associations can be considered a good measure of social capital and whether an increased number of associations necessarily allow for the increase of trust in hosting communities.

In a number of empirical studies, trust has been considered as a good measure of social capital. This, in turn, has been positively associated with economic growth, and more efficient provision of public goods.[52] Trust is considered as an element that can cope with market imperfections and moral hazard in uncertain environment, especially in economies where contracts are not sufficiently reinforced by formal institutions. Very often in the literature, membership in voluntary associations has been systematically linked to the notion of social capital as the basis of trust.[53] For instance attitudes of trust may be determined by social relations in associations and clubs recognised as important vectors of interactions. Moreover, voluntary organisations are considered as contributing to build people's capacities to participate in political life. Finally, participation in a voluntary organisation can mean an adherence to some values and social norms.

However, some authors[54] question the existence of a relationship between social capital and membership in groups and voluntary associations, and emphasise the fact that the promotion of associations and participation in groups can be counterproductive and even reduce the level of trust in the community.

In short, whereas some scholars equate the level of participation to voluntary association to the stock of social capital,[55] others measure social capital in terms of trust and civic cooperation [56] without linking it to the number of voluntary associations present in a given society at a given historical moment.

To support the first interpretation, a study by Brehm and Rahn [57] based on data from the US General Survey found that interpersonal trust and participation in voluntary associations are positively related to each other. The study also highlighted how this relationship is skewed in favour of membership. Indeed, group members are found to strongly trust the other members of the same group whereas trust in other people positively affects the respondents' availability to participate in a group, but only to a more limited extent. However, some authors criticise the idea that membership of voluntary association is always associated with more trust and a more positive predisposition towards public good issues. Indeed, they underline how highly selective entry policies can lead to the emergence of exclusive groups and consequently to the formation of negative social capital. For that matter, it could be possible to identify associations which are based on values and rules contrary to trust and civic behaviour, and therefore constitute by themselves negative social capital, as for example, Mafia organisations or organised crime. Knack and Keefer[58] made an empirical investigation into the relationship between social capital measured as trust and respect of civic norms, and membership of voluntary associations. They used as an indicator of trust at the country level the percentage of respondents who believed the others would adopt a co-operative behaviour in a prisoner's dilemma kind of situation. Data were taken from World Values Surveys. Respect for civic norms was measured on the basis of positive responses given to questions relating to the willingness of people to co-operate with strangers in relation to various issues involving public goods (like cheating on taxes). They concluded that there is no relation between trust and participation in voluntary associations.

When applied to the case of Political Islam or, more generally, the existence of a multitude of Muslim voluntary associations, we see that membership of those associations does not represent a good measure of social capital and can indeed create diversity and reduce trust among host communities instead of increasing it. This can help to explain, for example, why, despite a growing number of Muslim associations, as ascertained above through the 'Muslim voices' project, the level of hostility towards Muslim communities has not decreased, and, vice versa, the likelihood of violence and social unrest by young Muslims has increased.

In the next section the attention is turned precisely to the question of whether an increased level of diversity lowers the level of trust among the citizens.

5 The consequences of the lack of social capital among immigrant Muslim communities: The case of France

An example of how diversity and lack of integration has reduced the level of trust in host communities is clearly represented by the wave of social unrest that hit the French suburbs in 2005. The media and television extensively broadcast the events that spread from Paris to many French provinces in October/November 2005 and involved the disruption of public and private property by young Muslim migrants.

The initial spark of the event were the deaths of two Muslim teenagers on 27 October 2005 in Clichy-sous-Bois. The French police was considered responsible for the event and that produced the first wave of protest and disruption in the neighbourhood. After a few days, a tear gas canister, allegedly belonging to the police, fell into the entrance of a mosque: seven localities in France experienced disorders. Further unrest occurred in the following days involving the police and the youngsters, leading to 21 nights of unrest in 300 neighbourhoods in 200 cities: 10,346 vehicles were burnt; 233 public buildings, 74 private buildings, 255 schools and 18 religious sites were vandalised or damaged; 4,770 persons were stopped, 4,400 detained in custody, 763 incarcerated (including over 100 juveniles); 11,500 civil servants were mobilised of which 271 were injured. The three French regions mostly concerned in the outbursts were Ile-de-France, Rhone-Alpes, and Nord-Pas-de-Calais: 60 per cent of immigrant families live in these three regions.[59]

So, is there a relationship between migration, Muslim migration and social unrest? How is social capital related to social unrest?

The work of Sophie Body-Gendrot is path-breaking in this context. As she correctly points out: 'It is not every death of a youth which causes civil unrest and it is not every banlieue which is a springboard for violent reactions. Every locality is differentiated by accumulated and/or lack of social capital'.[60] This mobilisation was not politically motivated or religiously defined. It was a casual, unplanned outburst of social disease. Therefore it is more appropriate to call the disorders 'social unrest' instead of 'riots', a term which is normally used for politically motivated outbursts of violence. In the case of French unrest two dimensions were interacting: first, frustrated teenagers acting out collectively and, second, a few individuals instrumentalising them. The reasons why it happened, from the social capital perspective, are weak social networks and fragmentation in the local context, despite the existence of many Muslim associations at the national level. This is the case, as reported in Worms's and Putnam's studies on the subject, for the French marginalised migrant underclass.[61]

Indeed, the areas which remained calm during the outbursts (like Marseille and Saint-Denis) were those with a strong local culture and social control exerted by families and local community organisations or where social work had been done. Sophie Body-Gendrot adds a further dimension to the social capital argument by underlining that space is also an important factor to consider as it can facilitate or limit social relations. Some of the reasons why social relations are less dense in the Banlieues of the Parisian, Lyon and Marseille regions are related to territorial variables like poor urban planning, insufficient and costly public transportation, and scarce public services.[62]

In conclusion, there seems to be a great correlation between the lack of social capital and the likelihood of social unrest. This would also point towards the necessity of boosting social networks and organisations to facilitate the integration of minority communities in the French Banlieue and, consequently, in French society. What could be missing is the institutional link between private social endeavours and political institutions. This leads to the question of whether there should there be public policy aimed at increasing the social capital stock.

There is a thriving debate in France about the role of public policy and the state in promoting the development of social capital. Social capital in France used to be a function of state intervention and its promotion used to be considered one of the main tasks of public policy. However the advent of globalisation is substantially changing the terms of state intervention in society and creating anxiety.

France is often described as the most state-centred of all post-industrialist democracies.[63] The French nation-state is the oldest in Europe and has represented the point of reference of French political, social, cultural and economic life for centuries. French citizens are used to having the same legal system, the same political institutions and the same rights and duties which are all derived from the French State.

However with globalisation the role of the state is changing and its institutions are acquiring new and different functions. In particular, transformation of the state concerns the following two dimensions:

1 there is a different perception of the role of the state in the economy and of the notion of 'public goods';
2 there is a re-orientation as to how the states interact economically with each other, which creates interdependence and international linkages.[64]

As regards the first dimension, given the complex and multilayered institutional framework which is the consequence of denser international/transnational interactions and their relations, it becomes harder to identify which institution should provide which public good, as well as becoming harder to define the notion of public good as such.

The new approach taken by state intervention to the economy is no longer the welfare state but what scholars have termed the 'competition state'.[65] This is a state able to provide a dynamic 'competitive' advantage in the international economy (as opposed to a static notion of 'comparative' advantage), promoting a favourable investment climate to transnational economic actors through the provision of public goods defined as 'immobile factors of capital',[66] for example, human capital, infrastructure, support for new technologies, protection of the environment or maintenance of the standards of life of the middle classes.

The transformation of the state from the domestically oriented welfare state to the externally orientated competition state leads to the second dimension of the change in the position of the state as a consequence of globalisation: the reorientation of the way it interacts in the international arena and with the other states. The state changes its international role, shifting its priorities from defence and security to business. The competition state, both in the developed and in the less developed world, attracts business by:

1 shifting its public policy making from the macro- to the micro-level: e.g. reduction of labour costs;
2 pursuing a 'dynamic competitive' advantage and thus rendering its structure more flexible;

3 keeping inflation low and the economy stable to attract foreign investment (neo-liberal macro-economic policies);
4 promoting enterprise innovation and profitability at the private and public level.[67]

French civil society has been nurtured by the state for centuries, therefore the transformation of the state within globalisation is a threat to the identity of the French civil society and, as a consequence, of French social capital at least to the extent to which this has been created through public intervention.[68]

Jean Pierre Worms claims that France is facing two interlocking crises as a consequence of globalisation:

- a crisis of socio-economic inequality, affecting especially, although not only, Muslim migrants concentrated in suburban slums;
- a crisis of political representation of the French lower classes.[69]

The French class divide, between the more educated class and the marginalised underclass, both national and migrant, is reflected in the dynamics of the development of social capital.

As Putnam notes,[70] for the educated classes, whereas the traditional social and political organisations of the unions, political parties and the Church have indeed witnessed a decline of membership in France, like in any other industrial country, overall membership in associations has been stable. In a way, there is a sort of 'privatisation of social capital formation'[71] which is centred on two developments:

1 a rapid growth in organisations defending sectoral interests;
2 a growth of the associations aimed at broader more altruistic objectives.

In the French underclass, Worms also notes the persistence of important forms of bonding social capital, but this is not enough to integrate marginal groups in the wider society.[72]

To explore the dynamic of social capital among the French national communities it is worth having a look at the French ministry of domestic affairs (*Ministere de l'interieur*). Online access is possible for the following annual registries:

- registry of recognised public utility associations;[73]
- registry of recognised public utility foundations;[74]

- registry of business foundations;[75]
- report of the inter-ministerial mission on surveillance and fight against sectarian tendencies.[76]

As far as the relationship with local authorities is concerned, the ministry of domestic affairs produces regular reports on their activities.[77]

The French National Institute of Statistics (INSEE) is extremely useful in identifying indexes of social capital relating to standards of life. Online access is available for the following indicators:[78]

- household consumption and ownership rates;
- evolution of household consumption by purpose;
- household ownership of durable goods by age of reference person;
- housing;
- main residences by tenure status;
- dwelling amenities;
- justice;
- crimes and misdemeanours reported and resolution rates;
- holidays/leisure;
- proportion of people taking vacations by age.

Another very useful indicator, especially given the position of France in the global economy, is represented by the kind and conditions of employment as specified in the figures provided by the National Institute of Statistics. Finally, the institute provides data relating to education, health and population.[79]

As far as political participation is concerned, the main point of reference is Science Po. The Centre for Political Research of Science Po published an extremely informative report on the relation between French citizens and politics.[80]

Table 9.2 Political interest from 1978 to 2006

% of those who show political interest	
1978, 1998: Post-legislative	46
1988: Post-presidential	42
1995: Post-presidential	49
1997: Post-legislative	48
2002: Post-presidential	41
2002: Post-presidential	54
2004: Post-European	46
2005: Pre-referendum	53

As a simple indicator of the level of participation of the French citizens to political life, the table above details the percentage of those who showed some interest in politics (see Table 9.2):

Finally, in France, the value of volunteering is relatively high as it formed 2.66 per cent of GDP in 1995–2000.[81] The French nonprofit sector counts more than 700,000 voluntary organisations, with more than 7 million volunteers. According to the French National Institute of Statistics,[82] 55 per cent of members benefit from common activities, 29 per cent pay fees without participating, while 17 per cent exert responsibilities and 9 per cent take part in organisation.

As far as migrant communities in France are concerned, although research shows the existence of a high number of Muslim associations (see above), scholars question their capacity to constitute social capital, to facilitate the integration of Muslim communities in French society and to increase the level of trust.[83]

This leaves us with the question of what kind of social engagement is required to increase the quality of life in French suburbs. How can more social capital be created? The debate is ongoing in the scholarly community, but there is some evidence that spatial intervention and the redefinition of urban spaces can help. Social unrest in France was an urban phenomenon. Social unbalances and inequalities are mirrored by spatial differences; social unrest is generated in spaces which are isolated from the rest of the city, in marginalised settings where social interactions are closer to social struggles and social problems are exacerbated by spatial constraints. Social marginalisation becomes spatial marginalisation as people living in the banlieues find it difficult to reach the centre, to enjoy public spaces, to meet in pleasant environments, or to participate to the life of the city. On the basis of these considerations, scholars like Saskia Sassen, Sophie Body-Gendrot, Richard Sennet and Zygmunt Bauman have advocated urban planning and redesigning of neighbourhoods as the solution to the problem of social integration of marginalised communities, both migrant and local ones.[84]

Can architects, urban planners and local authorities produce integration through a careful redesigning of social and living spaces? Or is this a task that has to be performed through more substantial state policies of integration? According to Sophie Body-Gendrot, 'One of the great tasks of urban design lies in creating spaces which do not foreground fear'.[85] More emphasis on a self-managed process by local communities in changing their surrounding spaces is supported by Saskia Sassen, who would advocate only a limited intervention by urban planners, like the establishment of an open market place or a recreation centre.[86] Richard Sennet is straightforwardly against creating a logical, functional or legible city place as this would not benefit the people who lived there.[87] Predictable planning deprives residents of the opportunity to define their own way to find meanings and solve problems in their neighbourhood. Solutions must come from the people themselves and cannot be imposed from above, neither by rational urban planning nor by imposition of policies of integration. The solution to these issues lies in the creation of a feeling of trust in and belonging to a shared urban space and in a community of people sharing the same problems and devising common solutions to them. Ultimately the solution lies in the creation of social capital. However, social capital cannot be identified only with the number of Muslim associations or organisations, but has to be related to the development of trust between settlers' communities and existing local ones. This can be helped by the creation of common spaces and places of meeting and integration.

In conclusion, the result of these dynamics in France therefore is not so much a decline in social capital, but ' … a general pattern of increase in self directed, fragmented social capital and a decrease in institutional, other directed social capital'.[89] What is really worrying is the lack of an institutional link between private sociability and the wider public sphere. This is very clear if we analyse the reactions of the French state and of French local authorities to the social unrest of 2005.

The French state reacted strongly to the outburst of social unrest to the extent that in the autumn of 2006, one year after the 'riots', Segolene Royal, the Presidential candidate for the left in France, supported the idea of calling on the army to take care of juvenile violence in the French suburbs. At the national level, on 9 November 2005, a state of emergency was declared. It lasted for three months and was terminated after 4 January 2006 by President Jacques Chirac. The state of emergency was outlined by a law passed in 1955 at the beginning of the Algerian war, and was therefore often interpreted as a 'post-colonial' measure. It allowed for the imposition of curfews and round-the-clock home searches all over the territory; however, only 5 per cent of localities resorted to curfews. Ban of group gatherings were extensively used and, in the sensitive zones of 25 departments, public places and entertainment zones were closed on various occasions. The attitude towards the migrant communities was especially tough, with prefects required to deport undocumented foreigners implicated in the unrest.[89]

The national judicial system also reacted strongly to the crisis. 2,808 people were stopped during the crisis, 800 were incarcerated, with more than 100 less than 18 years old. The government insisted that the prosecutions were 'tough'. However the evidence against the culprits was not strong enough and those convicted were sentenced on average to four months of jail, with more than two months of suspended sentencing.[90]

Why did the State adopt such a 'zero tolerance' approach to the social problems of 2005? The reasons for the reaction of the French State are very stratified and profound. By acting in the banlieues, the French State was trying to regain part of the authority lost in the global and in the European Political Economy as a consequence of globalisation and Europeanisation processes. Pressures to intervene were also related to the perception of a seemingly endless massive urbanisation process. Prominent amongst those reasons, however, was the crisis of social capital and shared collective norms in multicultural urban areas, characterised by their anonymity, segregation and global insecurity about jobs, as well as a political instrumentalisation of the fear of radicalised Muslim migrants.[91]

However, the reaction of local authorities was by far less severe than that of the central State, especially in those areas where social capital was more abundant and mayors used it to solve the crisis. Indeed, the explanation for the calm observed in many areas at risk comes from the presence of volunteers, religious leaders, strong families and strong communities ties. Marseilles, for example, which has numerous and accumulated civil resources and know-how in deprived areas has been able to avoid social unrest.[92]

It appears therefore imperative to rebuild the connections between private social capital and institutional intervention.

6 Conclusion

Primary research shows that in European countries forms of discrimination targeting Muslim communities as such predate the events of September 11. The ensemble of these discriminatory practices, ranging from education to political representation and from general legislation to gender has often been referred to as 'Islamophobia'.

The research established that instances of Islamophobia cover a wide number of issues and areas. The main manifestations of this phenomenon are represented by:

- the perception of Islam as a threat both in the domestic and in the international arena;
- religious hatred adding to xenophobia and racism;
- the identification of Muslims as 'the others';
- a lack of consideration of the Muslim viewpoint in the general debate.

Even before September 11, in political debates (especially international ones), the so-called 'Islamic threat' had replaced the threat of communism for Western societies. Islam was perceived 'to be the "enemy" both without and within'. Muslim communities were found to be completely different from other migrants' communities and thus represented 'the other'. Another instance of Islamophobia was given by the frequent dismissal of Muslims' contribution to general social, political or cultural debates, resulting in the marginalisation of the Muslim perspective in scholarly debates. Moreover, anti-Muslim behaviours seemed so embedded in the discourse of the countries analysed as to appear perfectly normal and acceptable.

A number of 'Muslim voices' emerged across Europe as a consequence of the discrimination against Muslim communities in EU member countries. These 'Muslim voices' started making demands for equal access to social, economic and cultural resources, thus articulating the need for the recognition of a 'Political Islam' not only at the national but also at the European level.

A network of social organisations represented Muslims in each country and their political leaders. These organisations have complex structures and it is difficult to differentiate between social, cultural, religious, and political groups. It is however debatable whether the high number of similar Muslim associations can be considered a good measure of social capital.

The core idea of social capital is that a person's social assets – family, friends, associates – are not irrelevant in that person's life. On the contrary, they are crucial to solve situations of crisis or to obtain economic or other advantages. This is not only true for individuals but for communities too, to the extent that the density of social capital in a given community can bring about material advantages and avoid or limit the impact of crises.

However, social capital cannot be identified only with the number of Muslim associations or organisations, but has to be related to the development of trust between settlers' communities and existing local ones.

An example of how diversity and lack of integration has reduced the level of trust in host communities is clearly represented by the wave of social unrest hitting the French suburbs in 2005. The reasons why it happened, from the social capital perspective, are weak social networks and fragmentation in the local context, despite the existence of many Muslim associations at the national level. The solution to these issues lies in the creation of a feeling of trust in and belonging to a shared urban space and in a community of people sharing the same problems and devising common solutions to them. Ultimately the solution lies in the creation of social capital.

Conclusion

The main objective of this book has been to study the impact of globalisation on migratory flows from a distinct International Political Economy (IPE) perspective. The scope of the theoretical framework was outlined in the first section of the book (Chapters 1 and 2). Here, the author clarified the meaning of International Political Economy and assessed the different IPE approaches to international migration, so as to select the appropriate theoretical context in which to analyse the empirical case. The case study was represented by the dynamics of migration from the MENA area, especially Egypt, to the European Union (EU).

The theoretical aim of the book has been, first, to understand the problem of migration, both legal and illegal, in the context of globalisation; and second, to assess the relation between globalisation, marginalisation and the EU response to threats of mass immigration from less developed countries. The theoretical section addressed questions relating to how to explain the increase of international migration in recent times, and explored whether and how this can be related to the process of globalisation. It defined globalisation in qualitative terms, and provided for the identification of the main political economic causes and consequences of globalisation-induced migration. It also highlighted the tension between legal and illegal migration.

From the empirical point of view, the book has presented the case of Egyptian migration. It reconstructed the dynamics of migration from Egypt, and explained the increase of migration from the MENA area and from Egypt in particular.

Summing up, this book comprises an enquiry into the impact of globalisation on migration from the point of view of marginalised countries. The analysis leads to the conclusion that Egyptian migration is a consequence of globalisation, and therefore is a relatively new phenomenon. This was achieved by first looking at the history of Egyptian migration (Chapter 4), and then at the profile of the Egyptian migrant both in theory and in practice

(Chapter 7). Egypt is increasingly becoming a source of permanent migration to the EU. This stands in contrast with a long tradition of stability of Egyptians, as well as a more recent tendency to migrate mainly within the regional borders of the Arab world.

To define the profile of the Egyptian migrant, the book has made reference to the results of field surveys conducted by the author on various occasions. The surveys have made it possible to claim that the characteristics of the Egyptian migrant are similar to those described by Piore/Bohning as the 'homo economicus' phase of the model of migration as a social process. This is typical of recent waves of migration. The Egyptian migrant to the EU is mainly a young man, motivated by economic considerations, and therefore more likely to take the risks of being smuggled illegally by organised crime into the host country. He is also willing to accept low standards of living, and jobs below his level of skills and education. This entails some consequences for the receiving countries.

The book shows that foreign born population in general, and people of Muslim religion in particular, live labour market conditions concealing instances of discrimination. They are indeed on average more unemployed than the native born population for each level of education. The most overrepresented in terms of unemployment rate are precisely migrants of Northern African origins. Moreover foreign-born labourers are on average employed in the low skilled agricultural and industrial sectors more than locally born workers, and they are also overqualified for their job placements (chapter 8).

The involvement of migrants in organised crime networks, and the fact that they do not care too much about their living conditions in the receiving countries, does increase the likelihood that migrants will find themselves embedded in illicit or illegal economic activities.

The findings of a research project financed by the EU support the hypothesis that the existence of the underground economy is a strong "pull" factor of migration to the EU. This is particularly true in the context of the "Fortress Europe" where borders are strictly closed (Chapter 3). There is a feedback process between undocumented migration and work opportunities in the underground economy which can hardly be underestimated. It is actually the engine allowing for the entry of illegal migrants to continue unhindered. Far from being an effect of illegal immigration, the submerged economy would appear to be one of its causes.

Moreover, the insertion of the vast majority of immigrants in the underground economy is one of the main reasons why European countries, especially southern ones, have adopted so quickly a very negative attitude towards a new phenomenon such as that of immigration. Working in an underground economy, as well as living without documents, contributes hugely both in marginalising migrants and in provoking migrants' negative attitudes towards local people.

This leads directly to the analysis of the issues relating to the myth and reality of migrants' "deviant behaviour".

In general, the fact that migrants can easily find work in the underground economy, as it is the case in Italy and in the other Mediterranean countries, is considered an incentive to "misbehave". In turn, however, the reaction of receiving societies is often a hostile one, to the extent that scholars have started talking about "Islamophobia" (chapter 9). Primary research shows that in European countries forms of discrimination hitting specifically Muslim communities as such predate the events of September the 11th. The ensemble of these discriminatory practices, ranging from education to political representation and from general legislation to gender has been referred to often as "Islamophobia".

A number of "Muslim voices" emerged across Europe as a consequence of the discrimination of Muslim communities in EU Member countries. These "Muslim voices" started making demands for equal access to social, economic and cultural resources, thus articulating the need for the recognition of a "Political Islam" not only at the national but also at the level of European Institutions.

It is however debatable whether the high number of similar Muslim associations can be considered a good measure of social capital.

Social capital cannot be identified uniquely with the number of Muslim associations or organisations, but has to be related to the development of trust between settlers' communities and existing local ones.

An example of how diversity and lack of integration has reduced the level of trust in host communities is clearly represented by the wave of social unrest hitting the French suburbs in 2005. The reasons why it happened, from the social capital perspective, are weak social networks and fragmentation in the local context, despite the existence of many Muslim associations at the national level. The solution to these issues have been identified by the creation of more social capital intended as a feeling of trust and belonging into a shared urban space and into a community of people sharing the same problems and devising common solutions to them.

Concluding, the roots of these new developments in the dynamics of migration from the MENA area are traced back in the paradox of marginalisation within globalisation, and in the paradox of regionalisation within globalisation (or lack of it). Indeed, Egypt has been progressively marginalised from the globalisation process (Chapter 6). This can be shown by looking at the main economic indicators of globalisation:

1. The level of FDI stock and flows
2. The amount of mergers and acquisition
3. The openness of the economy and the production for export.

The MENA area is certainly the one area of the world, together with Sub-Saharan Africa, that has experienced a decrease in its share of FDI stock in the last decades.

Despite an aggressive policy of liberalisation and privatisation that had begun in 1974 with the 'infitah' of Sadat, Egypt has to date been unable to attract substantial Foreign Direct Investment. Instead, both its share of FDI stock and its share of FDI inflows in the decade of the early 1990s/early 2000s have substantially decreased. Egypt is also very marginal in terms of mergers and acquisitions, and its trade openness remained very low indeed throughout the 1990s. This has occurred despite the country's undergoing a substantial process of reorganisation and stabilisation of its economy, under the supervision of the IMF and the World Bank, which has been successful to an extent in improving its macroeconomic performance. Nowadays, Egypt continues to rely heavily on remittances for the support of its economy, and these are coming increasingly from the most developed countries, firstly the US, and less and less from its Arab neighbours. Moreover, the MENA area is not integrated from the economic as well as political point of view. Also here, economic indicators are analysed in parallel with the account of the historical development of the creation of an integrated MENA area (Chapter 5).

The analysis of the attempts at regional economic integration as well as of the data presented leads to the conclusion that the integration of the MENA region is an oxymoron. Whereas other regions of the globe, most notably the three identified in the literature as the 'triad' – namely, Europe, the Americas and South Eastern Asia – have achieved high and increasing levels of economic and institutional integration, the Arab countries are still fundamentally divided between oil-exporting and labour-intense countries, as well as, within the first group, between the wealthy members of the GCC and other less affluent oil-exporters. Not even the solidarity among the Muslim 'Ummah' seems to have provided a stable path to integration. Indeed, aid capital flows within the region are mainly determined by geopolitical considerations and do not come exclusively, or even predominantly, from other Arab countries.

It seems possible to conclude that the MENA region is notably lacking economic and political integration in the wake of the globalisation era. The MENA region is a clear example of the paradox of lack of regionalisation within globalisation. Therefore, the wave of mass migration from the southern shores of the Mediterranean is very unlikely to cease in the near future.

At the macro level, the region would certainly benefit from the type of implementation by both destination and sending countries of policies which would allow MENA countries to catch up with the globalisation process. This may include education policies, especially as regards the use of new technologies in the creation of wealth, and policies aimed at attracting foreign business, such as infrastructural policies, as well as regional integration policies both from the economic and the political point of view. However, the implementation of similar policies may prove difficult.

Therefore, the best possible way to address the issue of illegal migration to Europe, in the impossibility of stopping migratory flows from marginalised countries, would be to legalise entry to the EU as a general rule. This is far from being the attitude adopted by the EU and by EU countries (chapter 3).

Notes

Introduction

1 See Chapter 3.
2 See Chapter 9.
3 See, for example, Boswell 2003; Guiraudon 2000; Huysmans 2000; Kostakopoulou 2001; Miles and Thränhardt 1995; Stetter 2000. See also Chapter 7 in this book.
4 See, for example, Gardezi 1995; Ghosh 1998; 2000; Sassen 1996; 1998; Weiner 1995.
5 See Chapter 1.
6 See Chapter 2.
7 The report of the project is available at the website of the Egyptian Ministry of Manpower and Migration, http://www.emigration.gov.eg/Publications/DisplayPublications.aspx/, as accessed on 1 September 2008.
8 See, for example, Gardezi 1995; Ghosh 1998; 2000; Sassen 1996; 1998.
9 A similar distinction is contained in Dicken 1998: 5.
10 See, for example, Hirst and Thompson 1999.
11 See, for example, Garret 1998.
12 See, for example, Mittleman 2000. For the relations between globalisation and migration, see, for example, Sassen 1998 and Weiner 1995.
13 For the debate on the definition of globalisation, see, for example, Hirst and Thompson 1999 and Mittleman 2000. For the relations between globalisation and migration, see, for example, Sassen 1998 and Weiner 1995. See also Chapters 1 and 2.
14 See Overbeek 2000.
15 Scholars refer to the 'triad' to indicate the three main zones of production of the globe: Asia-Pacific Region, America and Europe. See Hirst and Thompson 1999.
16 See Chapter 8.
17 See Geddes 2003.
18 See Huysmans 2000; also Ugur 2005.
19 For a detailed analysis of some EU member states' migratory policies, see Geddes 2003.
20 See Huysmans 2000; also, Guiraudon 2000.
21 See Cleland 1936: 36, 52.
22 For more information, see Eurostat 2000.

Chapter 1

1 See Brettel and Hollifield 2008.
2 Ibid.: Introduction and Ch. 1.
3 Ibid.: Introduction and Ch. 5.
4 Ibid.: Introduction and Ch. 3.
5 Ibid.: Introduction and Ch. 4.
6 Ibid.: Introduction and Ch. 2.
7 Ibid.: Introduction and Ch. 7.
8 Ibid.: Introduction and Ch. 7.
9 See Strange 1970.
10 For example, according to the Cumulative Book Index, the world bibliography of publication in the English language, in the period between 1953 and 1957, only three books were published under the label 'political economy'; see Whynes 1984: 1.
11 See Blake and Walters 1976.
12 See Spero 1977.
13 Ibid.
14 See Murphy and Tooze 1991: 4.
15 Ibid.: 3.
16 On the influence of perspectives in shaping policies, see also Gill and Law 1988.
17 Some noteworthy exceptions to this are represented, for example, by Cooper 1972; Paarlberg 1976; and Strange 1970.
18 See Gilpin's Preface to *The Political Economy of International Relations* (Gilpin 1987). See also Gill and Law 1988: xvii.
19 See Gilpin 1987: Preface.
20 Ibid.: 11.
21 See Milner 1993.
22 See Talani 2004.
23 See Putnam 1988.
24 See Keohane 1984: 18.
25 Ibid.: 22.
26 Ibid.: 25.
27 See Keohane 1986: 7.
28 See Milner 1992. For further details on the subject, see also Milner 1993.
29 See Gill and Law 1988.
30 Ibid.: 15.
31 Ibid.: 15.
32 In Murphy and Tooze 1991: 51–75.
33 For more details on this criticism, see ibid.: Ch. 1.
34 See Frey 1984.
35 See Murphy and Tooze 1991: 29.
36 Ibid.
37 See Strange 1991: 33.
38 Ibid.: 34.
39 See Cox 1981; also, Gill 1991.
40 '… the system under which credit is created, allocated and put to use' (Strange 1991: 35).

41 See Gill and Law (1988: 11): '... perspectives are not merely explanations of the global political economy, but are part of it.'
42 See Strange 1991.
43 See Cox 1983.
44 See Gill 1991.
45 Ibid.: 51.
46 Gramsci's historicism is characterised by three components: (i) transience – history and social change are cumulative, endless, yet non-repetitive processes; (ii) historical need – social interaction and political change take place within the *limiti del possibile* (limits of the possible), limits that, however, are not fixed and immutable, but exist within the dynamics of a given social structure; and (iii) a dialectical variant of philosophical realism which identifies the intellectual process as a creative, practical, yet open-ended and continuous engagement to explain an intractable social reality, not an ordered, perfectly rational one. Moreover, this process is dialectical, and is thus part of the historical process; it does not stand outside it. See Gill 1991: 56.
47 See Frey 1984.
48 See Gill 1991: 59.
49 See Börzel and Risse 2000.
50 For more details on this, see Risse-Kappen 1995: Introduction.
51 See Risse-Kappen 1996: 57.
52 Ibid.: 57.
53 See Weiner 1995.
54 Ibid.: 25.
55 Ibid.: 22.
56 See ibid.; also Brimlow 1995. For a different classification see Brettel and Hollifield 2008.
57 See Borjas 1990.
58 Ibid.
59 Contrary to the interpretation of Hollifield; see Brettel and Hollifield 2008: 202.
60 See Borjas 1990: Ch. 13.
61 Ibid.: 58.
62 For a similar criticism, see Brettel and Hollifield 2008.
63 See Freeman and Kessler 2008.
64 See Freeman 2008: 3.
65 See Freeman and Jupp 1992: 83.
66 Ibid.: 84.
67 See Freeman 1979: 255.
68 See Freeman and Jupp 1992: 17.
69 See Freeman 2008: Table 1.
70 Ibid.: 4.
71 See Freeman and Kessler 2008: 671.
72 See Freeman 2008: 11.
73 Ibid.: Conclusions and Implications.
74 See Freeman and Kessler 2008.
75 See Hollifield 2000.
76 See next section and Chapter 2.
77 See Hollifield 1992; 1998; 2000.

78 See Brettel and Hollifield 2008.
79 Ibid.: 195.
80 Ibid.: 196.
81 See Hollifield 2000.
82 Ibid.: 105.
83 See Soysal 1998.
84 See Soysal 2000.
85 See Ghosh 2000.
86 For a survey of the literature on migration and the EU, see: Boswell 2003; Geddes 2000a; 2000b; 2003; Guiraudon 2000; 2003; Huysmans 2000; Lahav 2004; Lavenex 2001; Lavenex and Ucarer 2002; Stetter 2000; Thielemann 2003; 2004.
87 See Thielemann 2008, lecture given at LSE.
88 See Geddes 2000b: 633.
89 'Securitisation' here means the transformation of migration and refugee policy into a security issue and the adoption of security-related tools to deal with it. See Huysmans 2000.
90 See Geddes 2000b: 646.
91 See Guiraudon 2000.
92 Ibid.: 264.
93 See Huysmans 2000.
94 See Lavenex 2001.
95 See the first section of this chapter.
96 See Castels and Davidson 2000; Castels and Miller 1998; Cornelius *et al.* 2004; Sassen 1991; 1996; 1999; 2006.
97 See Brettel and Hollifield 2008: 195.
98 See, for example, Sassen 1988; also, Castells 1975; Sassen 1981.
99 See Sassen 1988; also Sassen 1981: Ch. 4.

Chapter 2

1 UCLA, 7 November 2005.
2 A similar distinction is contained in Dicken 1998: 5.
3 See, for example, Hirst and Thompson 1999a.
4 See, for example, Garret 1998.
5 See, for example, Mittleman 2000. For the relationship between globalisation and migration, see, for example, Sassen 1998 and Weiner 1995.
6 See Holm and Sørensen 1995: 12.
7 See Mittleman 2000: Title.
8 For a more detailed analysis of this approach to globalisation, see the Conclusions in Talani 2004. See also Overbeek 2000.
9 For a similar interpretation, see Held and McGrew 2000: Introduction.
10 A particularly noteworthy example of this attitude may be found in Gilpin 2000.
11 See Gilpin 2001.
12 Ibid.: 364.
13 These claims are contained, albeit without data, ibid.: 368.
14 See Hirst and Thompson 1999a. In their Chapter 8, the authors set out

their position within the European Integration debate, clearly endorsing an intergovernmentalist vision of the EU. In particular: 'Some nation states will remain the crucial actors in constructing a political basis of consent for the macroeconomic policies of the Community': 253. See also Thompson 1993.

15 See Hirst and Thompson 1999a: Introduction.
16 See Hirst and Thompson 1999b: 140.
17 Ibid.: 141.
18 All relevant data may be found in Hirst and Thompson 1999a: Ch. 3.
19 Ibid.: Ch. 3.
20 See figures in Hirst and Thompson 1999b: 152.
21 Ibid.: 152.
22 Ibid.
23 See Hirst and Thompson 1999a: Ch. 3.
24 A similar interpretation is presented in Held and McGrew 2000: Introduction.
25 See Hirst and Thompson 1999b.
26 For a similar distinction, see Held and McGrew 2000: Introduction.
27 See Keohane 2000.
28 See Held and McGrew 2000: 3.
29 See Cerny 1999.
30 Ibid.
31 Ibid.
32 Ibid.: 99.
33 See Held *et al.* 1999.
34 See Cerny 1999: 101.
35 Ibid.
36 See Cerny 1999.
37 See Held and McGrew 2000: 12.
38 See Mittleman 2000; also Dicken 1998 and Overbeek 2000.
39 See Dicken 1998: 5.
40 See Mittleman 2000.
41 See Hirst and Thompson 1999a.
42 Giddens's lecture at UCLA on 7 November 2005 made clear that some technological transformations, such as the Internet, were devised outside the economic world – in this case, by the military and only after they became attractive for the markets.
43 See Overbeek 1995.
44 Ibid.
45 Ibid.
46 For the debate about commodification see, for example, Ertman and Williams 2005. See also Muchie and Li Xing 2006.
47 See Overbeek 2000.
48 See Shafik 1999.
49 See Overbeek 1995.
50 See, for example, Garret 1998.
51 See, for example, Held and McGrew 2000.
52 See Overbeek 2000.
53 See Dicken 2003.
54 As mentioned above, scholars refer to the 'triad' to indicate the three main

zones of production of the globe: the Asia-Pacific region, America and Europe.

55 See, for example, Breslin *et al.* 2002 and Hettne *et al.* 1999.
56 On this subject, see, for example, Murshed 2002.
57 See Chapter 8.
58 For a detailed analysis of the number of migrants necessary to cover the needs of EU member states, see United Nations 2001.
59 For a detailed analysis of some EU member states' migratory policies, see Geddes 2003.
60 See Geddes 2003. See also Chapter 3 in this book.
61 By 'securitisation', the experts mean the development of migration into a 'security issue', which has to be managed by security agencies such as, for example, Europol. See Huysmans 2000; also Guiraudon 2000.
62 See, for example, BBC 2004. See also Chapter 9 in this book.
63 See Overbeek 2000.
64 For data, see Ghosh 1999; also Harris 1995.
65 See Sassen 1998: xiii.
66 See Overbeek 2000.
67 See Ch. 5.

Chapter 3

1 See Geddes 2003.
2 See Huysmans 2000, also Ugur 1995.
3 For a detailed analysis of some EU Member States' migratory policies, see Geddes 2003.
4 See Huysmans 2000, also Guiraudon 2000.
5 See Huysmans 2000, also Guiraudon 2000 and Kostakopoulou 2000.
6 See Hollifield 1992; see also Baldwin-Edwards 1999: 9.
7 See Boswell 2003: 10.
8 Ibid.: 12.
9 See Hollifield 1992; see also Baldwin-Edwards 1999: 9.
10 See Boswell 2003: 15.
11 See Boswell 2003, Stetter 2000. For a different categorisation of the phases in the evolution of a common EU approach to migratory policy see Kostakopoulou 2000: 498.
12 See Stetter 2000.
13 See Ugur 1995: 967; see also Huysmans 2000.
14 See Ugur 1995: 974.
15 See Stetter 2000.
16 Ibid.: 86.
17 See http://ec.europa.eu/justice_home/fsj/customs/printer/fsj_customs_intro_en.htm, accessed 14 October 2008.
18 See Stetter 2000: 86.
19 See Supplement 3/76 to the Bulletin of the EC.
20 See www.europa.eu, accessed 14 October 2008.
21 Ibid.
22 Ibid.

23 Ibid.
24 See Stetter 2000.
25 See Guiraudon 2000: 256.
26 See Thielemann 2005/06 lecture at the LSE
27 See Kostakopoulou 2000; see also Huysmans 2000, Miles and Thränhardt 1995, and Ugur 1995.
28 For the text of the Convention see http://eur-lex.europa.eu/LexUriServ/LexUriServ.do?uri=CELEX:42000A0922(02):EN:HTML, accessed 11 November 2008.
29 See Huysmans 2000: 757.
30 See Preamble of the Schengen Agreement (http://www.garanteprivacy.it/garante/document?ID=33372, accessed 11 November 2008).
31 Ibid.: Article 30.
32 Ibid.: Articles 6/9.
33 Ibid.: Article 30.
34 See www.europa.eu, accessed 15 October 2008.
35 See Preamble of the Schengen Agreement.
36 Ibid: various Articles .
37 See www.europa.eu, accessed 15 October 2008.
38 For more details see the text of the Dublin Convention, available at http://www.europaworld.org/DEVPOLAWAR/Eng/Refugees/Refugees_DocC_eng.htm, accessed 14 October 2008.
39 See Huysmans 2000: 756.
40 For the full text see http://eur-lex.europa.eu/LexUriServ/LexUriServ.do?uri=CELEX:32003R0343:EN:HTML, accessed 15 October 2008.
41 See www.europa.eu, accessed 15 October 2008.
42 Ibid.
43 See Kostakopoulou 2001: 130.
44 See Geddes 2003: 135. This distinction, according to Geddes, is important; see also Geddes 2000: 94.
45 See art K1 of the TEU (Official Journal C 191, 29 July 1992), available at http://eur-lex.europa.eu/en/treaties/dat/11992M/htm/11992M.html#0001000001, accessed 11 November 2008.
46 See Guiraudon 2000: 257.
47 See Title 6 TEU (Official Journal C 191, 29 July 1992), available at http://eur-lex.europa.eu/en/treaties/dat/11992M/htm/11992M.html#0001000001, accessed 11 November 2008.
48 Ibid: article K4 TEU.
49 See Guiraudon 2000: 257.
50 See Title 6 TEU (Official Journal C 191, 29 July 1992), available at http://eur-lex.europa.eu/en/treaties/dat/11992M/htm/11992M.html#0001000001, accessed 11 November 2008.
51 See Geddes 2000: 108, Kostakopoulou 2000: 499.
52 See Section 3 of this chapter.
53 See Geddes 2000: 108.
54 Ibid.
55 See Huysmans 2000: 766.
56 Ibid.
57 See Kostakopoulou 2000.

58 Ibid.: 498.
59 Ibid.: 499.
60 See Articles 61/62/63 of the EC Treaty as amended by the Amsterdam Treaty, available at http://eur-lex.europa.eu/en/treaties/dat/11997E/htm/11997E.html#0173010078, accessed 27 October 2008.
61 See http://europa.eu/scadplus/leg/en/s22000.htm, accessed 27 October 2008.
62 Ibid.
63 See http://eur-lex.europa.eu/en/treaties/dat/11997E/htm/11997E.html#0173010078, accessed 27 October 2008.
64 Ibid.
65 See http://europa.eu/scadplus/leg/en/s22000.htm, accessed 27 October 2008.
66 See art 29 of the TEU, at http://eur-lex.europa.eu/en/treaties/dat/11997M/htm/11997M.html#0145010077, accessed 27 October 2008.
67 Ibid.
68 For further information see http://europa.eu/scadplus/leg/en/s22000.htm, accessed 27 October 2008.
69 See Kostakopoulou 2000: 505. See also Ucarer 2002: 29.
70 See Geddes 2000: 129, Huysmans 2000: 756, Ucarer 2002: 29.
71 See Geddes 2000: 129.
72 See Huysmans 2000: 756.
73 See Geddes 2000: 130.
74 See Lavenex 1998.
75 For more information see http://europa.eu/scadplus/leg/en/lvb/l33105.htm, accessed 27 October 2008.
76 European Council and European Commission (1998): 1–2, quoted in Kostakoupolou 2000: 507.
77 See http://www.europarl.europa.eu/facts/4_11_1_en.htm, accessed 27 October 2008.
78 For more information see http://ec.europa.eu/justice_home/news/information_dossiers/the_hague_priorities/index_en.htm, accessed 27 October 2008.
79 See http://www.europarl.europa.eu/facts/4_11_1_en.htm, accessed 27 October 2008.
80 See Barnard 2007, Handoll 1995, Martin and Guild 1996, Peers 2001.
81 See Handoll 1995: 61.
82 See Peers 2001: 291. For more information see Handoll 1995: Chapters 3–8.
83 Ibid.: 292. For more information see Handoll 1995: Chapters 3–8.
84 Ibid. For more information see Handoll 1995: Chapters 3–8.
85 Ibid. For more information see Handoll 1995: Chapters 3–8.
86 Ibid.: 293. For more information see Handoll 1995: Chapters 3–8.
87 Ibid.: 292. For more information see Handoll 1995: Chapters 3–8.
88 Ibid.: 295. For more information see Handoll 1995: Chapters 3–8.
89 Ibid.: 296–297. For more information see Handoll 1995: Chapters 11–12
90 See Handoll 1995: 371.
91 Ibid.: 372.
92 Ibid.: 373.
93 Ibid.: 373–77.

94 Ibid.: 377–80.
95 See Peers 2001: 297.
96 See Handoll 1995: 369.
97 See Peers 2001: 297–98.
98 For more information see http://europa.eu/scadplus/leg/en/lvb/l33126.htm, accessed 6 November 2008.
99 For more information see http://europa.eu/scadplus/leg/en/lvb/l33118.htm, accessed 6 November 2008.
100 See Peers 2001.
101 See Handoll 1995: 317–23.
102 Ibid.: 323–29.
103 Ibid.: 329.
104 Ibid.: 329–36.
105 Ibid.: 336–40.
106 Ibid.: 340–43.
107 See Peers 2001: 299, note 28.
108 See art. 13 (Migration) of the Partnership agreement between the Members of the African, Caribbean and Pacific groups of States of the one part and the European Community and its Member States of the other part, available at http://ec.europa.eu/development/icenter/repository/agr01_en.pdf,accessed 6 November 2008.
109 See Huysmans 2000; see also Guiraudon 2000, Kostakopoulou 2000.
110 See Guiraudon 2000.
111 Ibid.: 264.
112 See Lavenex 2001.
113 See the first section of this chapter.
114 See Kostakopoulou 2000: 515.

Chapter 4

1 See Cleland 1936: 36, 52.
2 See Oweiss 1980.
3 As with all Egyptian emigration statistics, a wide range of estimates is available. Some report a figure of 100,000 working abroad in 1965. See Sell 1987.
4 Ibid.: 28.
5 See Ibrahim 1982: 66.
6 See Feiler 2003.
7 See Dessouki 1982, quoted in Feiler 2003: 105.
8 See Feiler 2003.
9 See Zohry and Harrell-Bond 2003.
10 See Sell 1987.
11 See Zohry and Harrell-Bond 2003.
12 See Egyptian Ministry of Manpower and Emigration 2008.
13 See Feiler 2003.
14 See Section 3 below.
15 For all information relating to the current institutions in charge of migration issues in Egypt, see Sawi 1995.
16 See Choucri 1978. There are occasional comments on the contrary: see Birks and Sinclair 1979, Bohning 1984: 67.

17 See Cleland 1936: 36.
18 See Amin 2000: 95.
19 See Amin 2000, Appleyard 1999, Dessouki 1982, Feiler 2003, Zohry and Harrell-Bond 2003.
20 For an analysis of internal social mobility in Egypt in the Nasser and Sadat era, see Binder 1978. For an analysis of the social background of Islamist movements in Egypt, see Kepel 1999.
21 See Amin 2000: 96–7.
22 For a review of the literature on Egyptian migration between 1974 and 1984, see Seccombe 1985.
23 See Sell 1987.
24 See Ibrahim 1982: 65.
25 See Zahlan 1999.
26 See Zohry and Harrell-Bond 2003.
27 See Amin 2000: 96–7.
28 See Zahlan 1999.
29 See Zohry and Harrell-Bond 2003.
30 Ibid.
31 See Zahlan 1999.
32 For a similar interpretation, see Russell 1992: 721.
33 See Zahlan 1999; Russell estimates this number to be a bit less than one million (1992).
34 See Zahlan 1999.
35 See Zohry and Harrell-Bond 2003.
36 See Russell 1992.
37 Russell (1992: 721) refers to the case of Egyptians substituting between 750,000 and 850,000 Yemeni migrants in Saudi Arabia after Yemen decided to back Iraq in the Gulf War.
38 See ILO 2008.
39 Nassar (2005) divides the period between 1989 and 2000 into three phases: one between 1989 and 1991; the second between 1992 and 1997 (characterised by a sharp increase in numbers of emigrants from Egypt); and the last between 1997 and 2000, witnessing a new decline. However, the author of this book does not agree with dividing such a short period into three phases, as the variations in numbers can be temporary and vary according to the sources.
40 On the lack of reliability of Egyptian statistics on migration, see Fargues 2007: Part 1.
41 The figures proposed by the ILO are the same as CAPMAS; see ILO 2008.
42 See Egyptian Ministry for Manpower and Emigration 2008.
43 See Zohry and Harrell-Bond 2003.
44 Personal source within the IOM/Egyptian Ministry of Manpower and Emigration.
45 See Egyptian Ministry of Manpower and Emigration 2008.
46 See OECD 2008.
47 See later discussions in this chapter.
48 See *Migration News*, 11/1, January 2004.
49 See *Migration News*, various issues (http://migration.ucdavis.edu/mn/pastissues_mn.html, accessed 15 October 2008).

50 See Ministeria del Interior 2001. See also *Migration News*, various issues.
51 See *Migration News*, various issues.
52 See El Pais 2001.
53 See *Migration News*, 8/1, January, 2001.
54 See *Migration News*, 13/4, October 2006.
55 See El Pais 2001.
56 See *Migration News*, various issues.
57 Ibid.
58 Ibid.
59 Acuerdo Sobre Mano de Obra Entre al Reino de Espagna y el Reino de Marrueccos BOE no. 226 20.09.2001.
60 See Collyer 2004: 39.
61 See *Migration News* , various issues.
62 See Eurostat 2001.
63 See IOM 2005.
64 See Panorama 2003.
65 See *The New York Times*, 4 January 2001.
66 Ibid.
67 Ibid.
68 See *Panorama* 2003.
69 Personal experience of the author.
70 See IOM 2005: 55.
71 For news on deportation of Egyptians from Lampedusa and Sicily, see VR Sicilia 2008.
72 See IOM 2005: 55.
73 See *La Repubblica* 2008.
74 See Zohry 2007.
75 See IOM 2005.
76 See *The New York Times* 2000.
77 Ibid.
78 Ibid.
79 See Morris 2001.
80 See *The New York Times* 2000.
81 Ibid.
82 Ibid.
83 For more details on the smuggling of Chinese nationals via Belgrade see IOM 2000.
84 Ibid.
85 See Bomford 2001.
86 See IOM 2000.
87 See Carroll 2001.
88 See Skeldon 2000.
89 For more information on the subject see IOM 2000.
90 See Morris, Kaya and Beaumont 2001. See also Travis 2001.
91 Ibid.
92 See BBC 2007.
93 IOM 2005; for more information on Egypt as a transit country for illegal migrants, see Roman 2006.

Chapter 5

1 See Chapters 1 and 2 of this book.
2 See Hirst and Thompson 1999.
3 See Chapter 2 of this book.
4 See, for example, Dodge and Higgot 2002; also Hakimian and Moshaver 2001 and Hudson 1999.
5 Following the World Economic Outlook (IMF) convention, a country is classified as an oil exporter if its oil export earnings during the period 1994–98 constituted more than 50 per cent of total export earnings.
6 See IMF 2003.
7 For an analysis of the reasons underlying the lack of integration of the ME area, see Kubursi 1999.
8 For a useful reference on this issue, see Hudson 1999.
9 Ibid.: 1.
10 For an historical account of the development of intraregional economic relations in the Middle East and North Africa, see Owen 1999: Ch. 10; also Owen and Pamuk 1999.
11 See Dodge and Higgot 2002, Owen 1999, Owen and Pamuk 1999.
12 See Owen 1999, Owen and Pamuk 1999.
13 See Owen 1999.
14 See Diab 1963: Chs 1 and 2, Musrey 1969: Chs 5 and 6, quoted in Owen 1999.
15 See Owen and Pamuk 1999.
16 See Sayigh 1999: Ch. 11.
17 See Diab 1963: Ch. 4, as quoted in Owen 1999.
18 See Sayigh 1983: 147–55.
19 See next section.
20 See Owen and Pamuk 1999.
21 See Owen 1999.
22 See Owen and Pamuk 1999.
23 See Owen 1999.
24 Ibid.
25 See Sayigh 1999.
26 See Owen 1999.
27 See figures in section below.
28 See Sayigh 1999.
29 For a more detailed analysis of reasons behind the developments in the MENA region economic integration process, see Owen and Pamuk 1999.
30 See Owen 1999: 227.
31 See, for example, Junemann 2004a.
32 See Chapter 3. Securitisation here means the transformation of migration and refugee policy into a security issue, and the adoption of security-related tools to deal with it. See Huysmans 2000; also, Junemann 2004c.
33 See Grunert 2004.
34 See Gillespie 2004.
35 See Junemann 2004b.
36 See Stetter 2004; also, Asseburg 2004.
37 See Tovias 2004.

38 See Chorou 2004.
39 See Zahlan 1999: Ch. 12.
40 See UNCTAD 2008.
41 A review is presented in Fazio 2009.
42 See Al-Atreash and Yousef 1999.
43 See Honohan and Lane 2000, Masson 2007, Subramanian and Tamirisa 2003
44 See Fazio 2009.
45 See Zahlan 1999.
46 See Zahlan 1999; for an analysis of remittances to Egypt, see Chapter 5.
47 See Harrigan, Wang and Said 2005: 247–70.
48 See United Nations ESCWA 2007: 7.
49 See Arab Monetary Fund 2008.
50 See UN ESCWA 2007: 7.
51 Ibid. DAC countries are the members of the Development Assistance Committee (DAC).
52 Ibid.: 8.
53 Ibid.
54 Ibid.
55 Ibid.

Chapter 6

1 For a detailed analysis of the issue of marginalisation of the Middle East within globalisation, see Dodge and Higgot 2002; also Hakimian and Moshaver 2001 and Fawcett and Sayigh 1999.
2 See Chapter 2.
3 See Ayubi 1999: 339; also, Owen and Pamuk 1999.
4 See Khyeda 2007: 73–104.
5 See Ayubi 1999.
6 See next section.
7 See Khyeda 2007.
8 See Ayubi 1999: 346–7.
9 See next section.
10 Lending arrangements, which are similar to a line of credit, are approved by the IMF Executive Board to support a country's adjustment programme. The arrangement requires the member to observe specific terms in order to be eligible to receive a disbursement. The IMF lends under Stand-by and Extended arrangements, and, at reduced rates, under Poverty Reduction and Growth Facility arrangements. See IMF 2008.
11 See Ayubi 1999: 346–7.
12 The crisis following 11 September 2001 led to a marked devaluation of the Egyptian pound (see Figure 6.6). Hence, from January 2003, the Egyptian pound was allowed to float. On 1 February 2005, Egypt's exchange rate was reclassified to a conventional peg from a managed float with no predetermined path for the exchange rate. Since July 2007, the de facto exchange arrangement has been akin to a managed float. See IMF 2008.
13 For reasons why FDI did not materialise, see Ayubi 1999: 341.
14 See IMF 2008.

15 For an analysis of the relation between remittances and monetary aggregates in Egypt, see Nassar 2005.
16 See UNCTAD 2008.
17 See Chapter 2.
18 See Chapter 2.
19 See UN 2008. The UN identifies 41 core ICT indicators, divided into four groups as follows:

    1 ICT infrastructure and access (12 indicators, see Annex 2);
    2 access to, and use of, ICT by households and individuals (13 indicators, see Annex 3);
    3 use of ICT by businesses (12 indicators, see Annex 4);
    4 the ICT sector and trade in ICT goods (four indicators, see Annex 5).

Chapter 7

1 See Sell 1987; see also Bohning 1984, Castells 1975 and Piore 1979.
2 See Bohning 1984: 71.
3 Ibid.: 141; see also Piore 1979: 61.
4 See Castells 2000.
5 See Sell 1987: 37.
6 Ibid.: 45.
7 See Piore 1979.
8 See Bohning 1984.
9 See Talani 2003.
10 For more information, see Eurostat 2000.
11 See CAPMAS 1991. The author makes reference to the CAPMAS survey of 1987, as it is the most comprehensive. More recent data on the characteristics of the Egyptian migrant can be found in Eurostat 2000. The data of the more recent survey, which focuses only on return migrants, are very similar to those of CAPMAS 1991, however.
12 See Talani 2003: 39.
13 See IOM 2003.
14 For more detail on this see Chapter 8.
15 The survey is called 'Attitudes of Egyptian Youth toward Migration to Europe' (2006). The data reported in this article are based on the tables of the survey, which have been published at Egyptian Ministry of Manpower and Emigration 2006. A more extensive analysis of those data is contained in Zohry 2006.
16 See Egyptian Ministry of Manpower and Emigration 2006.
17 See also Chapter 4.
18 See Egyptian Ministry of Manpower and Emigration 2006.
19 For a general analysis of the insertion of migrants in the underground economies especially of southern European countries, see Chapter 8.
20 See Talani 2006.
21 Ibid.
22 Ibid.
23 See also Chapter 4
24 See Geddes 2000.

25 See Talani 2006.
26 Ibid.

Chapter 8

1 See, for example, Boswell 2003, Guiraudon 2000, Huysmans 2000, Kostakopoulou 2001, Miles and Thränhardt 1995, Stetter 2000.
2 See OECD 2008.
3 Ibid.: 150.
4 Ibid.: 114.
5 Ibid.
6 Ibid.: 138.
7 Ibid.
8 See Nassar 2005: 7.
9 Ibid.
10 Ibid.: 8.
11 They consider an informal or underground economy as 'all incoming earning activities not regulated by the state in social environments where similar activities are regulated'. The illegal economy is instead represented by those activities which are against the law. See Reyneri 1999a: 16.
12 Ibid.
13 Ibid.
14 Ibid.: 2.
15 Ibid.: 2.
16 All sources agree in estimating that the level of the underground economy in Greece, Italy and Portugal is much higher than in all the other European countries. See Reyneri 1999a: 19. See also Baldwin-Edwards and Arango 1999.
17 See Reyneri and Baganha 1999: 5–7.
18 See Esping-Anderson 1999.
19 See Esping-Anderson 1999, Rhodes 1997.
20 See Reyneri and Baganha 1999.
21 See Palidda, Frangoulis and Papantoniou 1999.
22 See Solé 1999.
23 See Wilpert and Laacher 1999.
24 See also Baldwin-Edwards and Arango 1999.
25 See also Reyneri 1999b: 84.
26 See Reyneri 1999a: 21.
27 Ibid.
28 Ibid.: 20–22.
29 See also Reyneri 1999b: 88.
30 Ibid.
31 See UN ODCCP 2001.
32 See *The New York Times* 2000.
33 See Talani 2004.
34 See also Zincone 1999.
35 See Reyneri 1999a: 24.
36 Ibid.

37 Ibid.: 25.
38 Ibid.: 21.
39 See Rowlands 1998.
40 See Reyneri 1999a: 7–14.
41 Ibid.: 26.
42 See Palidda, Frangouli and Papantoniou 1999: 123–83.
43 See Reyneri 1999a: 26.
44 See *Corriere Romano* 2008.
45 See Reyneri 1999: 27.
46 Ibid.
47 Ibid.
48 Ibid.: 1.
49 Ibid.: Conclusions.
50 These conclusions were contained in the evaluation report by the author: Talani 2002: 11.
51 Ibid.
52 See Reyneri 1999a: 29.
53 See Talani 2002: 12–13.

Chapter 9

1 See Glavanis 1999.
2 Ibid.: 7–12.
3 Ibid.: 12–15.
4 Ibid.
5 Ibid.: 25–38.
6 See Halliday 1996.
7 See Glavanis 1999: 38–61.
8 Ibid.: Conclusion.
9 Ibid.: 66–67.
10 Ibid.: 67.
11 Ibid.: 61–85.
12 Ibid.: 81.
13 See later in this chapter.
14 Glavanis 1999: Conclusion.
15 Ibid.: 71.
16 Ibid.: 71.
17 The Runnymede Trust Commission on British Muslims and Islamophobia (1997).
18 Ibid.
19 See Glavanis 1999: 72.
20 Ibid.: 75.
21 Ibid.
22 Ibid.: 81.
23 Ibid.
24 Ibid.
25 Ibid.: 85.
26 Ibid.

27 Ibid.: 86.
28 Ibid.: 93.
29 Ibid.: 99.
30 Ibid.
31 Ibid.: 100.
32 Ibid.: 103.
33 Ibid.: 104.
34 Ibid.: 107.
35 Ibid.
36 Ibid.
37 Ibid.: 110.
38 Ibid.: 111.
39 Ibid.
40 Ibid.
41 Ibid.
42 Ibid.: 112–15.
43 Ibid.: 111.
44 Ibid.: 115–19.
45 Ibid.: 115–19.
46 See Putnam 2000: 19.
47 See Bourdieu 1980: 2–3.
48 See Coleman 1988.
49 See Putnam 2002: 3.
50 Ibid.: 6.
51 See Worms 2002: 138.
52 See Knack and Keefer 1997, Tabellini 2005.
53 See Glaeser *et al.* 2002.
54 See Knack and Keefer 1997.
55 See Glaeser *et al.* 2002.
56 See Knack and Keefer 1997.
57 See Brehm and Rahn 1997.
58 See Knack and Keefer 1997.
59 See Body-Gendrot 2007a: 5.
60 Ibid.: 9.
61 See Worms 2002 and Putnam 2002.
62 See Body-Gendrot 2007b.
63 See Worms 2002: 136.
64 See Cerny 1999.
65 Ibid.: 101, Chapter 2.
66 Ibid.: 101.
67 Ibid.
68 See Worms 2002: 137.
69 Ibid.
70 See Putnam 2002: 398.
71 Ibid.
72 See Worms 2002.
73 See *Liste des Associations reconnues d'utilité publique*. Available at: http://www.interieur.gouv.fr/sections/a_la_une/publications/cultes-associations/associations200703/view, accessed 7 February 2007.

74 See *Liste des Fondations reconnues d'utilité publique*. Available at: http://www.interieur.gouv.fr/sections/a_la_une/publications/cultes-associations/fondations200703/view, accessed 7 February 2007.
75 See *Liste des fondations d'entreprise 2007*. Available at: http://www.interieur.gouv.fr/sections/a_la_une/publications/cultes-associations/liste-fondations-entreprise/view, accessed 7 February 2007.
76 See *Rapport 2006 de la Mission Interministerielle de Vigilance et de Lutte contre les Dérives Sectaires*. Available at: http://www.interieur.gouv.fr/sections/a_la_une/publications/cultes-associations/rapport-2006-miviludes/view, accessed 7 February 2007.
77 Available at: http://www.interieur.gouv.fr/misill/sections/a_la_une/publications/collectivites-locales/publications-dgcl/view, accessed 7 February 2007.
78 See http://www.insee.fr/en/ffc/accueil_ffc.asp?theme=5, accessed 7 February 2007.
79 Ibid.
80 See Baromètre Politique Français (2006–07).
81 See Salamon *et al.* 2004.
82 See Febvre and Muller 2003.
83 See Body-Gendrot 2007a.
84 See Body-Gendrot 2007b.
85 Ibid.: 12.
86 Ibid.: 15.
87 See Sennet 1996.
88 See Putnam 2002: 398.
89 See Body-Gendrot 2007b: 5.
90 Ibid.: 15.
91 Ibid.: 4–5.
92 See Body-Gendrot 2007a: 17–18.

References

Introduction

Boswell, C. (2003) *European Migration Policies in Flux: Changing Patterns of Inclusion and Exclusion*. Blackwell and RIIA, Oxford.

Cleland, W. (1936) *The Population Problem in Egypt: A Study of Population Trends and Conditions in Modern Egypt*. Science Press Printing Company, Lancaster, PA.

Dicken, P. (1998) *Global Shift*. Paul Chapman Publishing Ltd, London.

Dodge, T. and Higgot, R. (2002) *Globalisation and the Middle East*. The Royal Institute of International Affairs, London.

Eurostat (2000) Push and Pull Factors of International Migration. Country Report: Egypt, *Population and Social Conditions*, working paper 3/2000/E/n.7.

Gardezi, Hassan (1995) *The Political Economy of International Labor Migration*. Black Rose Books, Montreal.

Garret, G. (1998) *Partisan Politics in the Global Economy*. Cambridge University Press, Cambridge.

Geddes, A. (2003) *The Politics of Migration and Immigration in Europe*. Sage, London.

Ghosh, B. (1998) *Huddled Masses and Uncertain Shores: Insights into Irregular Migration*. Martinus Nijhoff Publishers, London.

Ghosh, B. (2000) *Managing Migration: Time for a New International Regime*. Oxford University Press, Oxford.

Giraudon, V. (2000) European Integration and Migration Policy, *JCMS*, 38/2, 251–72.

Hakimian, H. and Moshaver, Z. (2001) *The State and Global Change: The Political Economy of Transition in the Middle East and North Africa*. Curzon Press, Richmond.

Hirst, P. and Thompson, G. (1999) *Globalization in Question*. Polity Press, Cambridge.

Huysmans, J. (2000) The European Union and the Securitization of Migration, *JCMS*, 38/5, 751–77.

Kostakopoulou, D. (2001) *Citizenship, Identity, and Immigration in the European Union: Between Past and Future*. MUP, New York (MC: JN30 K81).

Miles, R. and Thränhardt, D. (eds) (1995) *Migration and European Integration: The Dynamics of Inclusion and Exclusion*. Pinter, London.

Mittleman, J.H. (2000) *The Globalization Syndrome: Transformation and Resistance*. Princeton University Press, Princeton.

Overbeek, H. (2000) Globalisation, Sovereignty and Transnational Regulation: Reshaping the Governance of International Migration. In: Ghosh, Bimal (ed.) *Managing Migration: Time for a New International Regime.* Oxford University Press, Oxford, pp. 48–74

Sassen, S. (1996) *Losing Control.* Columbia University Press, New York.

Sassen, S. (1998) *Globalization and its Discontents.* New York Press, New York.

Stetter, S. (2000) Regulating Migration: Authority Delegation in Justice and Home Affairs, *JEPP*, 7/1, 80–102.

Ugur, M. (1995) Freedom of Movement vs. Exclusion: A Reinterpretation of the 'Insider'–'Outsider' Divide in the European Union, *International Migration Review*, 29/4, 964–99.

Weiner, M. (1995) *The Global Migration Crisis: Challenge to States and Human Rights.* HarperCollins College Publishers, New York.

Chapter 1 Migration in theory

Blake, D.H. and Walters, R.S. (1976) *The Politics of Global Economic Relations.* Prentice Hall, Englewood Cliffs, NJ.

Borjas, G.J. (1990) *Friends or Strangers.* Basic Books, New York.

Börzel, T.A. and Risse, T. (2000) Who is Afraid of a European Federation? How to Constitutionalise a Multi-Level Governance System (paper part of contributions to the Jean Monnet Working Paper). At: http://www.jeanmonnetprogram.org/papers/00/00f0101.html, accessed 10 December 2008.

Boswell, C. (2003) *European Migration Policies in Flux: Changing Patterns of Inclusion and Exclusion.* Blackwell and RIIA, Oxford.

Brettel, C.B. and Hollifield, J.F. (2008) *Migration Theory: Talking Across Disciplines,* second edition. Routledge, London.

Brimlow, P. (1995) *Alien Nation.* Random House, New York.

Castells, M. (1975) Immigrant Workers and Class Struggles in Advanced Capitalism: The Western European Experience. *Politics and Society*, 5, 33–66.

Castels, S. and Davidson, A. (2000) *Citizenship and Migration: Globalisation and the Politics of Belonging.* Macmillan, London.

Castels, S. and Miller, M. (1998) *The Age of Migration: International Population Movements in the Modern World.* Guilford, New York.

Cooper, R.N. (1972) Trade Policy is Foreign Policy. *Foreign Policy*, 9, 18–26.

Cornelius, W.A., Tsuda, T., Martin, P.L. and Hollifield, J.F. (2004) *Controlling Immigration: A Global Perspective*, second edition. Stanford University Press, Stanford, CA.

Cox, R.W. (1981) Social Forces, States and World Orders: Beyond International Relations Theory. *Millennium: Journal of International Studies*, 10/2, 126–55.

Cox, R.W. (1983) Gramsci, Hegemony and International Relations: An Essay in Method. *Millennium: Journal of International Studies*, 12/2, 162–75.

Freeman, G.P. (1979) *Immigrant Labour and Racial Conflict in Industrial Societies.* Princeton University Press, Princeton.

Freeman, G.P. (2008) Migration and the Political Sustainability of Welfare States. At: http://cartss.colorado.edu/Freeman.doc, accessed on 23 June 2008.

Freeman, G.P. and Jupp, J. (1992) *Nations of Immigrants*. Oxford University Press, Oxford.

Freeman, G.P. and Kessler, A.K. (2008) Political Economy and Migration Policy. *Journal of Ethnic and Migration Studies*, 34/4, 655–78.

Frey, B.S. (1984) *International Political Economy*. Basil Blackwell, Oxford and New York.

Geddes, A. (2000a) *Immigration and European Integration: Towards the Fortress Europe?* Manchester University Press, Manchester.

Geddes, A. (2000b) Lobbying for Migrant Inclusion in the European Union. *JEPP*, 7/4, 632–49.

Geddes, A. (2003) *The Politics of Migration and Immigration in Europe*. Sage, London.

Ghosh, B. (2000) *Managing Migration*. Oxford University Press, Oxford.

Gill, S. (1991) Historical Materialism, Gramsci and International Political Economy. In: Murphy and Tooze (1991), pp. 51–75.

Gill, S. and Law, D. (1988) *The Global Political Economy: Perspectives, Problems and Policies*. Harvester-Wheatsheaf, London.

Gilpin, R. (1987) *The Political Economy of International Relations*. Princeton University Press, Princeton.

Guiraudon, V. (2000) European Integration and Migration Policy. *JCMS*, 38/2, 251–72.

Guiraudon, V. (2003) The Constitution of a European Immigration Policy Domain. *JEPP*, 10/2, 263–82.

Hollifield, J.F. (1992) *Immigrants, Markets and States: The Political Economy of Postwar Europe*. Harvard University Press, Cambridge, MA.

Hollifield, J.F. (1998) Migration, Trade and the Nation State: The Myth of Globalization. *UCLA Journal of International Law and Foreign Affairs*, 3/2, 595–636.

Hollifield, J.F. (2000) Migration and the 'New' International Order: The Missing Regime. In: Ghosh (2000).

Huysmans, J. (2000) The European Union and the Securitization of Migration. *JCMS*, 38/5, 751–77.

Keohane, R.O. (1984) *After Hegemony: Cooperation and Discord in the World Political Economy*. Princeton University Press, Princeton.

Keohane, R.O. (1986) Realism, Neorealism and the Study of World Politics. In: Keohane, R.O. (ed.), *Neorealism and its Critics*. Columbia University Press, New York, 1–26.

Lahav, G. (2004) *Immigration and Politics in the New Europe: Reinventing Borders*. Cambridge University Press, Cambridge.

Lavenex, S. (2001) Migration and the EU's New Eastern Border. *JEPP*, 8/1, 24–42.

Lavenex, S. and Ucarer, E. (eds) (2002) *Migration and the Externalities of European Integration*. Rowman & Littlefield, Lanham, MD.

Milner, H. (1992) Theories of Cooperation. *World Politics*, 44, 427–95.

Milner, H. (1993) The Assumption of Anarchy in International Relations Theory: A Critique. In: Baldwin, D.A. (1993) *Neo-realism and Neo-liberalism: The Contemporary Debate*. Columbia University Press, New York.

Murphy, C.N. and Tooze, R. (1991) *The New International Political Economy*. Lynne Rienner Publishers, Boulder, CO.

Paarlberg, R. (1976) Domesticating Global Management. *Foreign Affairs*, 54/3, 563–76.

Putnam, R. (1988) Diplomacy and Domestic Politics. *International Organization*, 42/3, 427–60.

Risse-Kappen, T. (1995) *Bringing Transnational Relations Back In: Non-State Actors, Domestic Structures and International Institutions*. Cambridge University Press, Cambridge.

Risse-Kappen, T. (1996) Exploring the Nature of the Beast: International Relations Theory and Comparative Policy Analysis meet the European Union. *Journal of Common Market Studies*, 34/1, 53-80.

Sassen, S. (1981) *Exporting Capital and Importing Labor: The Role of Caribbean Migration to New York City*. New York University Press, New York.

Sassen, S. (1988) *The Mobility of Labour and Capital.* Cambridge University Press, Cambridge.

Sassen, S. (1991) *The Global City: New York, London, Tokyo*. Princeton University Press, Princeton.

Sassen, S. (1996) *Losing Control? Sovereignty in the Age of Globalization*. Columbia University Press, New York.

Sassen, S. (1999) *Guests and Aliens*. The New Press, New York.

Sassen, S. (2006) *Territory, Authority, Rights: From Medieval to Global Assemblages*. Princeton University Press, Princeton.

Soysal, Y. (1998) Towards a Post-national Model of Membership. In: Shafir, G. (ed.) *The Citizenship Debates: A Reader*. University of Minnesota Press, Minneapolis, pp. 189–220.

Soysal, Y.N. (2000) Citizenship and Identity: Living in Diasporas in Post-war Europe? *Ethnic and Racial Studies*, 23/1, 1–15.

Spero, J.E. (1977) *The Politics of International Economic Relations*. George Allen & Unwin, London.

Stetter, S. (2000) Regulating Migration: Authority Delegation in JHA. *JEPP*, 7/1, 80–103.

Strange, S. (1970) International Economics and International Relations: A Case of Mutual Neglect. *International Affairs*, 46/2, 304–15.

Strange, S. (1991) An Eclectic Approach. In: Murphy and Tooze (1991), pp. 33-49.

Talani, L.S. (2004) *European Political Economy. Political Science Perspectives*. Ashgate, London.

Thielemann, E.R. (ed.) (2003) European Burden-Sharing and Forced Migration. *Journal of Refugee Studies* (special issue), 16/2.

Thielemann, E.R. (2004) Why European Policy Harmonization Undermines Refugee Burden-Sharing. *European Journal of Migration and Law*, 6/1, 43–61.

Thielemann, E.R. (2008) Various lectures given at the London School of Economics, author's notes.

Weiner, M. (1995) *The Global Migration Crisis: Challenge to States and Human Rights*. HarperCollins College Publishers, New York.

Whynes, D.K. (1984) *What is Political Economy? Eight Perspectives*. Basil Blackwell, Oxford.

Chapter 2 The globalisation thesis within the globalisation debate

BBC (2004) Children Ask: 'Is Terrorism Allowed in Islam?' The Attacks in America on 11th September 2001 Shocked the World. At: http://www.bbc.co.uk/print/bristol/content/faith/2004/03/11/911.shtml, accessed 17 May 2008.

Breslin, S., Hughes, C.W., Philis, N. and Rosamond, B. (2002) *New Regionalisms in the Global Political Economy*. Routledge, London.

Cerny, P. (1999) Reconstructing the Political in a Globalising World. In: Buelens, F., *Globalisation and the Nation State*. Edward Elgar, Cheltenham.

Dicken, P. (1998) *Global Shift: Transforming the World Economy*. Paul Chapman Publishing, London.

Dicken, P. (2003) *Global Shift: Reshaping the Global Economic Map in the 21st Century*. Sage, London.

Ertman, M.M. and Williams, J.C. (eds) (2005) *Rethinking Commodification: Cases and Readings in Law and Culture*, New York University Press, New York. At: http://ssrn.com/abstract=582641, accessed on 11 November 2008.

Garret, G. (1998) *Partisan Politics in the Global Economy*. Cambridge University Press, Cambridge.

Geddes, A. (2003) *The Politics of Migration and Immigration in Europe*. Sage Publications, London.

Ghosh, B. (1999) *Challenges and Opportunities of Economic Globalisation: Some Implications for Labour, Industry and Nation States*, paper prepared for Bundesanstalt für Arbeit workshop, 'Internationalisierung der Arbeitsmarkte', 27–28 April, Frankfurt a/M.

Gilpin, R. (2000) *The Challenges of Global Capitalism: The World Economy in the 21st Century*. Princeton University Press, Princeton.

Gilpin, R. (2001) *Global Political Economy: Understanding the Global Economic Order*. Princeton University Press, Princeton and Oxford.

Guiraudon, V. (2000) European Integration and Migration Policy: Vertical Policy-making as Venue Shopping. *Journal of Common Market Studies*, 38/2, 251–71.

Harris, N. (1995) *The New Untouchables: Immigration and the New World Worker*. Penguin, London.

Held, D. and McGrew, A. (2000) *The Global Transformations Reader*. Polity Press, Cambridge.

Held, D., McGrew, A., Goldblatt, D. and Perraton, J. (1999) *Global Transformation*. Polity Press, Cambridge.

Hettne, B., Inotai, A. and Sunkel, O. (1999) *Globalism and the New Regionalism.* Macmillan, London.

Hirst, P. and Thompson, G. (1999a) *Globalization in Question.* Polity Press, Cambridge.

Hirst, P. and Thompson, G. (1999b) The Tyranny of Globalization: Myth or Reality? In: Buelens, F., *Globalisation and the Nation State.* Edward Elgar, Cheltenham, pp. 139–178.

Holm, H.H. and Sørensen, G. (1995) *Whose World Order?: Uneven Globalization and the End of the Cold War.* Westview Press, Boulder, CO.

Huysmans, J. (2000) The European Union and the Securitisation of Migration. *Journal of Common Market Studies*, 38/5, 751–77.

Keohane, R.O. (2000) Sovereignty in International Society. In: Held and McGrew 2000.

Mittleman, J.H. (2000) *The Globalization Syndrome: Transformation and Resistance.* Princeton University Press, Princeton.

Muchie, M. and Li Xing (eds) (2006) *Globalisation, Inequality and the Commodification of Life and Wellbeing.* Adonis & Abbey, London.

Murshed, M.S. (2002) *Globalisation, Marginalisation and Development.* Routledge, London.

Overbeek, H.W. (1995) Globalisation and the Restructuring of the European Labour Markets: The Role of Migration. In: Simai, M. (ed.), *Global Employment: An International Investigation into the Future of Work.* Zed Books and United Nations University Press, London and Tokyo, pp. 204–218.

Overbeek, H.W. (2000) Globalisation, Sovereignty and Transnational Regulation: Reshaping the Governance of International Migration. In: Ghosh, B. (ed.), *Managing Migration: Time for a New International Regime.* Oxford University Press, Oxford, pp. 48–74.

Sassen, S. (1998) *Globalization and its Discontents: Essays on the New Mobility of People and Money.* New York Press, New York.

Shafik, N. (1999) Technology: A Disintegrative Factor in the Arab World. In: Hudson, C.M. (ed.), *The Middle East Dilemma.* Columbia University Press, New York, pp. 279-299.

Talani, L.S. (2004) *European Political Economy.* Ashgate, London.

Thompson, G. (1993) *The Economic Emergence of a New Europe?* Edward Elgar, Cheltenham.

UN [United Nations] (2001) Replacement Migration: Is it a Solution to Declining and Aging Population? At: www.un.org/esa/population/execsum.htm, accessed 7 May 2008.

Weiner, M. (1995) *The Global Migration Crisis: Challenge to States and Human Rights.* HarperCollins College Publishers, New York.

Chapter 3 'Fortress Europe'

Baldwin-Edwards, M. (1999) Where Free Market Reigns: Aliens in the Twilight Zone. In: Baldwin-Edwards, M. and Arango, J. (eds) *Immigrants and the Informal Economy in Southern Europe*, Frank Cass, London, pp. 1–16.

Barnard, C. (2007) *The Substantive Law of the EU: The Four Freedoms*, second edition. Oxford University Press, Oxford.

Boswell, C. (2003) *European Migration Policies in flux: Changing Patterns of Inclusion and Exclusion*. Blackwell, Oxford.

Geddes, A. (2000) *Immigration and European Integration: Towards Fortress Europe?*. Manchester University Press, Manchester.

Geddes, A. (2003) *The Politics of Migration and Immigration in Europe*. Sage, London.

Guiraudon, V. (2000) European Integration and Migration Policy. *Journal of Common Market Studies*, 38/2, 251–72.

Handoll, J. (1995) *Free Movement of Persons in the EU*. John Wiley & Sons, Chichester.

Hollifield, J.F. (1992) *Immigrants, Markets and States: The Political Economy of Postwar Europe*. Harvard University Press, Cambridge, MA.

Huysmans, J. (2000) The European Union and the Securitisation of Migration. *Journal of Common Market Studies*, 38/5, 751–77.

Kostakopoulou, T. (2000) The 'Protective Union': Change and Continuity in Migration Law and Policy in Post-Amsterdam Europe, *Journal of Common Market Studies*, 38/3, 497–518.

Kostakopoulou, T. (2001) *Citizenship, Identity and Immigration in the European Union*, Manchester University Press. Manchester.

Lavenex, S. (1998) 'Passing the buck': European Union refugee policies towards Central and Eastern Europe, *Journal of Refugee Studies*, 11/2, 126–45.

Lavenex, S. (2001) Migration and the EU's New Eastern Border. *JEPP*, 8/1, 24–42.

Martin, D. and Guild, E. (1996) *Free Movement of Persons in the European Union*, Butterworths, London.

Miles, R. and Thränhardt, D. (eds) (1995) *Migration and European Integration: The Dynamics of Inclusion and Exclusion*. Pinter, London.

Peers, S. (2001) Aliens, Workers, Citizens or Humans? Models for Community Immigration Law. In: Guild, E. and Harlow, C. (eds) *Implementing Amsterdam: Immigration and Asylum Rights in EC Law*. Hart Publishing, Oxford, pp. 291–309

Stetter, S. (2000) Regulating Migration: Authority Delegation in JHA. *JEPP*, 7/1, 80–103.

Thielemann, E. (2005/06), lecture given at the LSE, London.

Ucarer, E.M. (2002) Guarding the borders of the European Union: paths, portals and prerogatives. In: Lavenex, S. and Ucarer, E.M. (eds) *Migration and the Externalities of European Integration*. Lexington Books, Oxford, pp. 15–33.

Ugur, M. (1995) Freedom of Movement vs. Exclusion: A Reinterpretation of the 'Insider'–'Outsider' Divide in the European Union. *International Migration Review*, 29/4, 964–99.

Chapter 4 Migration in practice

Amin, G. (2000) *Whatever happened to Egyptians?* The American University in Cairo Press, Cairo.

Appleyard, R. (ed.) (1999) *Emigration Dynamics in Developing Countries*, Volume IV: *The Arab Region*. Ashgate, London.

BBC (2007) Egypt Pressed on Migrant Deaths, 8 August 2007. At: http://news bbc.co.uk/1/hi/world/middle_east/6937071.stm, accessed 10 July 2008.

Binder, L. (1978) *In a Moment of Enthusiasm: Political Power and the Second Stratum Egypt*. University of Chicago Press, Chicago and London.

Birks, J.S. and Sinclair, C.A. (1979) Egypt: A Frustrated Labour Exporter? *Mid East Journal*, 33/3, 288–303.

Bohning, R. (1984) *Studies in International Labour Migration*. Macmillan, London an Basingstoke.

Bomford, A. (2001) Sarajevo: Gateway to Europe, BBC News. At: http://news.bbc co.uk/1/hi/world/europe/1161989.stm, accessed 17 December 2008.

Choucri, N. (1978) *Migration Processes Among Developing Countries: The Middle East*. MIT Press, Cambridge, MA.

CARIM (2008) Euro-Mediterranean Consortium for Applied Research on International Migration, European University Institute, RSCAS, San Domenico in Fiesole, Florence. At: http://www.carim.org/, accessed 3 September 2008.

Carroll, R. (2001) Grim War on Human Traffickers, *The Guardian*, 5 February.

Collyer, M. (2004) *The Development Impact of Temporary International Labour Migration on Southern Mediterranean Sending Countries: Contrasting Examples of Morocco and Egypt*, Working Paper T6, Sussex Centre for Migration Research.

Cleland, W. (1936) *The Population Problem in Egypt: A Study of Population Trends and Conditions in Modern Egypt*. Science Press Printing Company, Lancaster, PA.

Dessouki, A.E.H. (1982) The Shift in Egypt's Migration Policy 1952–1977. *Middle Eastern Studies*, 18/1, 53–68.

Egyptian Ministry for Manpower and Emigration (2008) At: http://www.emigration.gov.eg/MigrationLaw/EgyptianMigrationLaw.aspx, accessed 7 July 2008.

El Pais (2001) Reportage on immigration. Un viaje desesperado hacia lo incierto. *El Pais*. At: http://www.elpais.com/global/, accessed 6 January 2009.

Eurostat (2001) Why Do People Migrate? *Eurostat Statistics in Focus: Population and Social Conditions, Theme 3*, 1/2001.

Fargues, P. (ed.) (2007) *Mediterranean Migration, 2006–2007*. European University Institute, RSCAS, San Domenico in Fiesole, Florence.

Feiler, G. (2003) *Economic Relations between Egypt and the Gulf Oil States, 1967–2000: Petro Wealth and Patterns of Influence*. Sussex Academic Press, Brighton.

Ibrahim, S.E. (1982) *The New Arab Social Order: A Study of the Social Impact of the Oil Wealth*. Westview Press, Boulder, CO.

ILO [International Labour Organization] (2008) At: http://laborsta.ilo.org/, accessed 6 January 2009.

International Office for Migration [IOM] (2000) Trafficking in Migrants: Focus on the Balkans, *IOM Quarterly Bulletin*, N.22, Autumn.

IOM [International Office for Migration] (2005) *World Migration 2005*. IOM, Cairo.

Kepel, G. (1999) Toward a Social Analysis of Islamist Movements. In: Binder, L. (ed.), *Ethnic Conflict and International Politics in the Middle East*. University Press of Florida, Gainesville, FL, pp. 181–207.

La Repubblica (2008) Immigrati: strage verso l'Italia, La Repubblica, 16 Giugno. At: http://www.repubblica.it/2008/02/sezioni/cronaca/sbarchi-immigrati/nuovi-sbarchi/nuovi-sbarchi.html, accessed 10 July 2008.

Ministeria del Interior, Delegacion del Gobierno para la extranjeria y la inmigracion (2001) La inmigracion en Espana: Evolucion y perspectivas. *Delegacion del Gobierno para la extranjeria y la inmigracion.* At: http://www.mir.es/, accessed 6 January 2009.

Morris, C. (2001) Turkey's Human Traffic: Rescuers deal with victims of the Turkish disaster, *BBC News.* At: http://news.bbc.co.uk/1/hi/programmes/from_our_own_correspondent/1100986.stm, accessed 17 December 2008.

Morris, C., Kaye, M. and Beaumont, P. (2001) Bosnia's Corrupt Elite Grow Fat on Human Cargo smuggled to West, *The Observer*, 28 January.

Nassar, H. (2005) *Migration, Transfers and Development in Egypt.* European University Institute, RSCAS, Research Reports 2005/01.

The New York Times (2000) Illegal Migration Rises Sharply in European Union, 25 December.

OECD [Organisation for Economic Co-operation and Development] (2008) International Migration Statistics. At: http://www.oecd.org/statsportal/0,3352,en_2825_293564_1_1_1_1_1,00.html, accessed 17 December 2008.

Oweiss, I. (1980) Migration of Egyptians. *L'Egypte Contemporaine*, 381, 5–16.

Panorama (2003) Li manda Gheddafi, 16 June.

Roman, H. (2006) *Transit Migration in Egypt.* European University Institute, RSCAS, Research Reports, 2006/1.

Russell, S.S. (1992) International Migration and Political Turmoil in the Middle East. *Population and Development Review*, 18/4, 719–27.

Sawi, A. (1995) *Migration-related Institutions and Policies in Egypt.* European University Institute, RSCAS, Analytic and Syntetic notes, 2005/08.

Seccombe, I.J. (1985) International Labor Migration in the Middle East: A Review of Literature and Research, 1974–84. *International Migration Review*, 19/2, 335–52.

Sell, R. (1987) Gone for Good? Egyptian Migration Processes in the Arab World. *Cairo Papers in Social Sciences*, The American University in Cairo Press, Cairo.

Skeldon, R. (2000) *Myths and Realities of Chinese Irregular Migration.* IOM, Geneva.

Travis, A. (2001) A Joint Anglo-Italian initiative to Stem the Flow from the Balkans, *The Guardian*, 5 February.

VR Sicilia (2008) Rimpatriati 35 Egiziani da Lampedusa. At: http://www.vrsicilia.it/index.php?option=com_content&Itemid=11&id=3821&task=view, accessed 10 July 2008.

Zahlan, A.B. (1999) Labor Migration and Economic Integration in the Middle East. In: Hudson, M.C. (ed.) *Middle East Dilemma.* Tauris & Co. Ltd, New York, pp. 259–79.

Zohry, A. (2007) Egyptian Irregular Migration to Europe. *Migration Letters*, 4/1, 53–63.

Zohry, A. and Harrell-Bond, B. (2003) *Contemporary Egyptian Migration: An Overview of Voluntary and Forced Migration.* University of Sussex working papers, C3.

Chapter 5 Why do Egyptians migrate now?

Al-Atreash, H.M. and Yousef, T. (1999) *Intra-Arab Trade – Is It too Little?* IMF Working Paper, WP/00/10.

Arab Monetary Fund (2008) Statistics. At: http://www.amf.org.ae/pages/, accessed 22 July 2008.

Asseburg, M. (2004) The EU and the Middle East Conflict: Tackling the Main Obstacle to Euro-Mediterranean Partnership. In: Junemann 2004a, pp. 174–94.

Chorou, B. (2004) Arab Regional Integration as a prerequisite for a successful Euro-Mediterranean Partnership. In: Junemann 2004a, pp. 194–214.

Diab, M.A. (1963) *Inter-Arab Cooperation 1951–1960*. Economic Research Institute, American University of Beirut, Beirut.

Dodge, T. and Higgot, R. (2002) *Globalisation and the Middle East*. The Royal Institute of International Affairs, London.

Fazio, G. (2009) EMU and the Euro-Mediterranean Dialogue: Trade Interdependence between Mediterranean and Euro-area Countries. In: Talani, L.S. (ed.), *The Future of EMU*. Palgrave, Basingstoke.

Gillespie, R. (2004) Reshaping the Agenda? The Internal Politics of the Barcelona Process after September 11. In: Junemann 2004a, pp. 21–37.

Grunert, A. (2004) Loss of Guiding Values and Support: September 11 and the Isolation of Human Rights Organizations in Egypt. In: Junemann 2004a, pp. 133–53.

Hakimian, H. and Moshaver, Z. (2001) *The State and Global Change: The Political Economy of Transition in the Middle East and North Africa*. Curzon Press, Richmond.

Harrigan, J., Wang, C. and Said, H. (2005) The Economic and Political Determinants of IMF and World Bank Lending in the Middle East and North Africa. *World Development*, 34/2, 247–70.

Hirst, P. and Thompson, G. (1999) *Globalization in Question*. Polity Press, Cambridge.

Honohan, P. and Lane, P.R. (2000) *Will the Euro Trigger More Monetary Unions in Africa?* World Bank Policy Research Working Paper, no. 2393.

Hudson, M.C. (ed.) (1999) *Middle East Dilemma: The Politics and Economics of Arab Integration*. Columbia University Press, New York.

Huysmans, J. (2000) The European Union and the Securitization of Migration. *JCMS*, 38/5, 751–77.

IMF [International Monetary Fund] (2003) World Economic and Financial Surveys, World Economic Outlook Public Debt in Emerging Markets, September 2003. At: http://www.imf.org/external/pubs/ft/weo/2003/02/index.htm, accessed 20 November 2005.

Junemann, A. (ed.) (2004a) *Euro-Mediterranean Relations after September the 11th: International, Regional and Domestic Dynamics*. Frank Cass, London.

Junemann, A. (2004b) Repercussions of the Emerging European Security and Defence Policy on the Civil Character of the Euro-Mediterranean Partnership. In: Junemann 2004a, pp. 37–54.

Junemann, A. (2004c) Security Building in the Mediterranean after September the 11th. In: Junemann 2004a, pp. 1–21.

Kubursi, A.A. (1999) Prospects for Arab Economic Integration After Oslo. In: Hudson 1999, pp. 299–321.

Masson, P. (2007) Currency Unions in Africa: Is the Trade Effect Substantial Enough to Justify their Formation? *The World Economy*, 1-15, doi: 10.1111/j.1467-9701.01028.x.

Musrey, A.G. (1969) *An Arab Common Market: A Study in Inter-Arab Trade Flows.* Frederick J. Praeger, New York–Washington–London.

Owen, R. (1999) Inter-Arab Economic Relations during the 20th Century: World Market vs Regional Market? In: Hudson 1999, pp. 217–33.

Owen, R. and Pamuk, S. (1999) *A History of Middle East Economies in the 20th Century.* Harvard University Press, Cambridge, MA.

Sayigh, Y.A. (1983) A New Framework for Complementarity among the Arab Economies. In: Ibrahim Ibrahim (ed.) *Arab Resources: The Transformation of a Society.* Center for Contemporary Arab Studies, Washington DC and London; Croom Helm, Washington DC and London, pp. 147–55.

Sayigh, Y.A. (1999) Arab Economic Integration: The Poor Harvest of the 1980s. In: Hudson 1999, pp. 233–259.

Stetter, S. (2004) Democratization without Democracy? The Assistance of the European Union for Democratization Processes in Palestine. In: Junemann 2004a, pp. 153–74.

Subramanian, A. and Tamirisa, N.T. (2003) Is Africa Integrated in the Global Economy? *IMF Staff Papers*, 50, 352–72.

Tovias, A. (2004) Israeli Policy Perspectives on the Euro-Mediterranean Partnership in the Context of EU Enlargement. In: Junemann 2004a, pp. 214–33.

UN Economic and Social Commission for Western Asia [ESCWA] (2007) *Economic Trends and Impacts: Foreign Aid and Development in the Arab Region*, 4, United Nations E/Escwa/Ead/2007/1, 4 January.

UNCTAD [United Nations Conference on Trade and Development] (2008) Statistics. At: http://www.unctad.org, accessed 4 September 2008.

Zahlan, A.B. (1999) Labor Migration and Economic Integration in the Middle East. In: Hudson 1999, pp. 259–279.

Chapter 6 Why do Egyptians migrate now?

Ayubi, N. (1999) *Overstating the Arab State: Politics and Society in the Middle East.* IB Tauris, London.

Dodge, T. and Higgot, R. (2002) *Globalisation and the Middle East.* The Royal Institute of International Affairs, London.

Fawcett, L. and Sayigh, Y. (1999) *The Third World Beyond the Cold War: Continuity and Change.* Oxford University Press, Oxford.

Hakimian, H. and Moshaver, Z. (2001) *The State and Global Change: The Political Economy of Transition in the Middle East and North Africa*. Curzon Press, Richmond.
IMF [International Monetary Fund] (2008) Data and Statistics. At: http://www.imf.org, accessed 23 July 2008.
Khyeda, S. (2007) Foreign Direct Investment in the Middle East: Major Regulatory Restrictions. *Insight Turkey*, 9/2, 73–104.
Nassar, H. (2005) *Migration, Transfers and Development in Egypt*. European University Institute, RSCAS, Research Reports 2005/01.
Owen, R. and Pamuk, S. (1999) *A History of Middle East Economies in the 20th Century*. Harvard University Press, Cambridge, MA.
UN [United Nations] (2008) The Global Information Society: A Statistical View – Partnership on Measuring ICT for Development, April 2008, LC/W.190. At: http://www.itu.int/ITU-D/ict/material/LCW190_en.pdf, accessed 22 December 2008.
UNCTAD [United Nations Conference on Trade and Development] (2008) *Globalisation and Development*. At: http://www.unctad.org/Templates/StartPage.asp?intItemID=2874&lang=1, accessed 28 July 2008.
World Bank (2001) *The Little Data Book*. World Bank, Washington DC.

Chapter 7 Who is the Egyptian migrant?

Bohning, W.R. (1984) *Studies in International Labour Migration*. Macmillan Press, London.
CAPMAS [Central Agency for Public Mobilization and Statistics] (1991) *External Migration Survey in Egypt, 1987*. CAPMAS, Cairo.
Castells, M. (1975) Immigrant Workers and Class Struggle in Advanced Capitalism: The Western European Experience. *Politics and Society*, 5, 33–66.
Castells, M. (2000) *The Rise of the Network Society*. Blackwell, Oxford.
Egyptian Ministry of Manpower and Emigration (2006) Attitudes of Egyptian Youth toward Migration to Europe. At: http://www.emigration.gov.eg/idomsite/Upload/Researches/72/Attitudes of Egyptian youth towards Migration to Europe.pdf, accessed 8 November 2006.
Eurostat (2000) Push and Pull Factors of International Migration. Country Report: *Egypt, Population and Social Conditions*, 3/2000/E/n.7.
Geddes, A. (2000) *Immigration and European Integration: Towards Fortress Europe?* Manchester University Press, Manchester.
IOM [International Organization for Migration] (2003) *Egyptian Migration 2003*. IOM, Cairo.
Piore, Michael J. (1979) *Birds of Passage: Migrant Labor and Industrial Societies*. Cambridge University Press, Cambridge.
Sell, R. (1987) Gone for Good? Egyptian Migration Processes in the Arab World. *Cairo Papers in Social Sciences*. The American University in Cairo Press, Cairo.
Talani, L.S. (2003) Why do Migrants Leave their Countries? Motivations to Migrate at the Point of Departure, the Case of Egypt. At: http://www.files.emigration.

gov.eg/Upload/Publications/English/11/why_do_migrants.pdf, accessed 18 August 2008.

Talani, L.S. (2006) *Motivations for Migration at the Point of Departure: The case of Morocco.* Project financed by the British Academy.

Zohry, A. (2006) *Egyptian Irregular Migration to Europe.* Paper presented at the European Population Conference, University of Liverpool, UK, 21–24 June.

Chapter 8 What do Muslim migrants do in receiving countries?

Baldwin-Edwards, M. and Arango, J. (1999) *Immigrants and the Informal Economy in Southern Europe.* Frank Cass, London.

Boswell, C. (2003) *European Migration Policies in Flux: Changing Patterns of Inclusion and Exclusion.* Blackwell and RIIA, Oxford.

CARIM (2008) *Euro-Mediterranean Consortium for Applied Research on International Migration,* European University Institute, RSCAS, San Domenico in Fiesole, Florence, At: http://www.carim.org/, accessed 3 September 2008.

Corriere Romano (2008) Immigrazione e Campi Rom, 30 April.

Esping-Anderson, G. (1999) *Social Foundations of Post-Industrial Economies.* Oxford University Press, Oxford.

Guiraudon, V. (2000) European Integration and Migration Policy. *JCMS*, 38/2, 251–72.

Huysmans, J. (2000) The European Union and the Securitization of Migration. *JCMS*, 38/5, 751–77.

Kostakopoulou, D. (2001) *Citizenship, Identity, and Immigration in the European Union: Between Past and Future.* MUP, New York.

Miles, R. and Thränhardt, D. (eds) (1995) *Migration and European Integration: The Dynamics of Inclusion and Exclusion.* Pinter, London.

Nassar, H. (2005) *Migration, Transfers and Development in Egypt.* European University Institute, RSCAS, Research Reports 2005/01.

The New York Times (2000) Illegal Migration Rises Sharply In European Union. 25 December.

OECD (2008) *A Profile of Immigrant Populations in the 21st Century: Data from OECD Countries.* OECD, Paris.

Palidda, S., Frangoulis, M. and Papantoniou, A. (1999) *Deviant Behaviour and the Criminalisation of Immigrants.* European Commission, Brussels.

Reyneri, E. (1999a) *Immigration and the Underground Economy in New Receiving South European Countries: Manifold Negative Effects, Manifold Deep-Rooted Causes*, Final Report of the Project 'Migrants' Insertion in the Informal Economy, Deviant Behaviour and the Impact on Receiving Societies'. CE/DGXII-Science, Research and Development, TSR Program, SOE2-CT95-3005.

Reyneri, E. (1999b) The Mass Legalisation of Migrants in Italy: Permanent or Temporary Emergence from the Underground Economy?. In: Baldwin-Edwards and Arango 1999, pp. 84–104.

Reyneri, E. (2003) Illegal Immigration and the Underground Economy. *National Europe Centre Paper No. 68*. Paper presented to conference entitled The Challenges of Immigration and Integration in the European Union and Australia, 18–20 February, University of Sydney.

Reyneri, E. and Baganha, M. (1999) New Migrants in South European Countries and Their Insertion in the Underground Economy. In: Reyneri 1999a.

Rhodes, M. (1997) Globalisation, Labour Markets And Welfare States: A Future Of 'Competitive Corporatism?'. *EUI Working Papers*, No. 97/36.

Rowlands, D. (1998) Poverty and Environmental Degradation as Root Causes of International Migration: A Critical Assessment. In: UN–IOM, *Technical Symposium on International Migration and Development*, The Hague, 29 June–3 July.

Solé, C. (1999) The Impact of Immigration on South European New Receiving Societies. In: Reyneri 1999a.

Stetter, S. (2000) Regulating Migration: Authority Delegation in Justice and Home Affairs. *JEPP*, 7/1, 80–102.

Talani, L.S. (2002) Final Evaluation Report of the Project 'Migrants' Insertion in the Informal Economy: Deviant Behaviour and the Impact on Receiving Societies'. CE/DGXII–Science, Research and Development, TSR Program, SOE2-CT95-3005.

Talani, L.S. (2004) *European Political Economy: Political Science Perspectives*. Ashgate, London.

UN ODCCP (2001) Global Programme against Smuggling of Migrants. At: http://unodc.org/, accessed 15 January 2009.

Wilpert, C. and Laacher, S. (1999) New Forms of Immigration and the Informal Labour Market in Old Receiving Countries: France and Germany. In: Reyneri 1999a.

Zincone, G. (1999) Illegality, Enlightenment and Ambiguity: A Hot Italian Recipe. In: Baldwin-Edwards and Arango 1999, pp. 43–83.

Chapter 9 Islamophobia and social capital

Baromètre Politique Français (2006–07) CEVIPOF–Ministère de l'Intérieur, *Le Rapport à la Politique des Français*. Available at: http://www.cevipof.msh-paris.fr/bpf/barometre/vague1/synthese/BPF-V1_R03_DB-BC-JC.pdf, accessed 7 February 2007.

Bauman, Z. (2000) *Liquid Modernity*. Polity Press, Cambridge.

Body-Gendrot, S. (2007a) Urban "riots" in France: anything new?. In: Ponsaert, Paul (ed.) *Local Security Policy in the Netherlands and Belgium*, Boom Juridische Utig, Den Haag, Netherlands.

Body-Gendrot, S. (2007b) Order and Disorder in the Urban Landscape. In: Burdett, R. and Sudjik, D. (eds) *The Urban Age Book*. Tashent

Bourdieu, P. (1980) Le Capital Social: Notes Provisoires. *Actes de la Recherche in Sciences Sociales*, 31, 2–3.

Brehm, J. and Rahn, W. (1997) Individual-Level Evidence for the Causes and Consequences of Social Capital. *American Journal of Political Science*, 41/3, 999–1023.

Cerny, P. (1999) Reconstructing the Political in a Globalising World. In: Buelens, F., *Globalisation and the Nation State*. Edward Elgar, Cheltenham.

Coleman, J. (1988) Social Capital in the Creation of Human Capital. *American Journal of Sociology*, 94, 95–120.

Febvre, M. and Muller, L. (2003) *Une Personne sur Deux est Membre d'une Association en 2002*, INSEE Première, 920.

Glaeser, E.L., Laibson, D. and Sacerdote, B. (2002) An Economic Approach to Social Capital. *Economic Journal*, 112/483, 437–58.

Glavanis, M.P. (1999) *'Muslim voices' in the European Union: The Stranger Within – Community, Identity and Employment*, Project No. ERB-SOE2-CT96-3024, CCSR/ University of Manchester.

Halliday, F. (1996) *Islam and the Myth of Confrontation*. I.B. Tauris, London.

Knack, S. and Keefer, P. (1997) Does Social Capital Have an Economic Payout? A Cross-Country Investigation. *The Quarterly Journal of Economics*, 112/4, 1251–88.

Putnam, R. (2000) *Bowling Alone: The Collapse and Revival of American Community*. Simon & Schuster, New York.

Putnam, R. (2002) *Democracies in Flux*. Oxford Scholarship online. Available at: www.oxfordscholarship.com, accessed 19 February 2007.

Runnymede Trust Commission on British Muslims and Islamophobia (1997) *Islamophobia: A Challenge For Us All*, Final Report. Available at: http://www.runnymedetrust.org/projects/commissionOnBritishMuslims.html, accessed 12 October 2008.

Salamon, L.M., Sokolowski, W.S. and Associates (2004) *Global Civil Society: Dimensions of the Nonprofit Sector*, Volume Two. Kumarian Press, Bloomfeld, CT.

Sennet, R. (1996) *Uses of Disorder: Personal Identity and City Life*. Faber and Faber, London.

Tabellini, G. (2005) Culture and Institutions: Economic Development in the Regions of Europe. *IGIER Working Paper* no. 292.

Worms, J. (2002) France: Old and New Civic and Social Ties in France. In: Putnam, R.D. (ed.) *Democracies in Flux: The Evolution of Social Capital in Contemporary Society*. Oxford University Press, New York, pp. 137–88.

Index